HOW TO BUILD SMALL BOATS

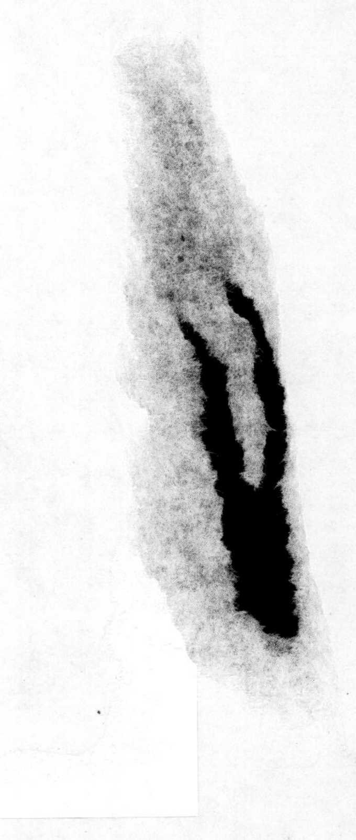

ELEVEN FOOT DINGHY "WEE NIP" SAILING

HOW TO BUILD SMALL BOATS

by Edson I. Schock

**South Brunswick and New York:
A. S. Barnes and Company
London: Thomas Yoseloff Ltd**

Library of Congress Catalogue Card Number: 52-7409

FIRST PAPERBACK EDITION 1979

A. S. Barnes and Co., Inc.
Cranbury, New Jersey 08512

Thomas Yoseloff Ltd
Magdalen House
136-148 Tooley Street
London SE1 2TT, England

ISBN 0-498-08142-7 (paperback)
Printed in the United States of America

ACKNOWLEDGEMENT

I am indebted to several friends for assistance in preparing this book, and I wish to take this opportunity to thank them; particularly Miss Josephine Lees, my wife Mary, and my son James.

Edson I. Schock

INTRODUCTION

THE DESIGNS IN THIS BOOK WERE SELECTED PRIMARILY AS BEING PARTICULARLY WELL suited for amateur building, and the complicated curved surfaces, common to certain types of boatbuilding, have been avoided as much as possible. Of the twelve designs shown, six have been built by the author in his cellar or back yard, while the others have been built by neighbors. All were amateur boatbuilders. So these designs have actually been tried out, not by professionals but by amateurs, in most cases they were a first attempt at boatbuilding. Thus, ease of construction is assured.

As important as ease of building is safety, and all these are safe boats. That means that they are harder to capsize than the average of their types. They are not what a sailor would call "cranky" and they won't sink even if swamped, and all of them handle and balance well. This is important, particularly in a sailing boat, since the beginner, learning to sail, should get the "feel" of a well-balanced boat. Also, a well-balanced boat makes a fast boat.

The next consideration in choosing the plans for this book was usefulness. For the youngster who is starting out on his first yacht there is the little "Half Shell," a 9½-ft. skiff with generous beam for maximum stability, or the "Beachcomber," a 12½-ft. catboat that is roomy, easy to handle, hard to upset, yet fast enough to beat most boats of her size and sail area. For the racing enthusiast there is the 15-ft. knockabout "Eager Beaver," that has shown her heels to the fleet, beating 18-ft. round-bottom knockabouts a minute a mile. This is a good performance for an amateur-built boat. There is also a 10½-ft. racing outboard, a small ice boat, and the 11½-ft. sailing dinghy, "Wee Nip," that would also make a good little racing class for club or camp. For the sportsman, there is an 11-ft. duck boat of very simple design, and three skiffs suitable for fishing. The 12½-ft. outboard runabout or the 16-ft. utility outboard would also be fine for fishing, and the latter would be quite safe even in fairly rough water.

For the yachtsman, the little 7-ft. pram would make an excellent tender since she is beamy and has good carrying capacity for so small a boat.

For a family boat the big skiffs, the outboard runabout, or the utility outboard would make perfect picnic boats, and would be fine for rides on lake or river. In fact, if you are planning to use them at your camp you had better build two boats, as one is likely to be in use all the time by the youngsters, consequently you will need a second boat for yourself.

CONTENTS

	INTRODUCTION	v
I.	*Thoughts on Building a Boat*	1
II.	*Tools and Materials*	3
III.	*Mold Loft Work*	9
IV.	*The Fabrication of Units Before Assembly*	12
V.	*Spar Making*	23
VI.	*Sails and Fittings*	26
VII.	*Painting and Varnishing*	38
VIII.	*Twelve Boats and How To Build Them*	41
IX.	*Care and Maintenance*	130
	BOATBUILDING TERMS	133

LIST OF PLATES

Photographs 1 ELEVEN FOOT DINGHY "WEE NIP" SAILING Frontispiece

2 SKIFF "HALF SHELL" UNDER WAY 51

3 SKIFF "SUZET" READY FOR LAUNCHING 53

4 SKIFF "PUDDLE DUCK" UNDER WAY 59

5 ELEVEN FOOT DINGHY AT BUILDER'S YARD 99

6 TWELVE FOOT CAT IN FRAME 109

7 TWELVE FOOT CAT AT THE DOCK 113

8 TWELVE FOOT CAT "BEACHCOMA" SAILING 115

9 "SHARON POTTS" UNDER CONSTRUCTION 127

10 FIFTEEN FOOT KNOCKABOUT "SHARON POTTS" SAILING 129

LIST OF ILLUSTRATIONS

Figure 1 TOOLS 5

2 FASTENINGS 7

3 STEM 12

4 DETAILS OF FLAT PLANK KEEL 13

5 ASSEMBLY OF KEEL REST, OR "HORSE" 14

6 FRAME DETAILS 15

7 CONSTRUCTION OF CENTERBOARD BOX 18

8 MAKING MAST 24

9 CHAINPLATE 28

10 BRONZE TANG 29

11 CLEATS 30

12 CENTERBOARD PLATES 31

13 CENTERBOARD PIN ASSEMBLY 32

14 BLOCK 33

15 STRAP TURNBUCKLE 34

16 SENSITIVE WIND VANE 35

17 BILGE PUMP 36

18 PLANK GAUGE* 37

19 MARKING THE WATERLINE 39

* *From Gadgets & Gilhickies by Ham de Fontaine.*

PLANS

1	7′4″ PLYWOOD PRAM	41
2	9′6″ PLYWOOD OUTBOARD SKIFF	46
3	11′6″ SKIFF	52
4	13′6″ SKIFF	56
5	12′6″ OUTBOARD RUNABOUT	62
6	10′6″ RACING OUTBOARD	70
7	16′ UTILITY OUTBOARD	76
8	11′3″ DUCK BOAT	86
9	75-SQUARE-FOOT ICEBOAT	90
10	"WEE NIP" 11′6″-CLASS SAILING DINGHY	94
11	12′6″ CATBOAT	102
12	15′ KNOCKABOUT	116

HOW TO BUILD SMALL BOATS

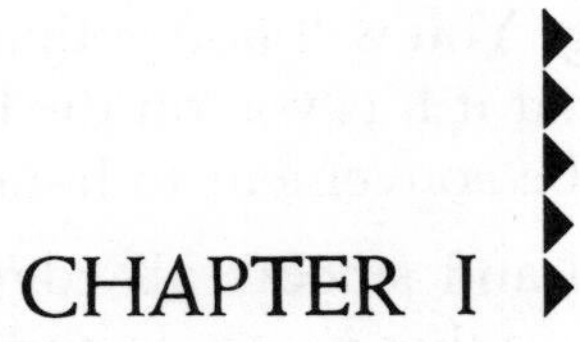

CHAPTER I

Thoughts on Building a Boat

In the building of any boat a certain amount of skill with hand tools is necessary. All boats have some curved surfaces so they are somewhat complicated things to construct. If you are not skilled in the use of common tools you should have someone who is willing to stand by to help if you get stuck. Nevertheless, some of the boats in this book have been built by beginners who were inexperienced carpenters but who by perseverance and care turned out very creditable jobs.

Keep in mind that a boat should be seaworthy. She must be able to take quite a beating by waves and strong winds, and must also take bumps from other boats when she is just tied up to the dock, minding her own business. You may take good care of your boat, but there is always someone who is careless and lets his boat take care of herself, which usually means that she damages other people's boats. So your boat must be strongly built.

In general, you will profit by planning ahead. Such operations as painting the bottom of floor boards before you screw them down will save you trouble. Try to think ahead. Also, keep in mind Rudyard Kipling's saying: "No sham survives the sea," and avoid building errors which would weaken the structure or harm the performance of your boat.

Some of these building errors are:

Use of poor lumber. There is so much hard work on a boat that it never pays to economize on lumber. Good well-seasoned wood is easier to work, and makes for a better finished job. Also it does not rot so easily.

Unfair curves. A fair curve is smooth and graceful for its entire length. An unfair curve has wobbles, kinks or bumps.

Boat not alike on both sides. No boat was ever exactly symmetrical, but a good builder can come mighty close to making it so. In general, differences should be kept to 1/8″

Leaks around the centerboard box. This is a place which is hard to get tight. We will talk more about this later.

Poor fits. These are caused by surfaces that are not true, resulting in open joints.

Centerboards that jam in the centerboard box. Provide enough clearance so the centerboard is free to go up and down easily.

Poor ventilation. Do not close in parts of your boat without allowing adequate openings for free air circulation. Poor ventilation will cause any wood to rot.

Crooked Spars. Make your mast and boom really straight.

Limber holes too small. Limber holes are notches through the frames next to the keel to allow water to pass freely from both ends of the boat to the lowest point. Make them generous in size.

Inconvenient rigging. You will notice that the booms on all these boats is shown quite high. Do not rig it so low that it hits you on the head when tacking. Also, the lead of the sheets and halyards should be convenient to hand.

Rough edges. Round and smooth all edges of frames, beams, and other parts of the boat. Cut off all nails or screws that protrude and file smooth the ends.

Poor rope. Do not use sash cord, or odd bits of old rope. Use good-grade Manila, and buy it large enough so that it will not cut your hands when you pull hard on it. Usually, for small boats 5/16″ or 3/8″ diameter is preferable to 1/4″. For mooring use at least 1/2″ diameter and treat with Cuprinol or a like preservative.

CHAPTER II

Tools and Materials

ALL THE BOATS IN THIS VOLUME CAN BE BUILT WITH HAND TOOLS. IT IS ALWAYS BETTER TO own your own tools than it is to borrow them. Keep all of them in good condition, and the cutting tools sharp. Never leave them lying about where dampness will get them rusty. Power tools will save you a lot of work and do the job quicker and better, but it is hardly worth while buying machinery just to build one boat. If you intend to build several boats, or have other use for motor-driven tools, by all means acquire an 8″ or 9″ circular saw and a 14″ band saw. Other power tools such as a drillpress and grinder are useful too, but the two saws are the most used for boatbuilding. In addition to any power tools, you should also have the following.

A LIST OF NEEDED TOOLS

Claw hammer, weight about 1¼ lbs. (1)*
Ripsaw, 6 point, about 26″ long.
Crosscut saw, 8 or 10 point, about 20″ long. (2)
Keyhole saw with a narrow blade, about 10″ long. (3)
Coping saw, with a package of a dozen 6″ blades. (4)
Hacksaw frame and several 10″ blades with fine teeth. (5)
Bit brace; the "Millers Falls" No. 322, 10″ is a good one. (6)
Bits. "Russell Jennings" ¼″, ⅜″, ½″, ⅞″ will suffice for most of the work. Buy them as required and you will soon have a good set. You can also use a **Screwdriver bit,** large and small to fit the bit brace, for driving screws in oak.
Countersink. Get one that will fit the bit brace, for wood screw heads.
Twist drills. Get one each of the following sizes to start: Nos. 3, 12, 20, 29, 32, 41, 44, ¼″, 9/32″, 5/16″, ⅜″.
Adjustable angle wrench. "Pexto" 8″ is a handy size. (7)
Monkey wrench, at least 9″ over-all length. (8)
Jack plane. The "Stanley" No. 603 "Bed Rock," 9″ is a good size.
Block plane, "Stanley" No. 100 which is a little fellow just fitting in the hand. Comes in handy for trimming off corners. (9)
Hand drill. A two-speed drill, with a chuck to hold ⅜″ round-shank drills. The "Yankee" No. 1445 is about the right size. (10)
Screwdrivers. A large one, 12″ over-all length, and a small one, 7″, will be needed. If you use

* Numbers in parenthesis refer to illustrations on page 5.

Phillips Head screws you will need screwdrivers to fit them. A ratchet screwdriver with several bits is a very useful tool to own. (11)

Pliers. The slip-joint kind, such as come in automobile tool kits are the most generally useful. (12)

Chisels. ½″ and a 1″ mortising chisels should be plenty. (13)

Mallet. For use with the chisels. Never strike the chisels with a hammer.

Adjustable bevel. The "Stanley" No. 25, 6″ is a handy size. (14)

Combination square with a 12″ blade.

Steel square, 18″ or 24″.

Clamps. Some prefer parallel-jaw woodworking clamps with steel screws, others like the malleable iron C clamps used by professional boatbuilders. You will need at least four of the size that opens about 4¼″. You can use a great number of clamps. If you are offered a barrel full, take them. You cannot have too many. On the other hand four or five clamps will get you by if you use them in the right places. For gluing wide assemblies, such as a transom, a pair of extension bar clamps are required, but temporary substitutes can be made (see text page 16, under "Making the Transom.") (15)

A ball of mason's twine and carpenter's chalk.

A plumb bob and line will be wanted.

Oilstone. For sharpening tools. Buy a good one with coarse grit on one side and fine on the other. An Arkansas stone is useful for putting an extra fine edge on cutting tools. Also get an **oil can** to use with the oilstone.

Files. You will need a 6″ and an 8″ mill, a 10″ half-round and an 8″ rat-tail file, all with handles. Double-cut files work well for boat jobs. Also buy a file card to keep your files clean.

Rule. A pull-out 6-ft. steel rule with a locking device is best but the folding wooden kind will do. A yardstick is also handy.

Jackknife. Get a strong one with the best steel blade you can buy.

Woodworking vise. One that opens 10″ or 12″, with 10″ wide jaws is big enough.

Metalworking vise. This is handy but not absolutely necessary. One with a 2″ wide jaw will do, but it should be of a heavy design that will stand abuse. It is sometimes necessary to screw the jaws very tight, and a light vise may break.

Dolly. This is a heavy tool for backing up work when riveting or hammering in nails on a thin board with nothing behind it. Holding a dolly behind the board will take up the spring and enable you to make a tight job. You can make a good dolly out of a piece of round steel shafting 1½″ in diameter by 10″ long, smoothed on the ends, but any suitable heavy object will do.

Batten or splines. These are long thin pieces of straight-grained wood used to guide the pencil in drawing smooth curves. You should have one about 5⁄16″ by ⅝″ in cross-section, and a foot longer than the boat you are building, also one about ⅛″ by 5⁄16″, 3 feet long. The long one should be of clear straight-grained white pine free from knots or kinks. It is difficult to find such a stick, and you may spend a lot of time locating one. It is worth the effort, however, for a good batten is a great help in getting curves smooth, fair and true. The short one should be of celluloid. They are sold by drafting supply dealers. The battens are held in place by small-diameter brads. It is not necessary to buy batten weights (ducks) such as draftsmen use, unless you are going to use the battens on a drawing board. Boatbuilders use battens on the mold loft floor, where small brads may be driven into the wood. The nails go alongside the stick, never through it.

FIGURE 1

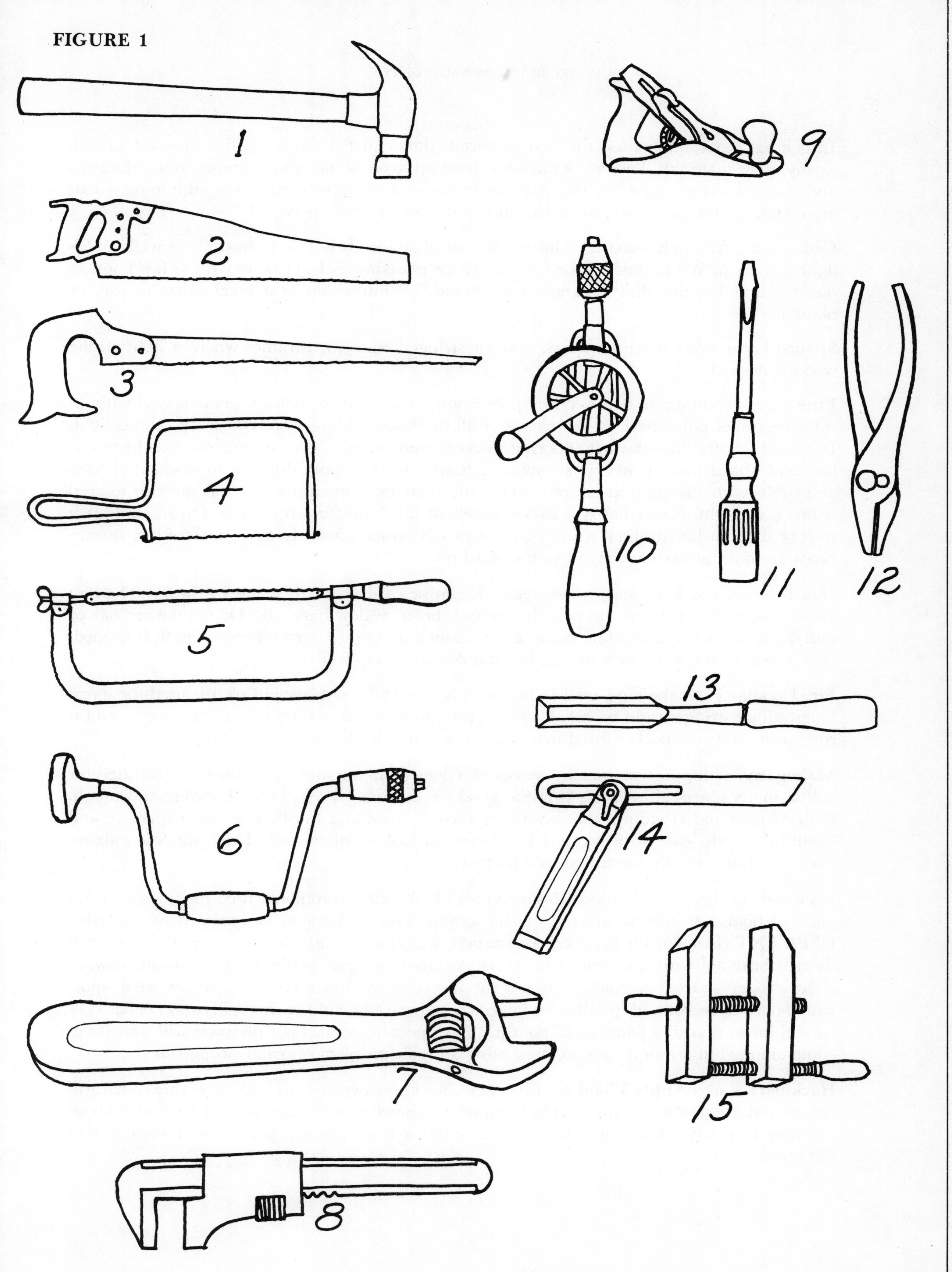

MATERIALS

In general, boatbuilders use the best materials they can get. This applies to wood as well as any other materials. Poor stock does not stand up to rough use and exposure to the elements and cheap wood is a poor boating investment. Some of the more common boatbuilding woods are cedar, spruce, pine, oak, fir, mahogany, and marine-grade plywood.

Cedar is a soft, tough wood used for small boat planking. It is easy to work, lasts well, and is light in weight. White cedar is the first choice for planking. Select planks with as few knots as possible and be sure that all knots are "sound." White cedar is a good wood to use for planking.

Spruce is the first choice for spars, also for stringers and sawn frames where a light strong wood is desired.

Pine is very common in boats. White pine is soft, even-grained, holds fastenings well without splitting, takes paint well, is the easiest of all the boatbuilding woods to work, and is light. It is used for decking, thwarts, flooring, lockers, and interior work in general. Southern yellow pine (hard pine) is heavy, strong and hard, but it is more difficult to work, it shrinks and swells with changing moisture content and therefore sometimes makes it difficult to keep seams watertight. Nevertheless it makes excellent planking for large boats. On small craft it may be used for longitudinal stringers, rudders and centerboards. In some parts of the country boats are built almost entirely of yellow hard pine.

Oak is tough and hard and, when steamed, can be easily bent. It is hard to work. The best variety for marine use is white oak, the second choice, yellow bark oak. Do not use red oak or kiln dried oak. Oak makes fine stems, keels, frames, and other parts where strength is needed. It is heavy, which is a disadvantage, but it holds fastenings well.

Fir. Douglas Fir is the kind used in boats. It is very stiff for its weight so it is used for spars, longitudinal stringers and beams. It splits easily, so care is necessary when fastening it, and it rots easily, so it should be stored in a place where it gets plenty of ventilation.

Mahogany. Philippine mahogany makes excellent planking and may also be substituted for oak in many places although it is not as good for bending as oak, but it is strong and tough. Both African and Honduras mahogany are used for trim and finish. They are expensive and beautiful woods, easy to work and handsome to look at afterward. They are fine cabinet woods and are usually varnished, not painted.

Plywood. Douglas fir plywood (marine grade) is the kind commonly used for the structural parts of boats. Be sure to get the marine grade. This is stamped or branded on the edge DFPA EXT (Douglas Fir Plywood Association, Exterior Grade). Do not accept it unless each sheet is branded with this symbol for there are many inferior grades on the market. Beware of little open spaces, or voids, between the layers of the inner plies. These are weak spots which may cause rot and usually can be seen along the edges of the sheet. Plywood needs very careful inspection; if a panel looks poor in this respect, reject it. Poor plywood will sometimes come unglued in a month or two, presenting a repair problem of major proportions.

Hackmatack and **Apple Wood** are first choice for knees because they are available in natural crooks and are tough and strong. Hackmatack is, unfortunately, hard to find. Oak or mahogany may be used for knees but should be cut with the grain running parallel with the chord of the knee.

FIGURE 2

FASTENINGS.

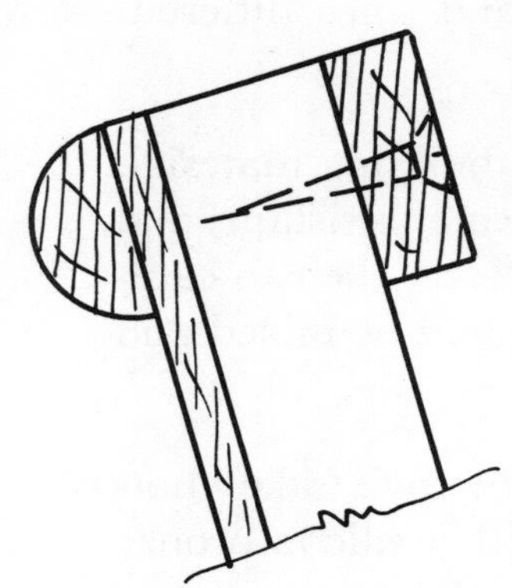

INWALE OR CLAMP SCREWED TO FRAME.

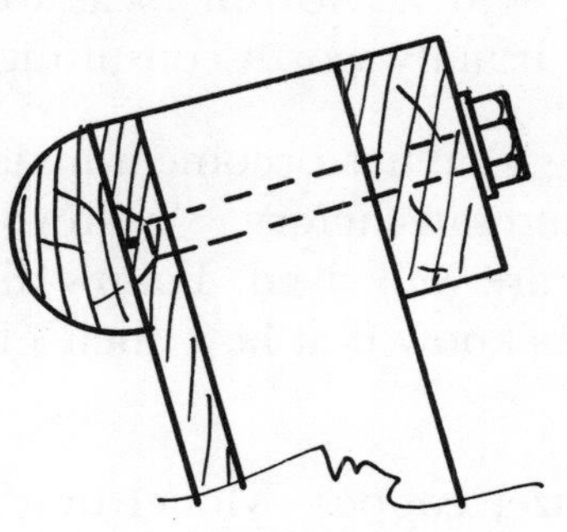

CLAMP BOLTED. GUARD COVERS BOLT HEADS. 1/4" BOLTS.

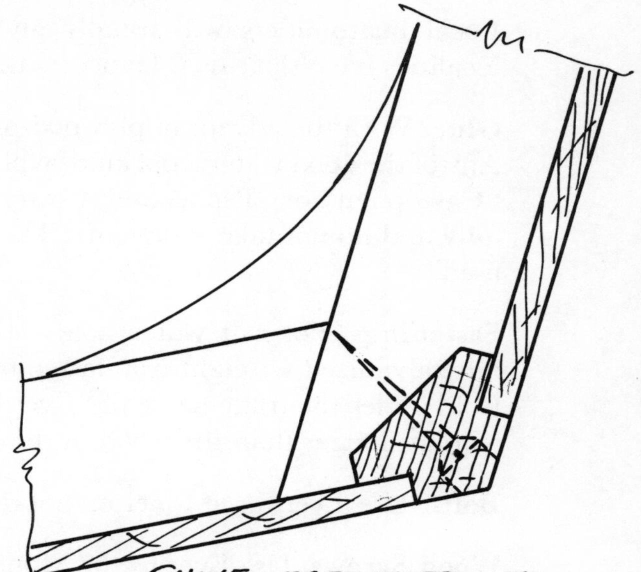

CHINE FASTENED TO FRAME WITH LONG SCREW: HEAD COUNTERSUNK; HOLE PLUGGED.

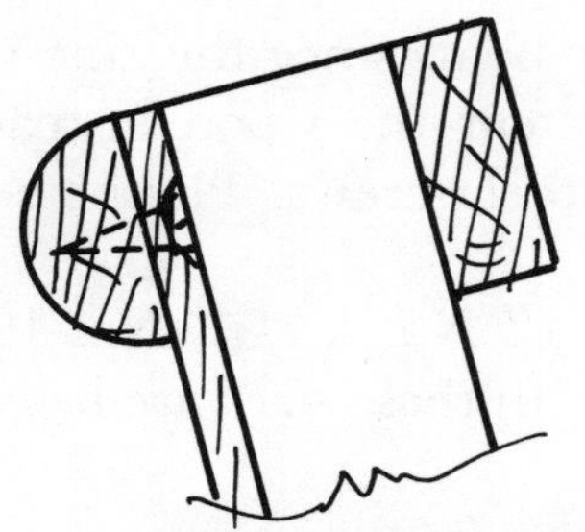

RUBBING STRIP OR GUARD SCREWED FROM INSIDE. SCREWS COME BETWEEN FRAMES, AND MUST BE DRIVEN BEFORE INWALE IS IN PLACE.

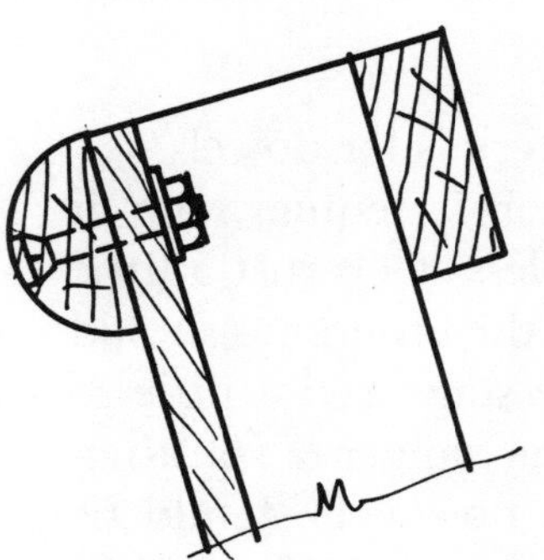

GUARD BOLTED. PUTTY OR PLUG COUNTERSINK HOLES OVER HEADS. THIS METHOD IS USED IF INWALE IS PUT IN BEFORE GUARD. USE 3/16" BOLTS, OR No. 10 MACH. SCRS.

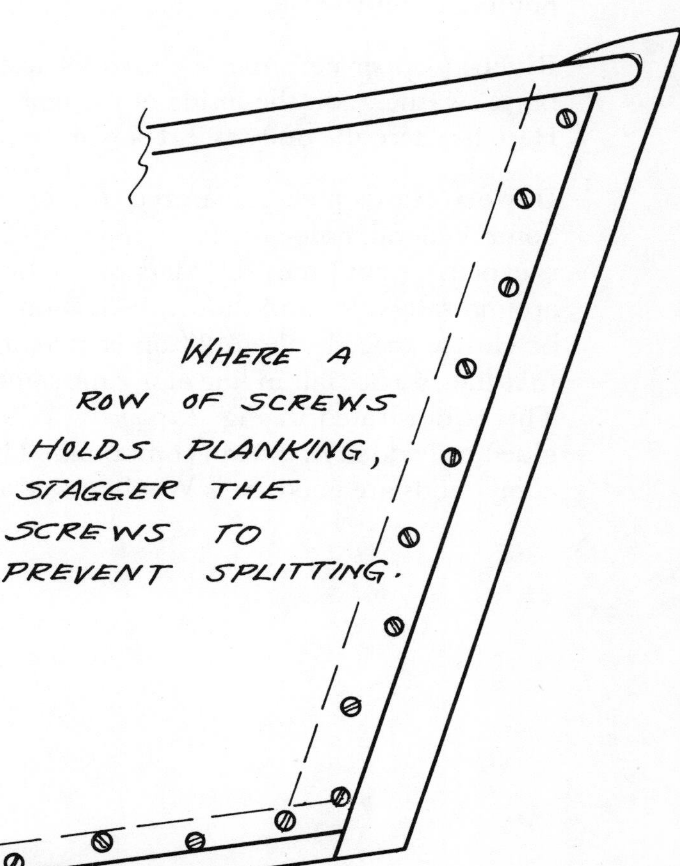

WHERE A ROW OF SCREWS HOLDS PLANKING, STAGGER THE SCREWS TO PREVENT SPLITTING.

Local boatbuilders will usually give you good advice on local woods, and since different localities have their own favorites, they are usually worth consulting.

Glue. With the advent of plywood planking glue has become a major boatbuilding material. Any of the good waterproof kinds will be found satisfactory. "Weldwood" (water resistant) and "Cascophen" or "Penacolite" (waterproof) are well liked. Follow directions on the can carefully and do not take short cuts. The makers know best how their glues should be mixed and used.

Fastenings. For salt water boats use bronze, copper, Monel or (for economy's sake) hot-dip galvanized wrought-iron fastenings. The best fastenings are made of either silicon bronze (sold under the trade name of "Everdur") or Monel metal, a nickel product. They are strong, will last longer than the wood in the boat, and will never show stains on the paint.

Bolts. Use Everdur, Monel or hot-dip galvanized wrought iron.

Wood Screws. Use Everdur or Monel. Do not use brass for salt water boats since the zinc in the metal leaches out, weakening the fastenings. Galvanized screws tear the wood instead of cutting a clean thread in it, and so do not hold as well as smoother screws. Plain steel fastenings should never be used on any boat since they soon rust.

The screw sizes commonly used for boats are: ¾″ No. 6, ⅞″ No. 7, 1″ No. 8, 1¼″ No. 10, 1½″ No. 12, 1¾″ No. 14, 2″ No. 14 or No. 16. Drills suitable for use with these sizes are listed under Tools.

Nails. Wrought-iron hot-dip galvanized boat nails, or "Stronghold" or "Anchorfast" (both serrated) of bronze or Monel are recommended. Do not use smooth bronze or copper nails, as they are likely to pull out too easily. The Independent Nail and Packing Co., Bridgewater, Mass., makes Stronghold and Anchorfast nails and will supply literature on their excellent holding qualities.

Rivets. Copper nails may be used for fastening planks to frames but they should always have burrs (washers) on the inside of the boat where the end of the nail is cut off and riveted over. Here is where the dolly (see Tools) is indispensable.

Dowels. Hardwood, galvanized iron or bronze rod are the common materials for dowels.

Some general notes on fastenings: Stainless steel is sometimes used for fastenings, but it is expensive, and most builders prefer bronze or Monel, also, most stainless steels rust a little around salt water and show brown stains on paint. For watertight seams the fastenings should be closely spaced (about 2″ on centers for ¼″ plywood), and should be staggered a little so that they do not fall in line along the same grain of the wood, to reduce the danger of splitting. This is illustrated in Fig. 2, page 7. Watertight joints (not plank edges, however) should be glued or bedded in a seam compound. The Minnesota Mining and Manufacturing Co. "3M" compounds are good, so is Woolsey's "Cawking."

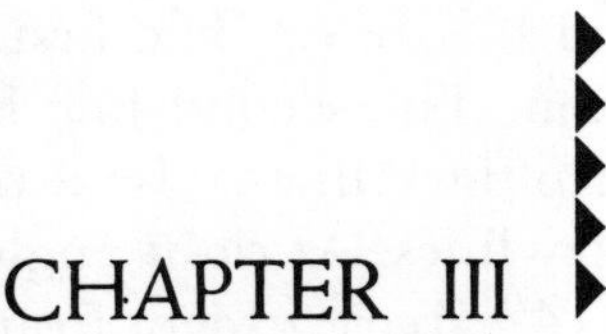

CHAPTER III

Mold Loft Work

Before any work is done on the construction of a boat, the "lines" are drawn full size on a large smooth floor, or on a piece of building paper. This process is known as "laying down the lines," and the floor on which it is done is called the mold loft floor. To the beginner this may look like an unnecessary step, but the better the loft drawing the easier it will be to do the rest of the work, from start to finish.

GENERAL PROCEDURE

In order to illustrate the process of laying down the lines, let us take the little catboat, on pages 102 to 114, as an example. You will find the drawings of this boat marked Plans 11. The mold loftman's job is to copy this drawing in detail, but making it full size, taking all important dimensions from the **offset table.** This will require a sheet of paper large enough to contain a full-size drawing of the boat and leave a little to spare all around. On this drawing should appear the **half breadth plan,** (top view) **elevation** (side view) and **body plan,** or **sections** (revealing the shape of the boat's ribs or frames), together with as much of the construction detail, that is details requiring special attention, as the builder thinks he will need. The more detail you show on this drawing the better.

Any kind of stiff paper good enough to draw on will do, but building paper, which may be had from your local lumber dealer, is what most of the small boatyards use. The size of the sheet required can be figured from the lines drawing and the offset table.

The greatest half breadth of the boat in question is 36⅜″. This is found at frame 7 in the offset table opposite the heading "half breadths, deck." The paper will of course have to be wider than this, say 40″ to 42″ wide.

On the lines drawing the plan view is shown at the bottom of the sheet with the elevation, or side view, above it, and the sections—called the "body plan"—at the right side of the sheet. In reproducing the lines full size it is convenient to draw the elevation on top of the plan, making the base line and center line the same, and using a different colored pencil for each view. Draw the sections (body plan) on a separate sheet of paper. If you draw the whole set of lines on one sheet, the paper usually will be too big to handle conveniently.

This brings us to the length of the paper. The big sheet will be as long as the boat, (in this case, 14′) plus a little extra at the bow, say 1′, and enough extra at the stern to show the rudder in place (as it is shown on the construction plan). For this boat this totals about 16′6″. The smaller sheet, for the body plan, should be equal to the beam of the boat (twice the half breadth) plus a bit extra on each side, say 7′. This makes:

1 large sheet, 42″ x 16′6″ for plan and elevation.

1 small sheet, 42″ x 7′ for the body plan (or sections).

SHEET LAYOUTS

Start with the large sheet. Lay it down smooth and flat and fasten it with weights, Scotch Tape, or thumb tacks. (If you are using the living room floor as a mold loft you had better use Scotch Tape, since thumb tacks will surely get you in trouble right at the start.) Along one 16′6″ side of the paper and 1″ from the edge, snap a chalk line. Snap another line exactly parallel to it and 8″ above. The first line serves as both centerline for the plan and base line for the elevation. The second line is the load waterline in the elevation. Go over these, making them sharp dark lines. Use a pencil sharpened to a chisel point and take care not to make wide or fuzzy lines. At right angles to these two lines draw the station lines, spacing them as indicated, (14″ apart, except from 0 to 1).

To lay out the small sheet for the body plan it is only necessary to draw a centerline up the middle of the 7-foot length of the paper, and a waterline (9 inches from the lower edge) at right angles to the centerline. In all this layout work be sure your right angles are true; a small error can make lots of trouble later on. Label all lines as you draw them.

DRAWING THE FULL-SIZE LINES

Since both sides of a boat are supposed to be symmetrical, designers usually represent only one side when preparing a set of lines. In laying down, or lofting the lines, it is sufficient to do likewise, except in the case of the body plan. Here it is more convenient to show both port and starboard sides of each frame so they can be checked for accuracy before assembly with the keel.

Commence with the body plan. First draw the midship frame, No. 6. From the offset table read the distance of keel below the waterline which is −7¾″ at frame No. 6. (The minus sign means it is below the waterline.) Measure down 7¾″ along the centerline and mark the point. The half breadth of the rabbet at frame No. 6 is 3″. Measure out 3″ from the center line and mark the rabbet point. A line between these points represents the bottom of the keel at frame No. 6. Next lay out the chine point, 1¼″ below the waterline, and 32⅞″ out from the centerline. Draw a line from rabbet point to chine point. Now mark the deck point (up from the waterline 14⅜″, out from centerline 36)″. Connect deck point to chine point. This completes one half of frame No. 6, the lines representing the outside of the planking. Draw all lines lightly at first, and go over them a second time, to darken them, thus it is easy to erase any errors which may occur. Duplicate the lines just drawn on the opposite side of the centerline so that your body plan will show both sides of the boat. To avoid confusion, you had better draw the forward frames in one color and the after ones in another.

There is one more step in laying down the body plan. This is left until the plan and elevation on the large piece of paper are finished, and the body plan has been checked for possible errors. This step, when you come to it, consists of "taking off the planking." This is necessary because your drawing shows the shape and size of the frames to the outside of the planking, while your frames, which are to be made from this drawing, have to fit the inside of the planks. The process is simple enough. You draw from deck to chine, and from chine to keel, lines parallel to the section lines, but ⅜″ inside them; this allows for ⅜″ thick planking. The frames are then made to these inside lines. Number each frame at the deck, chine, and keel, both sides. This prevents you from picking up the wrong point later on when you may be in a hurry.

Next draw the plan view and elevation. Tape down the large sheet of paper on your mold loft floor. (If the rules of the house can be set aside for a day the living room floor, or any other smooth floor, makes a good mold loft.) You already have ruled this sheet with centerline, waterline and frames or stations, so start with the plan view. From frame No. 1 measure forward 14½″ along the centerline and mark the point which represents the boat's bow. Measure out from the centerline ⅛″, and draw the face of the stem, as shown. Now mark on each frame the half breadths of the deck, chine and rabbet, taking dimensions from the offset table. For example, at frame No. 1, the rabbet is out from the centerline 1¼″, the chine 7⅛″, and the deck 11⅝″. Also make a mark at each frame $^{11}/_{16}$ out from the rabbet mark, to represent the half breadth of the keel at that frame. Bend your long batten around each of these sets of points, and draw the deck, chine, keel and rabbet lines duplicating, full size, those on the lines drawing. They should all be fair curves, if they are not, find the error and correct it. This is easier to say than to do and sometimes it takes quite a lot of study to locate the trouble.

Incidently, to hold the batten in place while you draw, some kind of weights will be needed if you don't want to drive brads into your floor. Draftsmen use lead weights (called ducks) of about 2½ lbs. each with brass fingers to engage the batten. These are excellent, but expensive, and for a single job you can get along by resting assorted bits of junk on the batten to hold it while you draw the line. Heavy books will sometimes do. Of course if you are working on a floor where the finish does not matter, you can hold the batten with brads driven into the floor alongside the batten.

Next, mark the points for the elevation drawing in the same manner, and draw the deck, chine, and rabbet using the dimensions shown in the offset table. Draw the plan one color, and elevation another, to prevent confusion. It is suggested that you use black for the elevation since it will have more lines than the plan. On this elevation drawing show the centerboard box, the rudder, mast step, mast, skeg, transom and knee, stem, deck, deck beams, frames, location of chainplates and any other details you may need. These can be put in as you work along or all drawn at first, as you wish. It is better to draw them all full size before you start building, then you can order material from full-size dimensions and know the pieces will fit (see Plan No. 11 Construction Plan). Some boatbuilders do it one way, and some the other, but those who don't lay out the parts full size run the risk of making mistakes. The more detail you put on the loft drawing, the faster the work will go later on.

SOME HINTS ON CHECKING

A little study of the plans will show you that each dimension on the lines appears twice on the finished loft drawing. The half breadths appear both on the body plan and on the longitudinal drawing of the plan, while the heights above or below the load waterline appear on both the profile and the body plan. Wherever a dimension appears twice, the two should agree on the full-size layout. This provides one check: another check of this set of lines can easily be made on the body plan alone; when all the frames have been drawn, the bottom lines should be parallel to one another, and the lines of the sides at each section are also supposed to be parallel. This is not true of all plans, of course. We generally try to get the lines accurate to within an ⅛″. This may not sound very accurate, but it is close enough.

RELY ON YOUR DRAWINGS

Once the loft drawing is made and checked, take your dimensions from it rather than from the small scale prints. The loft drawing should be easier to measure, more accurate and, if the parts fit together on the full-size drawing when you lay the pieces down on the paper, surely they will fit in the boat. If there are any errors on the small scale plans, you should catch them when you lay out the full-size loft drawing and thus save spoiling any wood parts.

CHAPTER IV

The Fabrication of Units Before Assembly

IF YOUR WORKSHOP IS SMALL IT IS FEASIBLE TO MAKE MANY PARTS OF YOUR BOAT DURING the "long winter evenings" in the shop and then, in the spring, to assemble the boat in the garage or even outdoors in the yard. Almost half the work can be done this way, so that once you start the final assembly of the hull, the work will go with encouraging speed. The following methods apply to the fabricating of individual units which will later be assembled into several of the boats in this book.

MAKING THE STEM

The oak for the stem should be the width and thickness shown on the plans you are using, and a couple of inches too long, to allow for final fitting. Figure 3 shows some of the steps

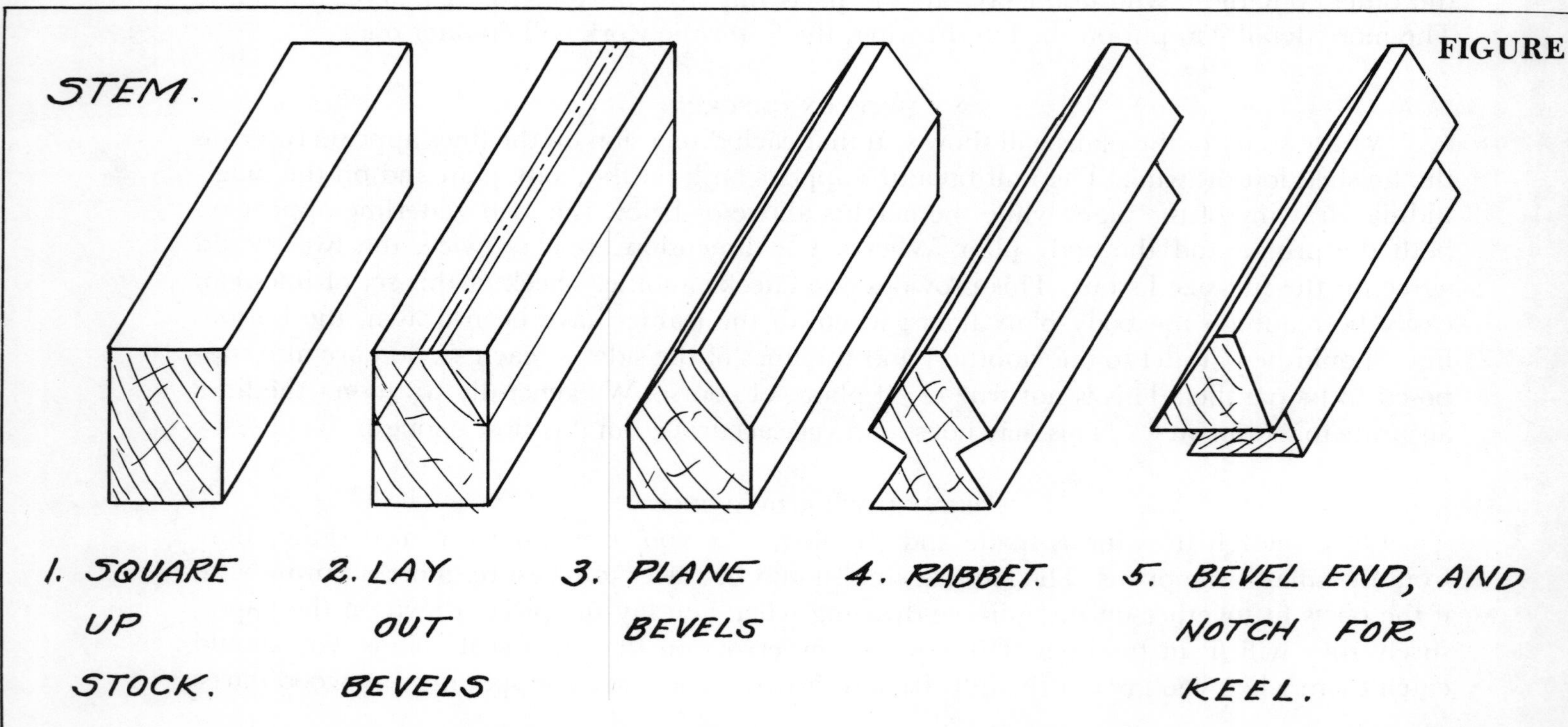

FIGURE
STEM.
1. SQUARE UP STOCK.
2. LAY OUT BEVELS
3. PLANE BEVELS
4. RABBET.
5. BEVEL END, AND NOTCH FOR KEEL.

in making a simple stem. First, square up the stock, then draw a centerline on the side you are going to use as the forward face of the stem. Second, lay out the bevels. Third, rough out the bevels, using chisel and mallet and keeping just outside the lines, but do not smooth the surfaces yet. The beveling can also be done with a hand plane or on a jointer or a circular saw.

Fourth, lay out the lines for the rabbet, and cut the rabbet either on a circular saw or by hand with chisel and mallet. Dimensions for the rabbet are given on the detail of the stem (see plans). Finish the bottom of the cut with a rabbet plane if you have one; if one is not available use a chisel and mallet, and work slowly and carefully. The exact bevel for the bottom should be taken from the loft drawing using an adjustable bevel square. Shellac the stem as soon as it is finished. The final smoothing is done after the boat is planked.

MAKING THE KEEL

The dimensions of the stock for the keel can be taken from the construction plan and the loft drawing. The thickness is specified on the construction plan, and the length and width are shown on the loft plan. Remember to measure length along the curve of the keel, not in a straight line.

Get a good oak plank for your keel, and have it run through the planer at the lumber mill to exact thickness, smooth on both sides but leave the edges rough. Draw a centerline on one of the planed sides. The chalk line does a good job on this. Along this centerline mark the stations for your frames. On the plans the frames are equally spaced, but due to the curve of the keel these distances will vary when measured along the actual line of the keel. If you lay a batten along the keel on the loft drawing and mark on it the exact location of each station, this batten may be laid on top of the keel and the marks transferred accurately. Draw station lines across the keel at right angles to the centerline using a square as a guide.

Mark the half breadth at each frame or station, of both the rabbet and the outside edge

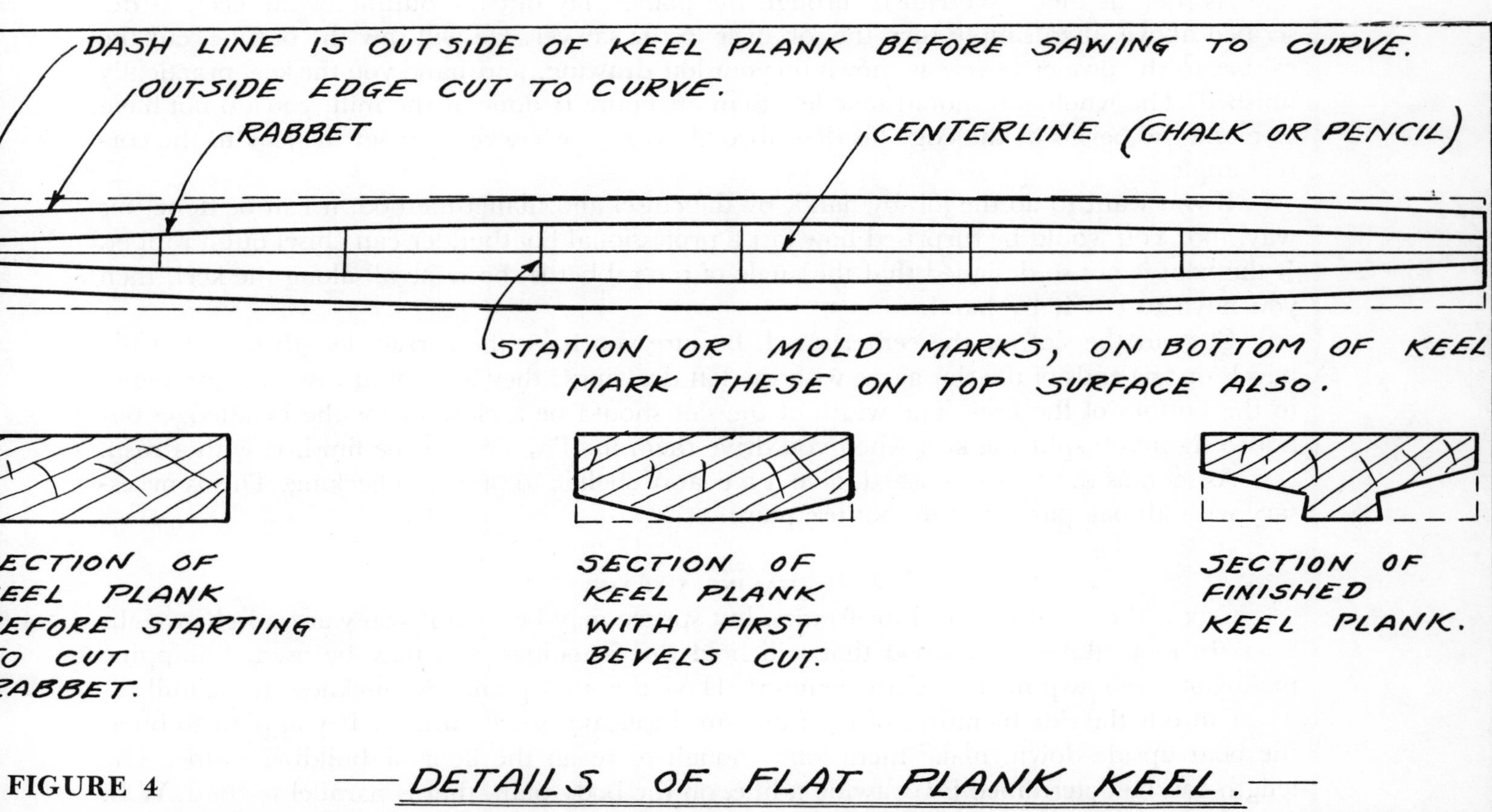

FIGURE 4 —DETAILS OF FLAT PLANK KEEL.—

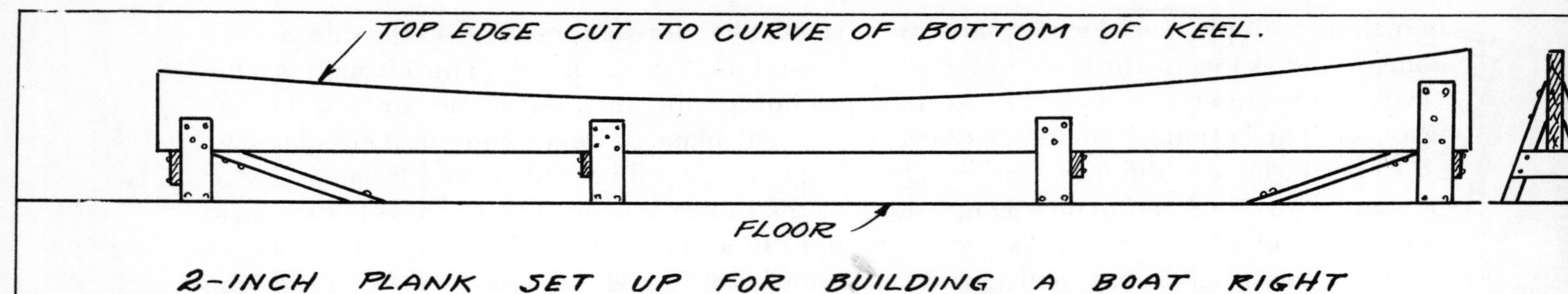
TOP EDGE CUT TO CURVE OF BOTTOM OF KEEL.
FLOOR
2-INCH PLANK SET UP FOR BUILDING A BOAT RIGHT SIDE UP. THE KEEL RESTS ON THIS PLANK, AND IS SCREWED OR WIRED DOWN TO IT DURING CONSTRUCTION.
FIGURE

of the keel. Draw the outline of the keel on the plank, using a batten and brads to hold it and a chisel-pointed pencil. If the boat has a centerboard, lay out the slot while you are working on the keel layout. Trim the keel plank to the outside lines, and cut the bevel on its forward end to fit the stem. Leave the after end about an inch too long, to trim off later.

Set the bevel square to the angle between the keel and bottom planking, and plane the bevel on each side from the rabbet line out. This gives you a flat surface parallel to the face of the boat's planking which later can be rested on the circular saw table when cutting the rabbet, thus making the saw cut at right angles to the hull planking. If your saw has an adjustable arbor or an adjustable table, this hand beveling will not be necessary.

If you do not have a circular saw, you can save yourself a lot of work and time by taking the keel to the mill and having them saw the rabbets on both sides for you. You will get a smooth job with good sharp corners, and the cost is not enough to worry about. In fact, the whole keel can be fabricated at the mill to advantage. Take your loft drawing and batten along with you when you go.

As soon as they have run it through the planer, lay out the outline of the keel, as described above, then simply turn the job over to the sawyer. He will saw the outline, cut the rabbet to the proper bevel, as shown on your loft drawing, and hand you the keel practically finished. The whole job should take less than an hour. If done at the mill, you do not have to plane the bevels at the edge (as described above)—the sawyer can set the saw to the correct angle.

If you want to do the job by hand, by the chisel and mallet method, it can be done this way, too. You would be surprised how fast a professional boatbuilder can chisel out a rabbet. If the boat is not so designed that the angle of the rabbet is the same all along the keel, then you have to cut it by hand.

Cut out the slot for the centerboard. Be sure you have the correct length and that the bevels on the ends of the slot agree with the loft drawings; they are not always at right angles to the bottom of the keel. The width of the slot should be a close fit for the headledges but not so tight you split the keel when you drive them in. The slot can be finished with a rasp.

As soon as the keel is finished, give it a coat of shellac to prevent checking. This is necessary with all oak parts, but do not use paint.

MAKING A FRAME

Oak is the usual material for frames, but spruce may be used if you want a light-weight boat. In fact, almost any wood that will hold the fastenings well may be used. Philippine mahogany, yellow pine, fir, all are common. Have the stock planed to thickness at the mill.

Cut out the side members of the frame in duplicate (see Figure 6). If you plan to build the boat upside down, make them long enough to reach the floor or building frame. The length can be determined by drawing a line, on the body plan, that is parallel to the L.W.L.

FIGURE 6

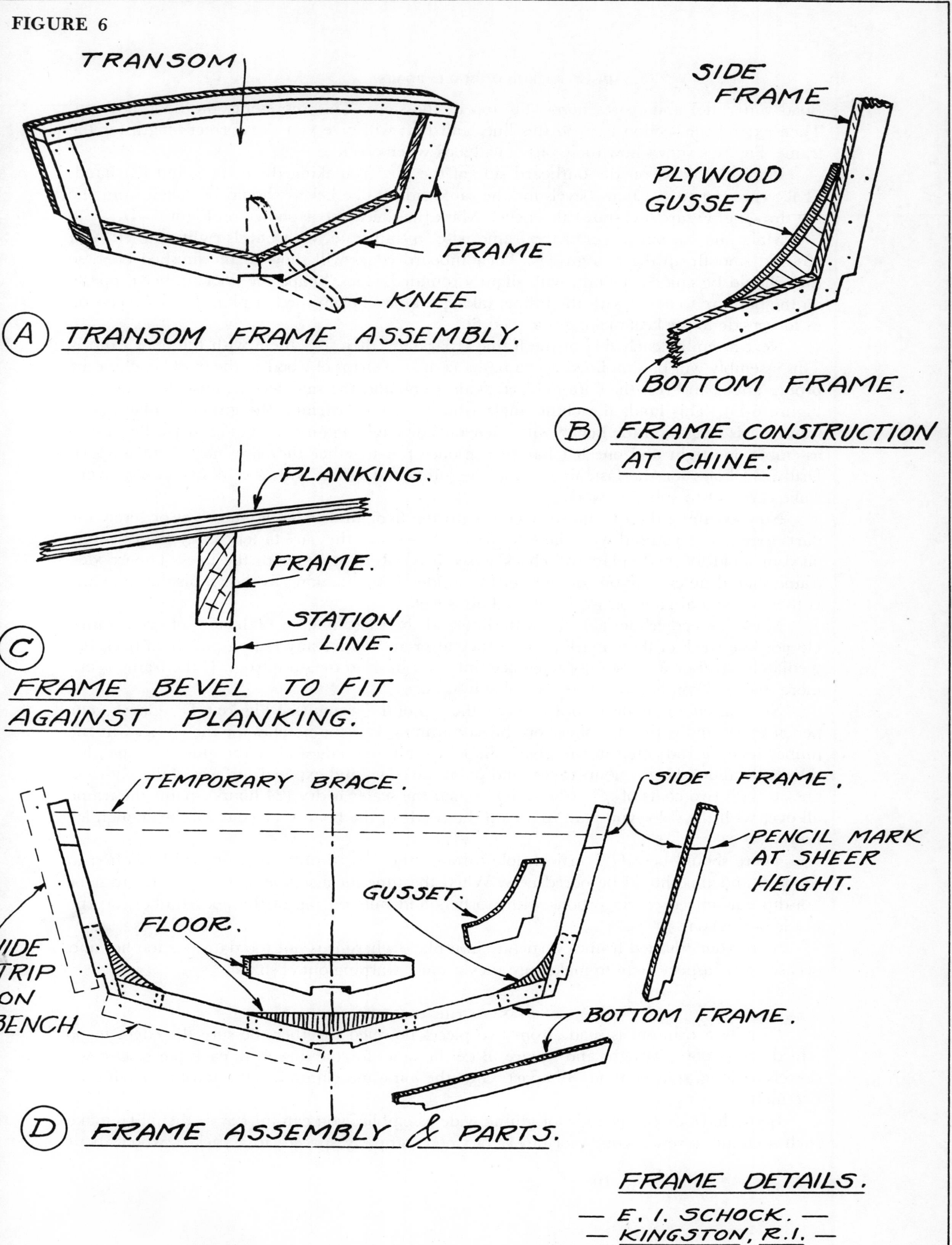
TRANSOM
FRAME
KNEE
A TRANSOM FRAME ASSEMBLY.
SIDE FRAME
PLYWOOD GUSSET
BOTTOM FRAME.
B FRAME CONSTRUCTION AT CHINE.
PLANKING.
FRAME.
STATION LINE.
C
FRAME BEVEL TO FIT AGAINST PLANKING.
TEMPORARY BRACE.
SIDE FRAME.
PENCIL MARK AT SHEER HEIGHT.
GUSSET.
FLOOR.
IDE
TRIP
ON
BENCH
BOTTOM FRAME.
D FRAME ASSEMBLY & PARTS.
FRAME DETAILS.
— E. I. SCHOCK. —
— KINGSTON, R.I. —

(load waterline) and passes across the top of the stem. This represents the floor position. Then extend the section lines to this line, and that will give you the correct length for the frame. Figure 6 shows how these pieces will look when erected.

Plane the bevel on the outboard side of the pieces, making them right and left hand. (Take care not to cut both bevels for the same side.) The bevels should be taken from the loft drawing. Figure 6-C shows this bevel. Mark the sheer line as shown on Figure 6-D.

Make the bottom pieces of the frame, also in duplicate, with bevels right and left. Cut out and smooth up the two gussets. Their inboard edges will show in the finished boat, so they should be sanded smooth, with slightly rounded edges. Shape the floor timber properly on the bottom, to agree with the frame, taking the bevel from the loft plan. Fit the recess on its lower side to the keel making it a good fit.

Next assemble each side of the frame separately, then join them with the floor timber. This assembly will be simplified if you nail a couple of strips of wood to the workbench at the proper angle, and rest the bottom piece against one and the sidepiece against the other (see Figure 6-D). This holds the chine angle while you are fastening the gusset in place. The frame parts lie flat on the bench with their outside edges against the guide strips. Be sure to assemble one right and one left hand since once put together they are hard to take apart. Drill lead holes for the fastenings, glue the joint, and fasten with screws or copper rivets. Take care not to split the wood.

Now assemble the two finished sides with the floor timber. Glue and rivet or screw the parts together as you did with the side pieces. As soon as they are fastened, lay the assembly on your mold loft body plan and check to see if the work agrees with the lines. The wooden frame should lie exactly on the lines of the inside of the planking as shown on the drawing. If they do, you are a good workman and all is well.

Mark the centerline, also the waterline and the sheer line on both sides of each frame. Do not lose track of these marks, and if they are removed for any reason put them back immediately, as they are the only reference lines you have to measure from. If the frame is out more than 1/8″ you had better re-assemble it at once.

Next fasten a temporary brace across the top of the frame (see Figure 6-D). Check your pencil marks indicating the sheer on the side frames. Cut the notches for the chine. Cut the limber holes as indicated in the plans. Smooth the rough edges after the glue sets (the glue should be allowed eight hours to set) and paint the edges and exposed surfaces of the plywood gussets with two coats of plywood sealer. When the sealer is dry (24 hours), paint the frame all over with the color you plan to use on the inside of the boat. One coat will be enough for now.

There should be a 1/4″ vertical hole through the floor timber where it will be bolted to the keel and this should be bored now. When the time for assembly comes, use Everdur or hot-dip galvanized carriage bolts with washers and nuts on top of the floor timber, on the inside of the boat.

Store your finished frames vertically in a place where it is not too damp or too hot and occasionally inspect them to make sure they are not warping out of shape.

MAKING THE TRANSOM

Usually a transom is made from two pieces doweled together. Be sure the edges to be joined are smooth, straight and square. Bore the holes for the dowels in each piece. Use 3/8″ dowels 6″ long, spaced about 8″ apart. Glue the joint and clamp it tight and let the glue set overnight.

If you have no bar clamps for gluing wide assemblies you can improvise them. To make such a clamp, screw a couple of blocks of wood, properly spaced, to a stick of wood about

1½″ by 2″. Make two or three clamps and have the blocks spaced about 1½″ further apart than the width of the transom assembly to be glued. Clamping action will be achieved by driving a pair of wedges between the transom edge and one of the blocks. Prevent the transom bending by securing with C clamps during the clamping period. Of course, if your transom is made from a single piece of wood this operation will not be necessary. A piece of mahogany plywood makes an excellent transom.

Mark the outline of the transom on your piece, working from a centerline, and taking the dimensions from the loft plan. Remember that the forward edge of the transom is wider than the after one (the plan shows the afterside) so you have to allow for this bevel when cutting. Plane the stock for the inner transom frame and cut it to fit. Figure 6-A shows this. Again watch out for bevels—allow enough wood and bevel in the right direction. Now plane the bevels on the sides and bottom, taking the angles from the loft plan with the bevel square. Use care to have the surfaces smooth, straight and flat. Good work here prevents leaks later on. Notch the transom to fit the keel.

Now make the transom knee, using natural hackmatack or apple if you can get it. If you have a good neighbor who has an apple orchard, a fine apple knee can often be had for the asking. If a natural knee is not to be had a piece of plywood with ¾″ square strips glued and riveted along its edges also makes a good knee, and it is strong and light. The transom knee on the construction plan of Plan No. 12 (page 123) is of this type. Secure the transom knee to the keel and transom when assembling them with 2½″ or 3″ Everdur screws driven from outside. Paint the transom when it is finished.

MAKING THE CENTERBOARD BOX, OR TRUNK

This is not a difficult job, but it must be exceptionally well fitted, strong and watertight. A poorly fitted centerboard box will leak, and it will be difficult to make it tight again once it starts leaking. So take your time and make this a masterpiece.

The box consists of bed logs at the bottom on each side, headledges or posts at each end, and the sides. Its construction is shown in Figure 7. Commence with the headledges, leaving them long enough to extend through the keel, to be sawed off later. Where they go through the keel they should fit the slot so that a light blow with a mallet is needed to drive them in. However, if they are too tight they will split the keel, if too lose they will leak. Next make the bed logs, carefully fitting the bottom edges to the curve of the keel as shown on the loft drawing, and planing these edges smooth and square across. Again remember that you are trying to make a watertight joint, and water can get through a surprisingly small crack. Temporarily assemble the two headledges in final position in the keel slot. Put the bed logs in position and clamp them to the headledges. Drill for the fastenings which will hold these four members together when finally assembled. Now drill ¼″-diam. holes, spaced about 5″ through bed logs and keel, to receive carriage bolts in the final assembly (see Fig. 7). The four members may then be removed, ready for final assembly of the whole box.

Cut the side pieces to shape, leaving them 1/16″ long at each end for planing smooth after assembly and fasten them to the bed logs. Glue the joints, or set them in seam compound, and bolt them with countersunk head machine screws, the countersink on the inside. When finished, the inside of the box must be smooth. Wood screws are sometimes used for this joint, but if they work loose you cannot get inside the box to tighten them; with bolts having nuts and washers on the outside, they may be tightened. Fig. 7 shows a detail of this joint. Now fasten one side to the headledges with screws and set the joint in glue or seam compound. (Seam compounds are made by several manufacturers and are specially intended for making seams watertight. The "3M" brand (made by Minnesota Mining & Mfg. Co.) is very good. Consult your paint store man.)

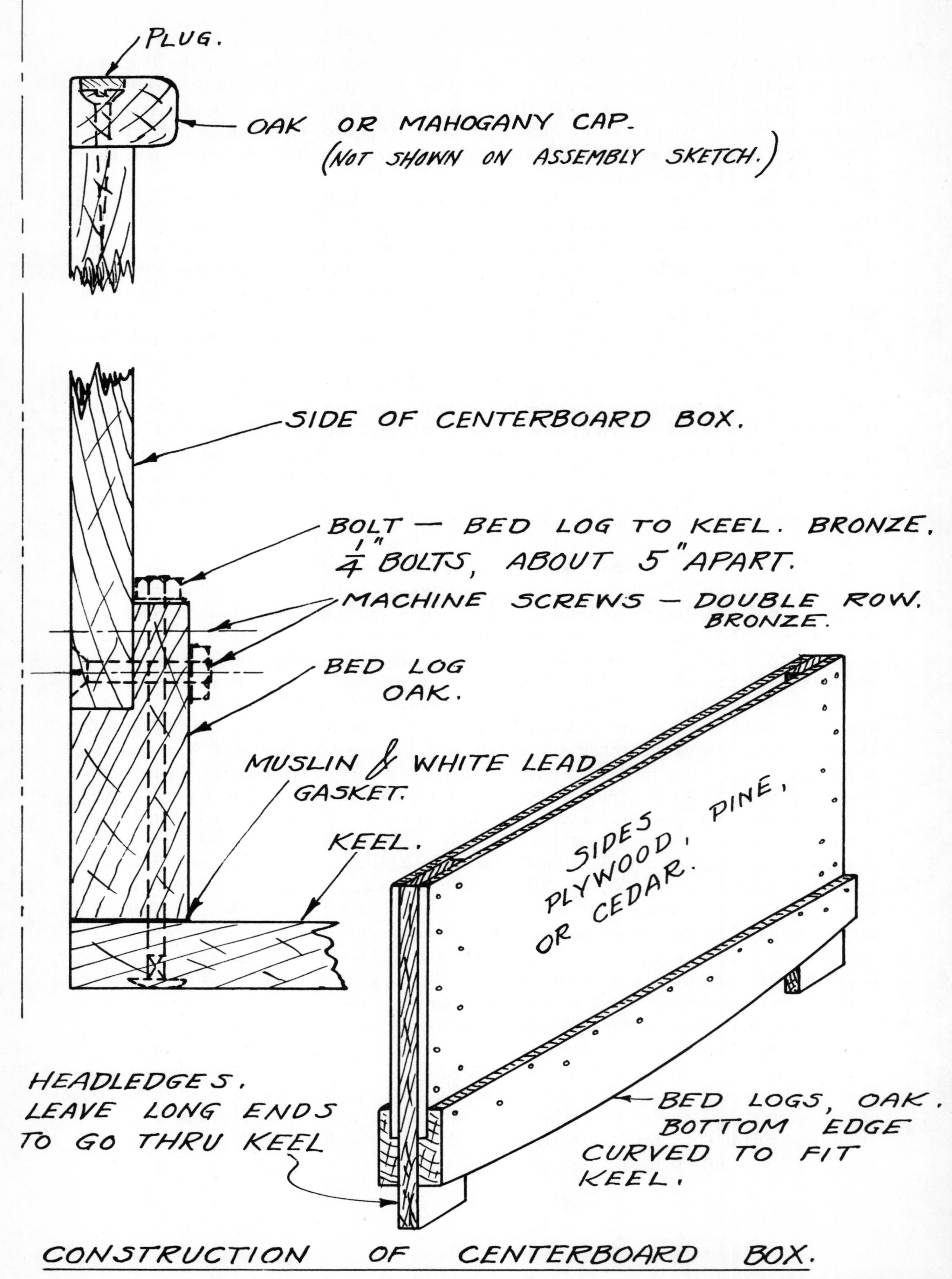

CONSTRUCTION OF CENTERBOARD BOX.

E. I. SCHOCK.

Before putting on the other side of the box, paint the whole inside with three coats of copper bottom paint. When painting the side not yet assembled, be sure you do not cover the area where the seam compound will go when you assemble it. Seam compound, or glue, will not stick as well to paint as to bare wood. Now complete the assembly quickly, before the glue sets. Screw the second side in place, and through-bolt the bed logs to the headledges. Tighten all screws and bolts until the glue, or seam compound, squeezes out all along the seams. Plane the ends of the centerboard box, sandpaper the whole thing, and paint it. If there are any bolt-ends protruding, saw them off, and file the ends smooth. Bore the hole for the centerboard hinge pin in the bed logs and fasten on the plates (shown in Fig. 12), setting them in seam compound, or white lead paste. The trunk cap, which is only a finish or decorative piece, is usually left until the boat is almost completed, so that there will be no danger of scarring it as you work.

Before installing the centerboard box in the boat, make full length gaskets of muslin to fit between the bed logs and the keel, cutting holes to line up with the bolt holes in the keel. Cover the gaskets with white lead paste on both sides and press them down lightly in their proper position on top of the keel. Gently lower the centerboard box into place, being careful not to disturb the gaskets. (By this time your hands, overalls, and much of the surrounding neighborhood probably will be covered with white lead paste, which is slippery, so do not drop things.) Drive the headledges gently into the keel slot until the bed logs rest firmly on the keel, with paste squeezing out, but with the gaskets still in place. Do not tackle this alone if you can avoid it, a helper is very useful here. Drive in the carriage bolts from below, put on the washers and nuts and pull the logs down tight. If your carriage bolts are too long to just reach through the keel, gasket, bed log, washer and nut, saw them off and file the ends smooth before driving them into position. When this is done you should feel as though you had accomplished something worth while. A well-built centerboard box should stay tight, and if you have done a good job, you will not be troubled by leaks.

MAKING THE CENTERBOARD

The centerboard may be of bronze, steel plate, or wood, but most people prefer the wooden ones. If they are well made of good material they do not warp, at least not enough to cause trouble by jamming in the centerboard box.

Oak or dense southern pine (long-leaf Georgia pine), in planks about 4″ or 5″ wide, will make a good board. Be sure to get seasoned wood and specify "edge grain" when you order, and have the stock planed to the required thickness. A centerboard detail is shown with the plans of the 15-foot knockabout, Plan 12 (page 119). Centerboards for the other boats in this book would be the same general type of construction.

Lay your stock on the mold loft plan, and mark the correct size and shape of the centerboard on it. It is easier to do if you cut out or trace the centerboard outline from the drawing and lay it on the wood. You can certainly see what you are doing better this way. If edge grain lumber is not to be had and you are forced to buy slash grain stock, be sure in placing the planks, to reverse the grain in alternate planks, as shown on the drawing. This reduces the tendency to warp. It is also important that the plank edges be square, so that the finished board will be flat. If the lumber is ordered S4-S (surfaced four sides), it will have square edges.

After the planks composing the centerboard have been cut a little oversize, and the outline of the board has been marked on them, comes the time to drill holes for the dowels which will hold them together. This is easier said than done. If you have a lathe, drill the individual pieces between centers, with the drill in the headstock and the tailstock center holding the board in line. With this set up drill half way through, then reverse and drill the rest of the hole from the opposite side. If you are drilling or boring by hand, do the best you can to go straight in. Sight along the edges of the board. With narrow boards you should not have trouble. For dowels you can use galvanized steel rods driven in tight. Remember to have no dowels in the way of the hole for the lead. Glue the plank edges with good waterproof glue, and clamp the whole assembly tight allowing overnight for the glue to set. Follow the same procedure as recommended for gluing the transom so the centerboard does not warp when you tighten the clamps. Inspect it half an hour later to be sure that it is behaving itself.

The next operation is to trim the edges with a saw and plane them smooth. The top and forward edges should be rounded and the bottom and after edges, where the board will reach below the keel, should be streamlined to a fairly sharp edge. This streamlined edge will improve the boat's speed and reduce any tendency of the centerboard to shimmy.

Cut out the hole for the lead and bevel the edges to a "V" to hold the lead casting in place after it has cooled. Do not drive nails into the edges of the hole to hold the lead. They will corrode or rust and allow the casting to drop out.

To cast the lead weight into the centerboard lay it on a flat, level surface with a piece of wood clamped tight to the under side of the hole. Tuck a little putty or modeling clay around the edges where the molten lead might leak out. Molten lead will run through the smallest crack. Do not test the hole with water, however, as any dampness will form steam and make the lead splatter, which might give you a nasty burn. Rub the exposed wood with chalk to keep the lead from scorching it.

The lead can be melted with almost any kind of fire, as it melts quite easily. An old saucepan will do for a crucible, but be sure its handle is strong enough to hold the weight of the lead. Be careful. Pour the molten lead into the hole in the centerboard, until it is full and bulging a little over the top edges. Again, be careful. Keep your hands covered with heavy work gloves, and your feet well back, where a little spilled lead will not burn them. Wear heavy shoes, not sneakers. When the casting is cold and hard, hammer the edges all around to make it a tight fit around the edge of the hole, using the dolly to back up your hammering. Now plane the lead smooth all over. The lead cuts easily and does not harm the plane iron, except to dull it a little. In fact lead is easier to plane than some hard woods. Use a light cut, and oil the bottom of the plane by wiping it on an oily rag.

Bore the hole for the centerboard pin. Make it 1/16″ larger in diameter than the pin, for a loose fit. Attach the lifting straps (located as shown on the construction plan) and the 3/8″ diameter manila rope pennant for lifting it. The correct length for the pennant can be determined as follows: let the board down until the after corner at the upper edge is even with the bottom of the keel. This is "all the way down." Put a stop on the pennant to prevent the board from going beyond this point. A good stop can be made by making a hole through a solid sponge rubber ball (go to the toy store for this), putting the rope through it and knotting it on both sides to keep the ball in place. This is better than a wooden block for a stop, as it won't hurt your bare feet if you step on it accidentally.

That part of the centerboard which is under the water when the boat is at anchor with the centerboard all the way up should have three coats of copper bottom paint. The rest should have three coats of deck paint. Store the board on edge, not flat. If stored flat someone might pile things on it, causing it to warp.

MAKING THE RUDDER

This is made in the same manner as the centerboard, but since it is smaller, it is less work. It should be made of strong hardwood such as oak or hard pine. For a varnished (stylish) rudder you can use Philippine mahogany. If the rudder is shallow and wide the boards should run horizontally and if it is deep and narrow they should be vertical or parallel to its leading edge. The deep type of rudder can often be made of a single board, and no doweling will be necessary. If rudders are well streamlined by sharpening both forward and after edges, they do not tend to warp. No matter what kind of rudder you make, do a good streamlining job on it. It will be a pleasure to see how smoothly the water passes the rudder, without eddies or bubbles.

While you are finishing the rudder you can be thinking about the tiller. This should be of straight-grain locust, oak, hickory, ash or elm, nicely sanded and varnished. No special instructions are needed for this, except to say that a heavy tiller is clumsy and unnecessary. A tiller tapered to 1″ diameter at the small (inboard) end is sufficiently strong and looks neat. Five coats of varnish are recommended for this piece, with light sandpapering between coats. The rudder itself gets three coats of bottom paint below the waterline and three of varnish or topside paint to match the boat above the water. The hardware can be attached after the boat is finished and you are ready to hang the rudder.

PLANKING

Fir plywood seems to be the best planking material for amateur boatbuilders to use. If a boat is properly designed for plywood, planking it is quick and easy, but if she is not so designed you had better plank her the conventional way. A few words are in order here on the design of plywood boats.

Plywood sheets bend easily in one direction, but if you try to bend them in two directions at once, they resist your efforts effectively. Therefore, a plywood boat should be so designed that the planking need be bent in only one direction. Two geometric forms may be produced by using single bends—the cylinder or the cone. Hence, the sides and bottom of these little plywood boats have to be segments of the surface of either a cylinder or a cone, and because of this characteristic it is easy to apply the planking. If the designer departs from these fundamental surfaces, the boat becomes hard, if not impossible, to build, and in some cases the plywood may require steaming to force it into a shape it does not want to assume. Most amateurs do not want to go to the trouble of rigging up a steam box, and for the boats in this book none is necessary. There is a note on the selection and purchasing of marine plywood in the chapter on materials. Read this again before you buy.

Now to lay out the plank for the side of a boat. Let us take Plan No. 11 as an example. You will find a drawing of the shape of the side plank among the plans of this boat, marked "true shape of sides before bending." This drawing is a geometric development of the cylindrical surface of the side of the boat, but don't let that worry you—just go ahead and use it. There is a straight line down the middle of the drawing. Start with this. Either on one of your plywood panels, or on a piece of paper, draw this line full size. Mark along it the station points for the frames, following the dimensions given on the development. At each frame station draw a cross line at right angles to the reference line. Measure the dimensioned distances on each of these lines, thus getting the points for the outline of the plank. Bend a batten around these points and draw the curve of the top and bottom of the plank. Mark and draw the diagonal cut for the bow.

Saw out this plank (use a fine tooth saw to minimize splintering), allowing about ¼″ extra all around for smoothing and fairing the edges later on. Cut one plank from each of your two panels. (Each panel will make one side and one bottom plank.) Do not cut both sides from one panel, or you will not have pieces left big enough for the bottom planks. After the sides and bottoms have been cut from the panels there will be sufficient scrap left to make all the knees and gussets required.

If the plywood looks better on one side than on the other, put the good side out and the poor side inside the boat. Mark the right-hand side S for Starboard—and the left-hand one P for Port. Draw the line of each frame on the inside of each plank. You will need these lines later to locate the frames when you come to assemble the boat. Paint the panels all over with plywood sealer and sandpaper them lightly. The sealer is like thin varnish and sufficiently transparent to leave the reference lines visible.

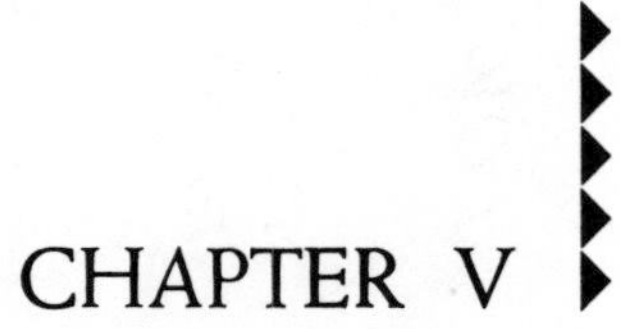

CHAPTER V

Spar Making

THE BEST SPAR MATERIAL IS STRAIGHT-GRAINED SITKA SPRUCE. THE MAST WE ARE ABOUT TO discuss is really a very long box, so try to get planks long enough so that scarphs will not be required. If long lengths are not available, the individual pieces may be scarphed as shown on the mast drawing for Plan No. 12, but do not scarph the mast unless it is necessary. Have your stock planed to the required thickness by the mill.

MAKING THE MAST

Lay out the two side pieces. These should be straight on the after edge, and have a long convex taper on the forward edge. Take dimensions from the mast drawings. Cut and plane these pieces to shape being sure the edges are square.

Lay out and saw the side pieces, smooth the edges and plane them square. The fit between the pieces of the mast must be good, as we rely entirely on the glued joint for strength, consequently this joint must be well fitted before it is glued if it is going to hold. Make the filler pieces to go inside, where shown on the plans. Chamfer the corners of all fillers (except the very top one) to act as drains if any water should get inside the mast.

To assemble the mast you need a level floor or bench. The best surface is a long, narrow, straight workbench. It should be absolutely level, and in one plane, not warped or twisted, as the mast will follow the shape of the bench, and the mast must be straight. If such a bench is not available (and probably it is not) the job can be done on a level floor.

Get your supplies together, and be sure you have enough of everything. Once you start you must work fast, and there is no time for running around getting organized. Boatbuilders use only glue to fasten a hollow spar together and this means it must be held with clamps while the glue sets. If you have enough clamps (one for every six inches of length of mast) get them all set at about the right opening. If you are short of clamps, you can nail the sides on with galvanized finish nails, six-penny size, spaced about 2″ or 2½″ apart. These hold the joint tight while the glue sets and may be left in the mast. When the glue has set, go around with a nailset and drive each in a little way and putty the holes. If you are nailing the joints instead of clamping them have the nails and the hammer handy to hand.

Round up three helpers and have a separate pot of glue and an old brush as a glue spreader for each to use. Have some old newspapers for the glued mast to rest on, and plenty of rags to wipe any glue off the floor, fingers, clothes, hammer handle, and any other places where it is likely to stick. Also have a piece of string longer than the mast ready to act as a guide. The brushes must have stiff bristles, like a toothbrush.

FIGURE 8

GLUING MAST.

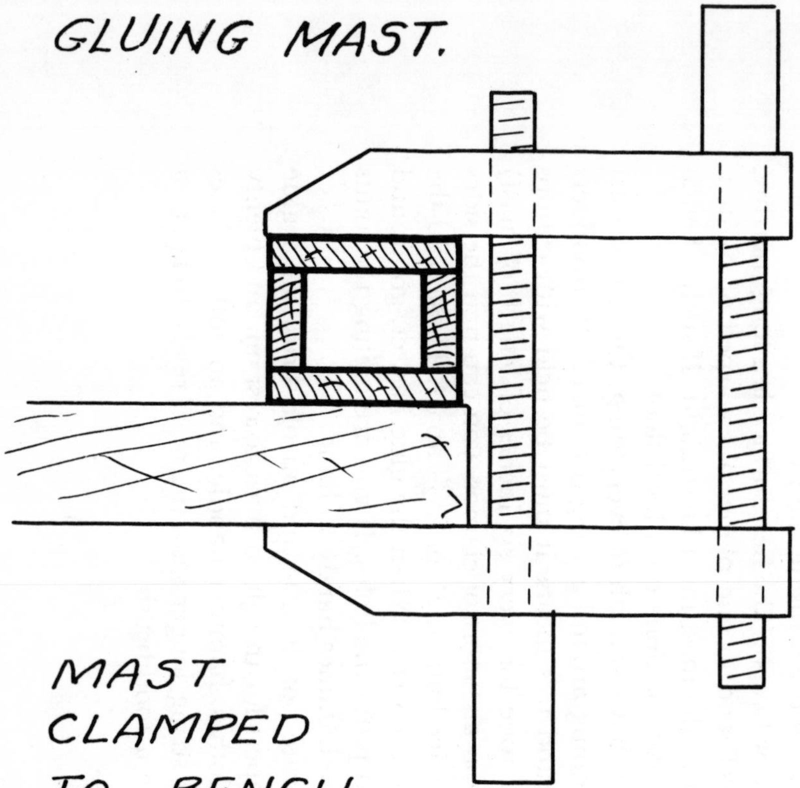

MAST
CLAMPED
TO BENCH.

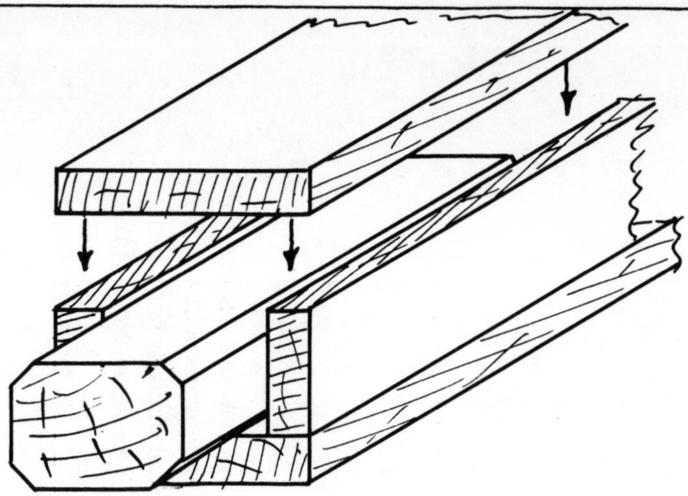

ASSEMBLY OF LOWER
END OF MAST.
NOTE BEVELS FOR DRAINS.

MASTHEAD.

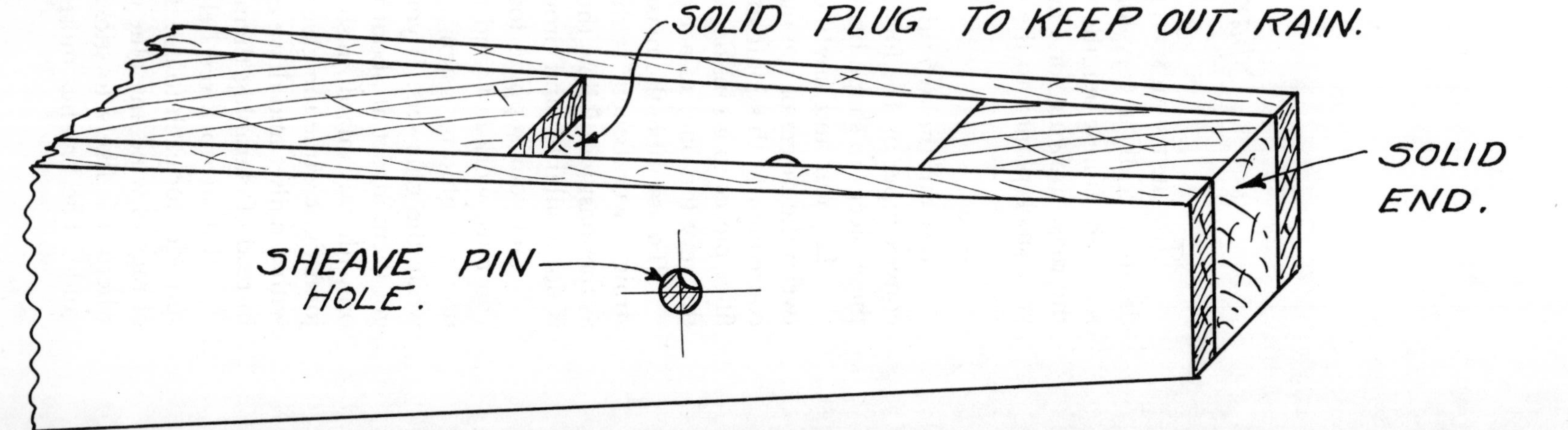

When everybody is ready, stand the two end pieces side by side, on edge on the bench while all hands spread glue on the top edges. Spread glue also on the side piece where it is to go on these edges. (When gluing two pieces of wood together, always put glue on both pieces.) While two helpers hold the string straight for a guide, you and the other helper nail the side piece on to the two upright end pieces, keeping the after edge straight with the string. Instead of using string, a chalk line can be snapped on the bench, but if you put newspapers under the work to protect the bench or floor, these will of course cover the chalk line. This is why the string is used. Turn the mast over and put the inside blocks in place where they belong, with a little dab of glue to hold them. Next spread the glue on the parts for the opposite side, and nail it on, keeping the after side straight as before. Let the glue set overnight or longer.

If you are using a bench where you can clamp the mast to the bench while the glue sets, the procedure will be about the same except that the first side you put on will be held with a few nails while you turn the mast over and clamp the whole assembly to the bench. These nails will be withdrawn and the holes plugged after the glue has set.

Plane the corners round all along each edge, but do not round them much. A quarter inch radius is enough, and in any case the radius should not be more than half the thickness of the mast wall.

Sandpaper well, and paint or varnish. If the spar is stored horizontally, be sure it is well supported at five points at least and that it is straight while in storage. Careless storage will warp and spoil the mast.

The hardware can be put on at any time after varnishing the spar. The gooseneck may be bolted through the mast with two ¼″ bolts, or screwed on with long screws. The masthead sheave must fit its slot closely, yet it must run freely and be straight in the throat, without rubbing on the sides. The track and cleats are put on with woodscrews, ⅝″ roundhead screws for the track, and 2″ flathead screws for cleats. If you plan to have a masthead wind vane do not put it on until the boat is overboard, and you are ready to step the mast. If put on ahead of time, it will probably be damaged. (See Fig. 16, page 35 for such a vane).

MAKING THE BOOM

The Boom is a little one-evening job. Get a good straight-grained stick of spruce, big enough to make a spar of the required dimensions. Lay out the side elevation on the side of the stick, having it straight along the edge which will be on top. Cut the curve of the bottom, and plane it smooth both top and bottom. Looking at it from the top it should taper a little toward each end. Plane this taper, then round the corners slightly, sandpaper smooth all over, and it is ready for varnish.

Three coats of varnish may do—four will be better. Sand very lightly with fine paper between each coat. Fit the outhaul, track, gooseneck, and sheet blocks according to the plans. Be careful to have the gooseneck securely fastened on: if it works loose you may tear your sail, and it has to take quite a beating at times when you are sailing.

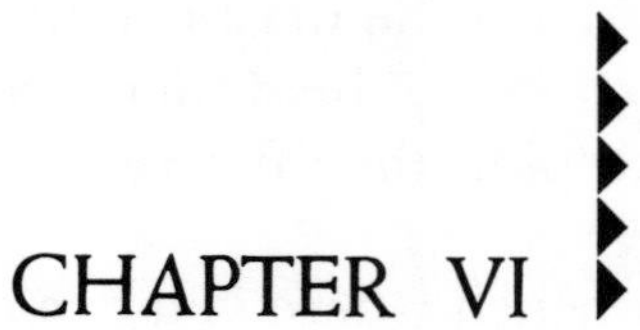

CHAPTER VI

Sails and Fittings

THERE IS AN OLD SAYING TO THE EFFECT THAT IT IS EASIER TO BUILD A BOAT THAN MAKE A sail. Whether this is true or not, a sailmaker can make a better sail than you can—unless you happen to be the exception that proves the rule. If your budget will allow it, have your sails professionally made since much of your boat's success depends on her sails and you should have the best you can afford. Names and addresses of sailmakers may be found in the advertising sections of such magazines as *Rudder* and *Yachting*.

Send the sailmaker a sketch or a freehand tracing of the sail plan of your boat, with full dimensions, and ask for an estimate. Light Egyptian cotton sailcloth is what is most desirable for small boat sails. Sailcloth made from American duck is also good, and is a little cheaper. Order your sails in the fall for spring delivery; the sailmaker then will have time to do a good job during the winter. If you wait until spring you will be caught in the rush of late orders, and you may be disappointed on delivery.

If you decide you want to make your own sails buy a copy of Alan Gray's book, *Sailmaking Simplified* and follow his directions. The author has made several sails from Gray's directions and they all came out very well. Don't take the advice of the local "experts" but do it just the way the book says. You may get a good job, but it will take you quite a lot of time, as there is some hand stitching to do that you will find goes pretty slowly.

Gray has a chapter on the care of sails, too. Don't skip it. Another good book on sails is *Yacht Sails: Their Care and Handling* by Ratsey and de Fontaine. Mr. Ratsey is one of our very best sailmakers, and Mr. de Fontaine is an editor of *Yachting*. Between them they have turned out a fine and useful book for old hand or amateur. Harvey Flint's book, *Winning Sailboat Races* also has a good chapter on the care of sails, both during the summer and while in winter storage. Put these books on your reading list. Whether you are using sails made by a professional or an amateur, take care of them.

For your first sail select a sunny day with a very light wind, and stretch your sails gently. Detailed instructions for this are in the books mentioned above. Never keep wet sails in a bag, but spread them out to dry each night, somewhere indoors. When storing them for the winter if they are soiled, wash them gently by hand with fresh water, and when dry, fold them carefully and store them in a clean, dry place where rats cannot reach them.

FITTINGS

Hardware

For the boatbuilder whose hobby shop is equipped to do machine work, making your own hardware is one of the most interesting parts of the job. Some wooden patterns will be required where castings have to be made, but much of the hardware can be made of flat or round stock, and bits of scrap brass or bronze. Make the fits loose since, if they are too tight, the salt water will corrode the parts and they may stick together.

Chainplates are made of Everdur flat stock, or equivalent, drilled for pins and screws and the ends filed to a neat round or oval. Smooth all rough edges. The tangs can be made the same way. These parts are really easy to make, yet are rather expensive to buy. See Fig. 9.

Cleats should be of a strong wood like locust, maple or oak. Saw out the outline from a piece of board of the proper thickness. Round the edges with a half round wood rasp, and finish shaping with a file. Hold the cleat in a vise during rasping and filing to make the job easier. Sandpaper all over, and give all cleats four coats of varnish. See Fig. 11.

Centerboard plates require castings, but the pattern is simple enough for you to make. The plates shown in Fig. 11 are installed with the 7/8″ diameter boss a tight fit in the bed logs of the centerboard box, and the finished surfaces tight against gaskets of muslin and white lead, like those under the centerboard box. Fasten these plates with wood screws. The advantages of this design of centerboard pin is that the centerboard may be removed by simply taking out the two pipe plugs and pushing the pin through either way. It can all be done in a few minutes instead of the customary struggle to get the old fashioned pin out. The centerboard pin assembly drawing, Fig. 13, shows its details.

Blocks like those in Fig. 14 are made of a piece of "sign brass" and some round stock. Cut the shell to shape by jig sawing and filing, and drill for the pin. Make the hole in the sheave a loose fit on the pin but the ends of the pin should be a tight fit in the holes in the shell, for riveting. To bend the shell, make a hardwood block to act as a form to be held in the vise; bend the brass blank over that. After assembling, rivet over the pin ends to lock the whole assembly. These blocks are light and strong. The author has a homemade set ten years old which is as good as ever.

Turnbuckles are a good project for the man who has a 3/8″ or a 5/16″ right and left hand, fine thread, tap and die set; but if you don't happen to have these tools it certainly will not pay to buy them to make only one set of turnbuckles.

The straps are flat stock, drilled and filed. The pins are a straightforward turning job. Make a pair, end-to-end, of one piece of stock, then cut them apart. Be careful to center the cotter pin hole in the pins nicely. The screws are round stock, with a piece of hexagonal stock soft soldered at the center point, to provide a grip for a wrench. See Fig. 15.

A feather wind vane, nicely balanced, is a great help when sailing, particularly when dead before the wind. Some sailors never use them, and of course these fellows like to make fun of those who do. But if you like a wind vane, or telltale, this is a good one.

The body may be whittled from white pine, then drilled for the feather, the counterbalance and the stem. A pheasant feather and a dab of Duco cement will take care of that end. The counter balance may be cut to the required length by trial, or may be balanced by wrapping fine wire around it and securing it with a touch of soft solder. The sleeve is cut from thin wall brass tubing and its end is fitted with a brass plug soldered in. This plug must be flat and smooth on the inside, as this surface is part of the bearing on which the telltale turns. The bearing end of the stem must also be smooth, and should be lathe turned so as to be exactly centered. The little strap at the bottom is to keep the telltale from flying off, and is soldered in place, leaving clearance all around the stop ring. These two pieces may be soldered at the same time, using a small torch and just a dab of solder. See Fig. 16.

FIGURE 9

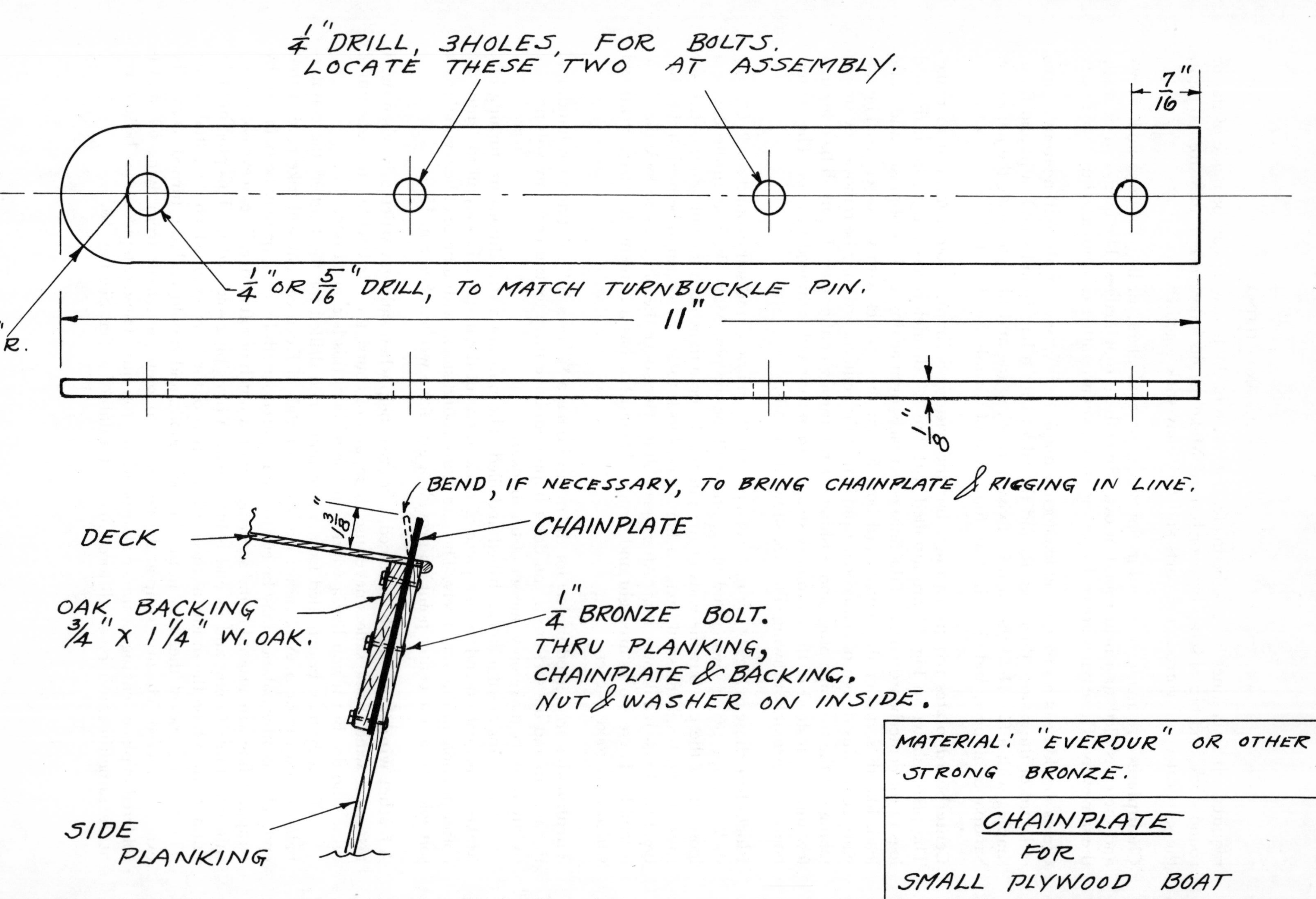

1/4" DRILL, 3HOLES, FOR BOLTS.
LOCATE THESE TWO AT ASSEMBLY.
7/16"
1/4" OR 5/16" DRILL, TO MATCH TURNBUCKLE PIN.
1/2" R.
11"
1/8"
BEND, IF NECESSARY, TO BRING CHAINPLATE & RIGGING IN LINE.
3/8"
DECK
CHAINPLATE
OAK BACKING
3/4" X 1 1/4" W. OAK.
1/4" BRONZE BOLT.
THRU PLANKING,
CHAINPLATE & BACKING.
NUT & WASHER ON INSIDE.
SIDE
PLANKING
METHOD OF ATTACHING TO HULL.
MATERIAL: "EVERDUR" OR OTHER
STRONG BRONZE.
CHAINPLATE
FOR
SMALL PLYWOOD BOAT
E. I. SCHOCK

FIGURE 10

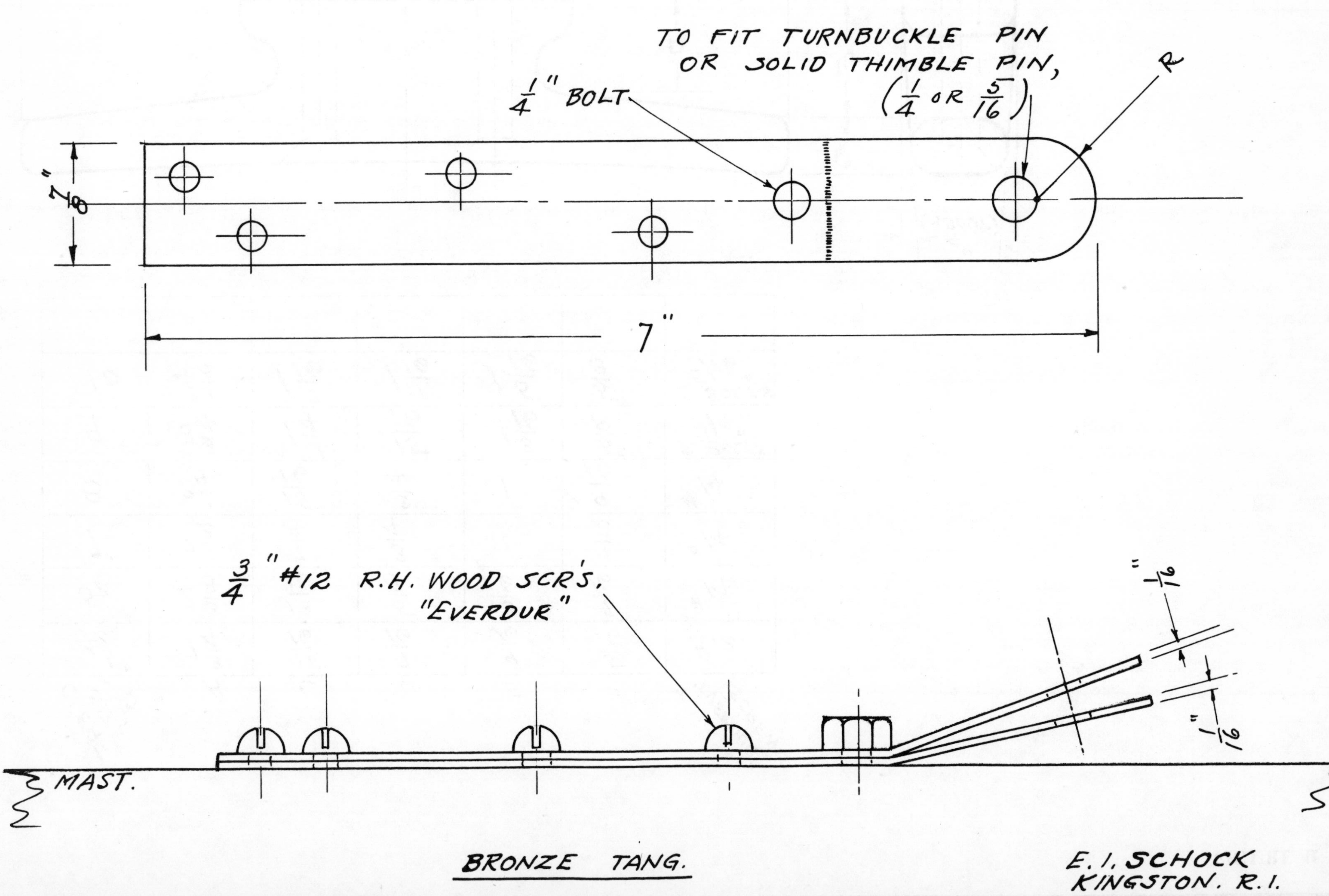

TO FIT TURNBUCKLE PIN
OR SOLID THIMBLE PIN,
(1/4 OR 5/16)
R
1/4" BOLT
7/8"
7"
3/4" #12 R.H. WOOD SCR'S.
"EVERDUE"
1/16"
1/16"
MAST.
BRONZE TANG.
E. I. SCHOCK
KINGSTON. R.I.

FIGURE 11

CLEAT SIZE "B"	A	C	D	E	F	TWO "EVERDUR" SCREWS
$4\frac{1}{2}$"	$1\frac{3}{4}$	$\frac{11}{16}$	$\frac{7}{16}$	$\frac{9}{16}$	$\frac{5}{16}$	#12
$5\frac{1}{2}$"	$2\frac{3}{8}$	$\frac{13}{16}$	$\frac{5}{8}$	$\frac{13}{16}$	$\frac{7}{16}$	#14
7"	$2\frac{1}{2}$	$\frac{7}{8}$	$\frac{3}{4}$	1	$\frac{1}{2}$	#14
8"	$3\frac{1}{4}$	$\frac{15}{16}$	$\frac{3}{4}$	1	$\frac{9}{16}$	#14
9	$3\frac{3}{4}$	$1\frac{1}{4}$	$\frac{15}{16}$	$1\frac{3}{16}$	$\frac{5}{8}$	2 BOLTS 1/4"
10	$4\frac{1}{4}$	$1\frac{7}{16}$	$1\frac{1}{16}$	$1\frac{5}{16}$	$\frac{5}{8}$	2 BOLTS 5/16"

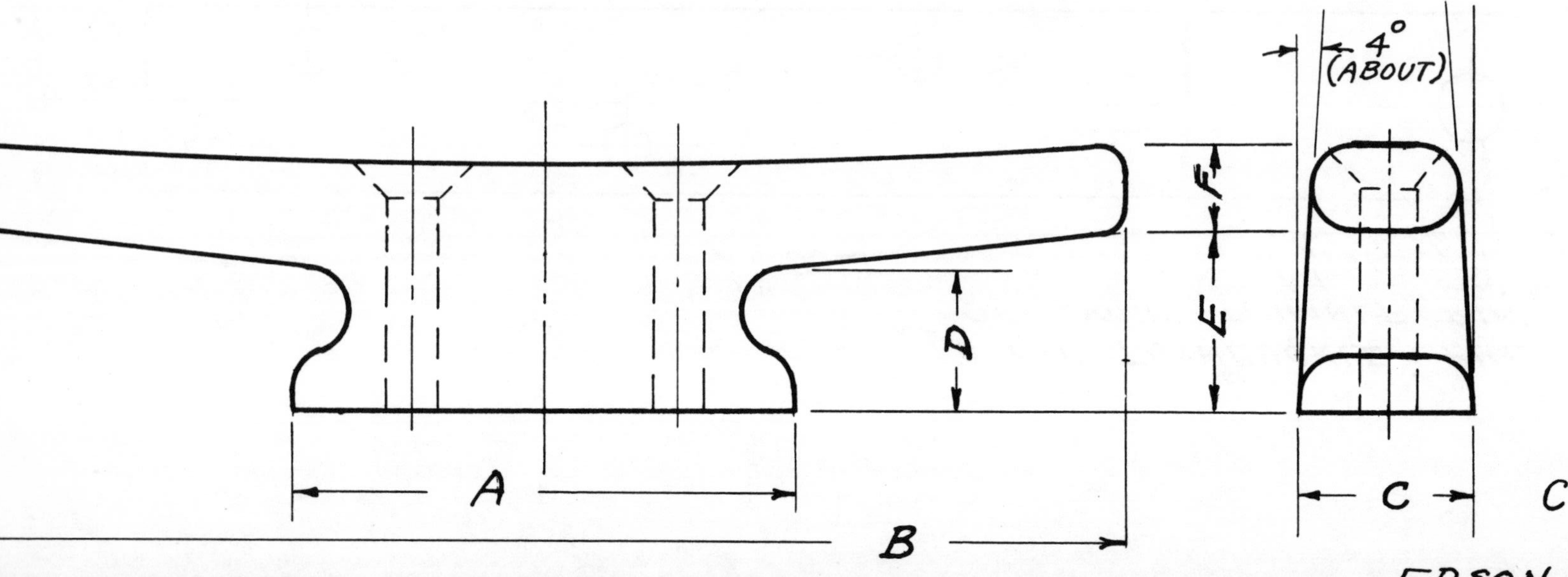

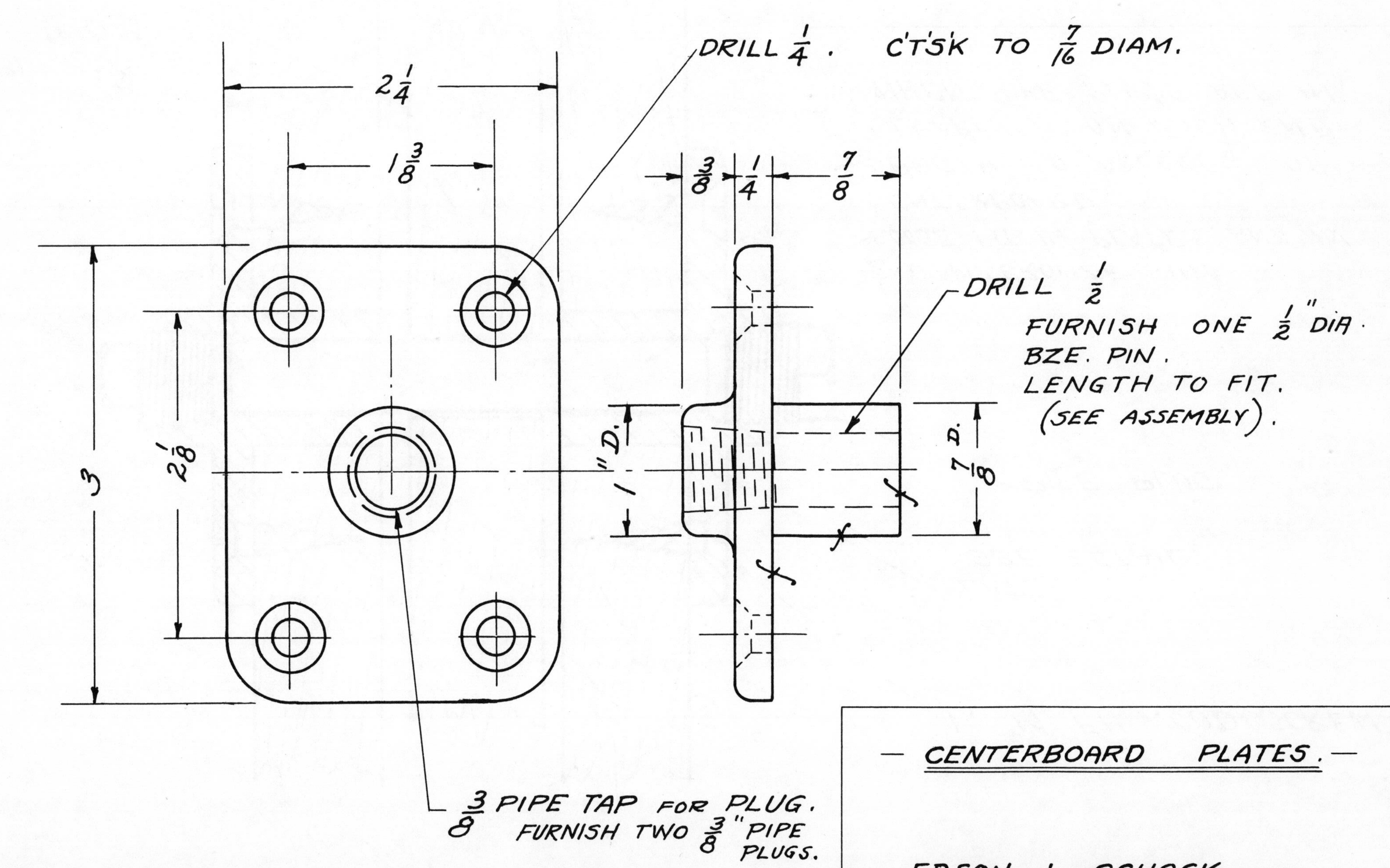

DRILL 1/4. C'T'S'K TO 7/16 DIAM.
2 1/4
1 3/8
3
2 1/8
3/8
1/4
7/8
1" D.
7/8 D.
DRILL 1/2
FURNISH ONE 1/2" DIA. BZE. PIN. LENGTH TO FIT. (SEE ASSEMBLY).
3/8 PIPE TAP FOR PLUG. FURNISH TWO 3/8" PIPE PLUGS.
2 REQ'D PER BOAT; CAST BRASS, OR BRONZE.
— CENTERBOARD PLATES. —
— EDSON I. SCHOCK. —
— KINGSTON. R.I. —

FIGURE 13

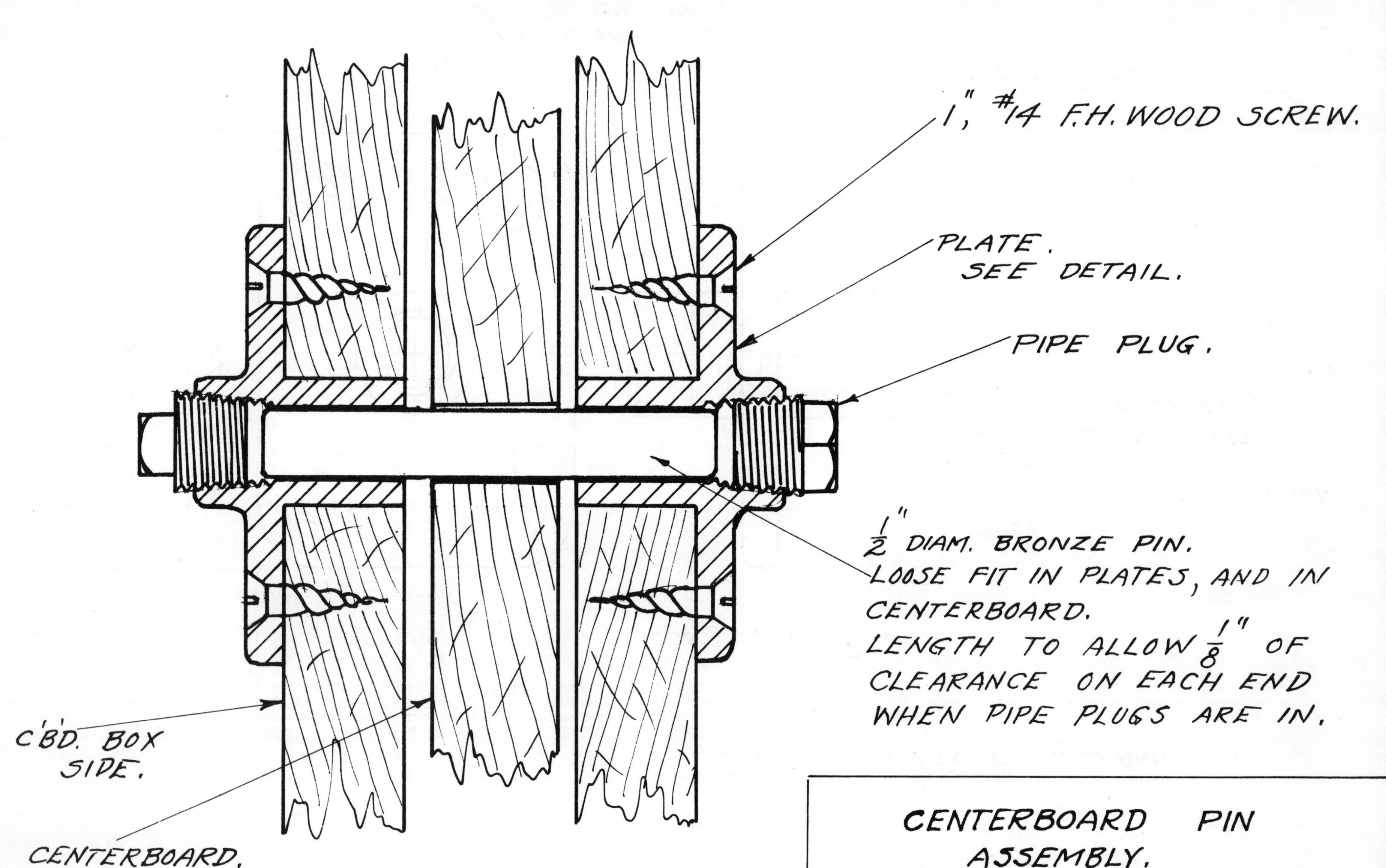

1", #14 F.H. WOOD SCREW.
PLATE. SEE DETAIL.
PIPE PLUG.
1/2" DIAM. BRONZE PIN.
LOOSE FIT IN PLATES, AND IN CENTERBOARD.
LENGTH TO ALLOW 1/8" OF CLEARANCE ON EACH END WHEN PIPE PLUGS ARE IN.
C'BD. BOX SIDE.
CENTERBOARD.
CENTERBOARD PIN ASSEMBLY.
E. I. SCHOCK.

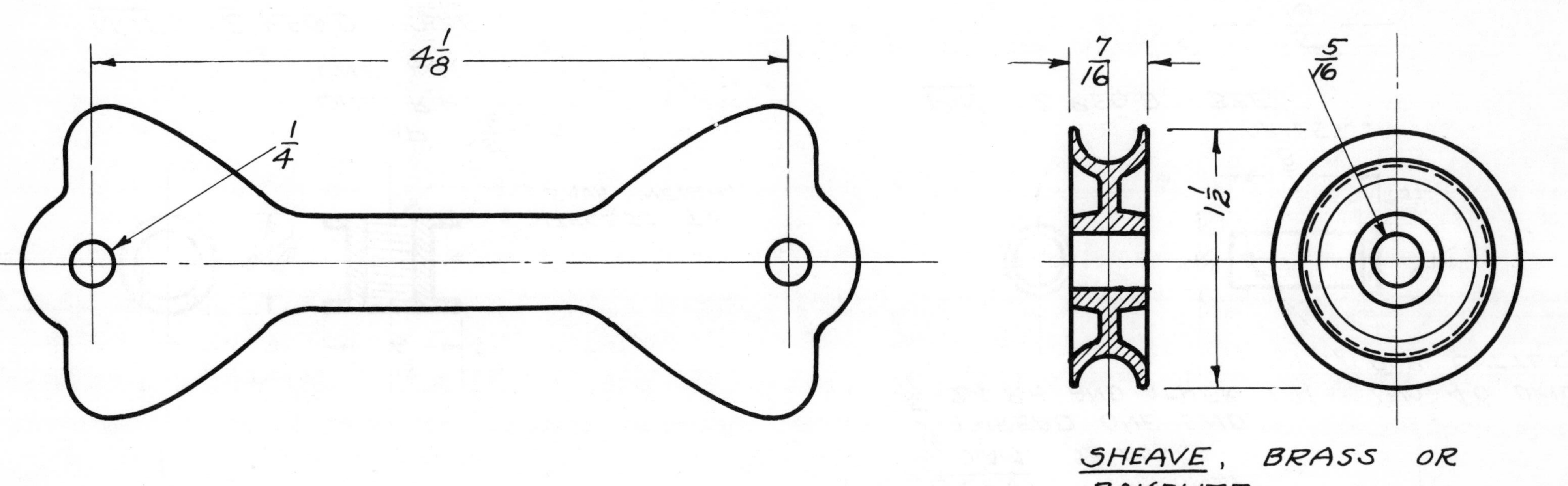

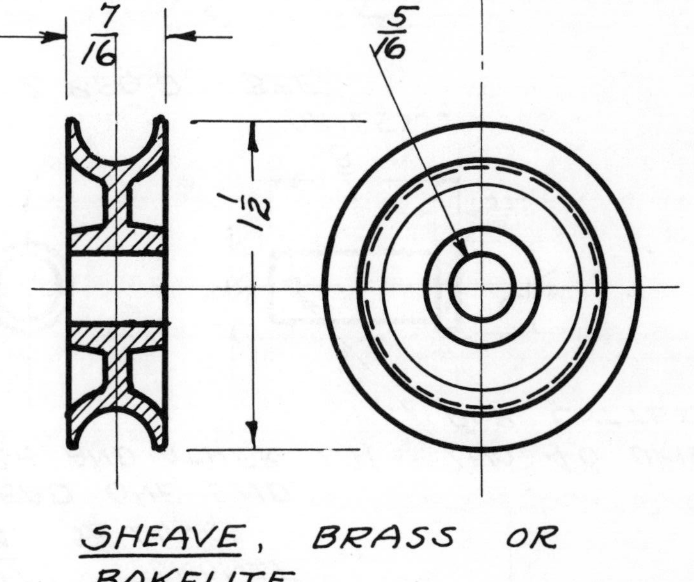

SHEAVE, BRASS OR BAKELITE.

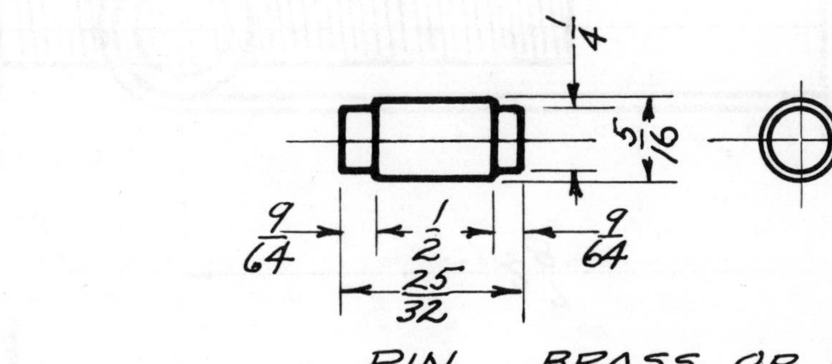

PIN. BRASS OR BRONZE.

BLOCK.

EDSON I. SCHOCK

KINGSTON, R.I.

FIGURE 15

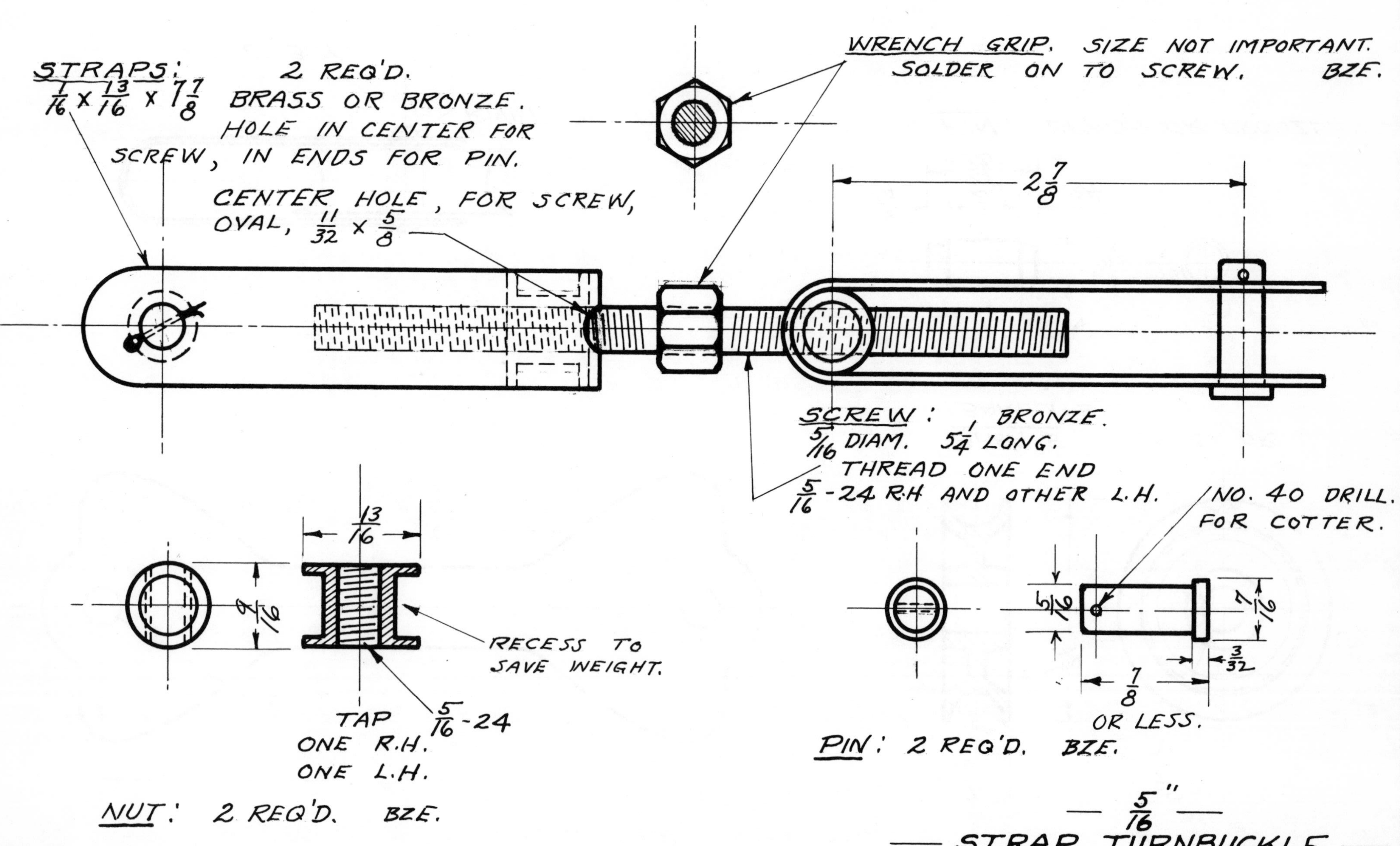
STRAPS: 2 REQ'D.
1/16 x 13/16 x 7 7/8 BRASS OR BRONZE.
HOLE IN CENTER FOR SCREW, IN ENDS FOR PIN.
CENTER HOLE, FOR SCREW, OVAL, 11/32 x 5/8
WRENCH GRIP. SIZE NOT IMPORTANT.
SOLDER ON TO SCREW. BZE.
2 7/8
SCREW: 5/16 DIAM. 5 1/4 LONG. BRONZE.
THREAD ONE END 5/16-24 R.H AND OTHER L.H.
NO. 40 DRILL.
FOR COTTER.
13/16
9/16
RECESS TO SAVE WEIGHT.
TAP 5/16-24
ONE R.H.
ONE L.H.
NUT: 2 REQ'D. BZE.
5/16
7/16
3/32
7/8
OR LESS.
PIN: 2 REQ'D. BZE.
5/16"
STRAP TURNBUCKLE.
EDSON I. SCHOCK

FIGURE 16

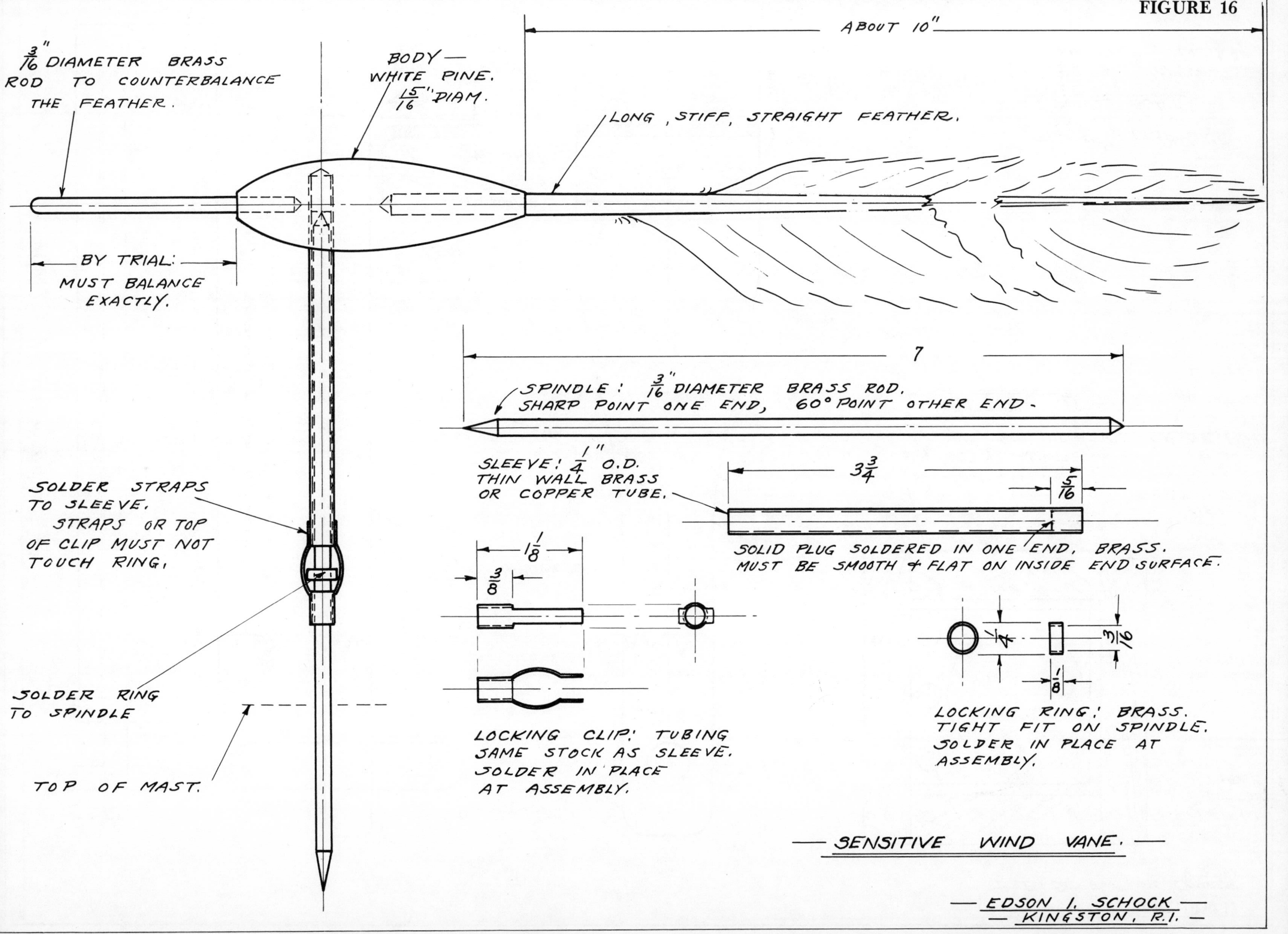

ABOUT 10"
3/16" DIAMETER BRASS ROD TO COUNTERBALANCE THE FEATHER.
BODY — WHITE PINE. 15/16" DIAM.
LONG, STIFF, STRAIGHT FEATHER.
BY TRIAL: MUST BALANCE EXACTLY.
7
SPINDLE: 3/16" DIAMETER BRASS ROD. SHARP POINT ONE END, 60° POINT OTHER END.
SLEEVE: 1/4" O.D. THIN WALL BRASS OR COPPER TUBE.
3 3/4
5/16
SOLID PLUG SOLDERED IN ONE END, BRASS. MUST BE SMOOTH & FLAT ON INSIDE END SURFACE.
SOLDER STRAPS TO SLEEVE, STRAPS OR TOP OF CLIP MUST NOT TOUCH RING.
1 1/8
3/8
LOCKING CLIP: TUBING SAME STOCK AS SLEEVE. SOLDER IN PLACE AT ASSEMBLY.
1/4
3/16
1/8
LOCKING RING: BRASS. TIGHT FIT ON SPINDLE. SOLDER IN PLACE AT ASSEMBLY.
SOLDER RING TO SPINDLE
TOP OF MAST.
— SENSITIVE WIND VANE. —
— EDSON I. SCHOCK —
— KINGSTON, R.I. —

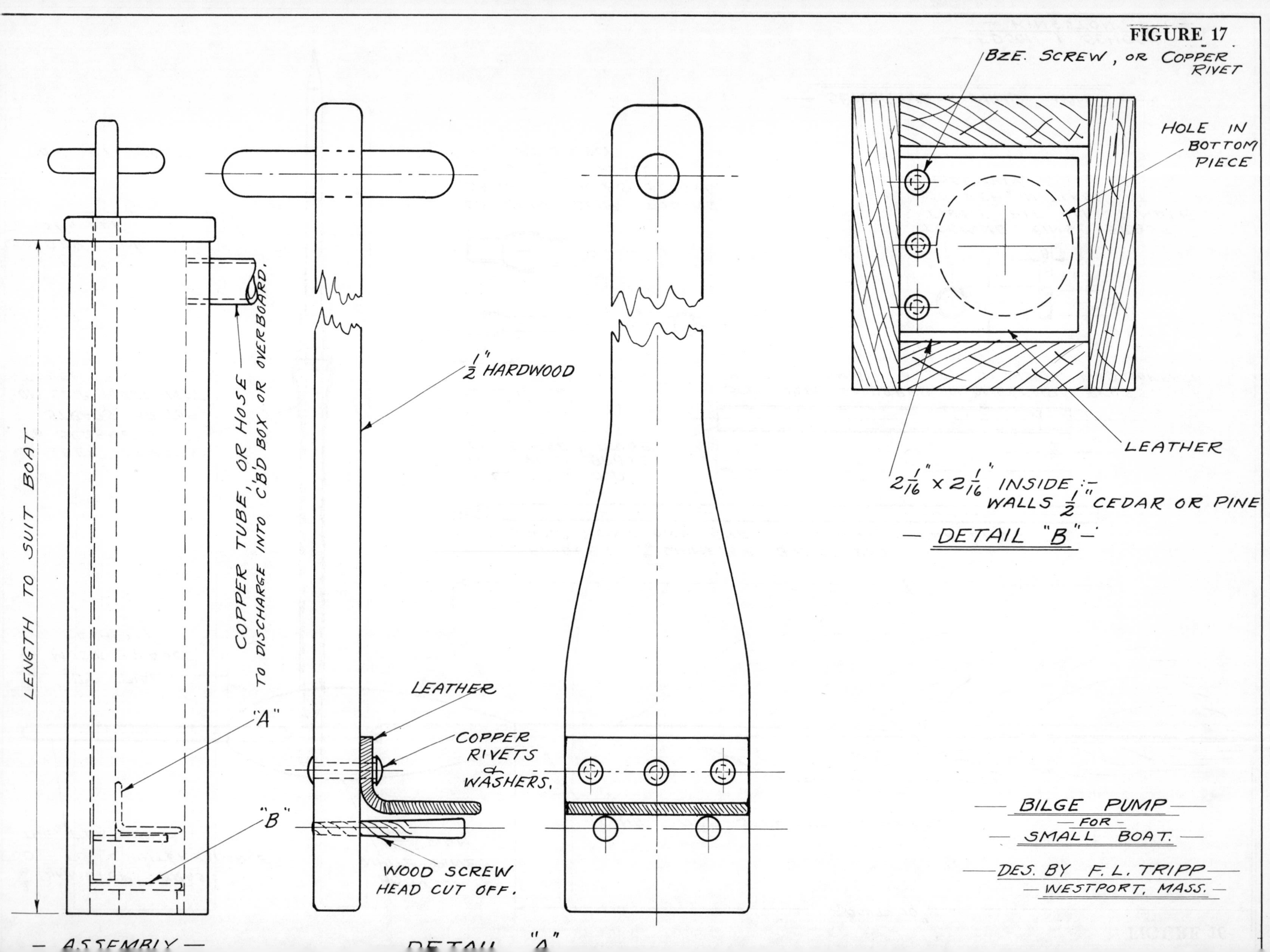
FIGURE 17
BZE. SCREW, OR COPPER RIVET
HOLE IN BOTTOM PIECE
LEATHER
$2\frac{1}{16}$" x $2\frac{1}{16}$" INSIDE :- WALLS $\frac{1}{2}$" CEDAR OR PINE
– DETAIL "B" –
BILGE PUMP
FOR
SMALL BOAT.
DES. BY F. L. TRIPP
WESTPORT, MASS.
$\frac{1}{2}$" HARDWOOD
LEATHER
COPPER RIVETS & WASHERS.
WOOD SCREW HEAD CUT OFF.
COPPER TUBE, OR HOSE
TO DISCHARGE INTO C'B'D BOX OR OVERBOARD.
LENGTH TO SUIT BOAT
"A"
"B"
– ASSEMBLY –

The bilge pump shown here is the kind the oldtimers used. It will pump more water with less effort than most expensive brass pumps, and it can be made in an evening. Credit for the design of this particular pump must go to F. L. Tripp, of Westport, Massachusetts, a boatbuilder whose boats are as nicely built as his pumps. One of these pumps was supplied with a 14-foot catboat of the author's design that Mr. Tripp built, and it worked so well that it is included here.

The construction is most simple; just a wooden box with a pair of leather valves and a handle. The leather should be flexible. The length of the main box of the pump should be just sufficient to bring the top even with the top of the centerboard box. Everyone who comes aboard your boat will want to try this little pump so you will never have to operate it yourself, unless you want to. It is truly a great labor-saving device. See Fig. 17.

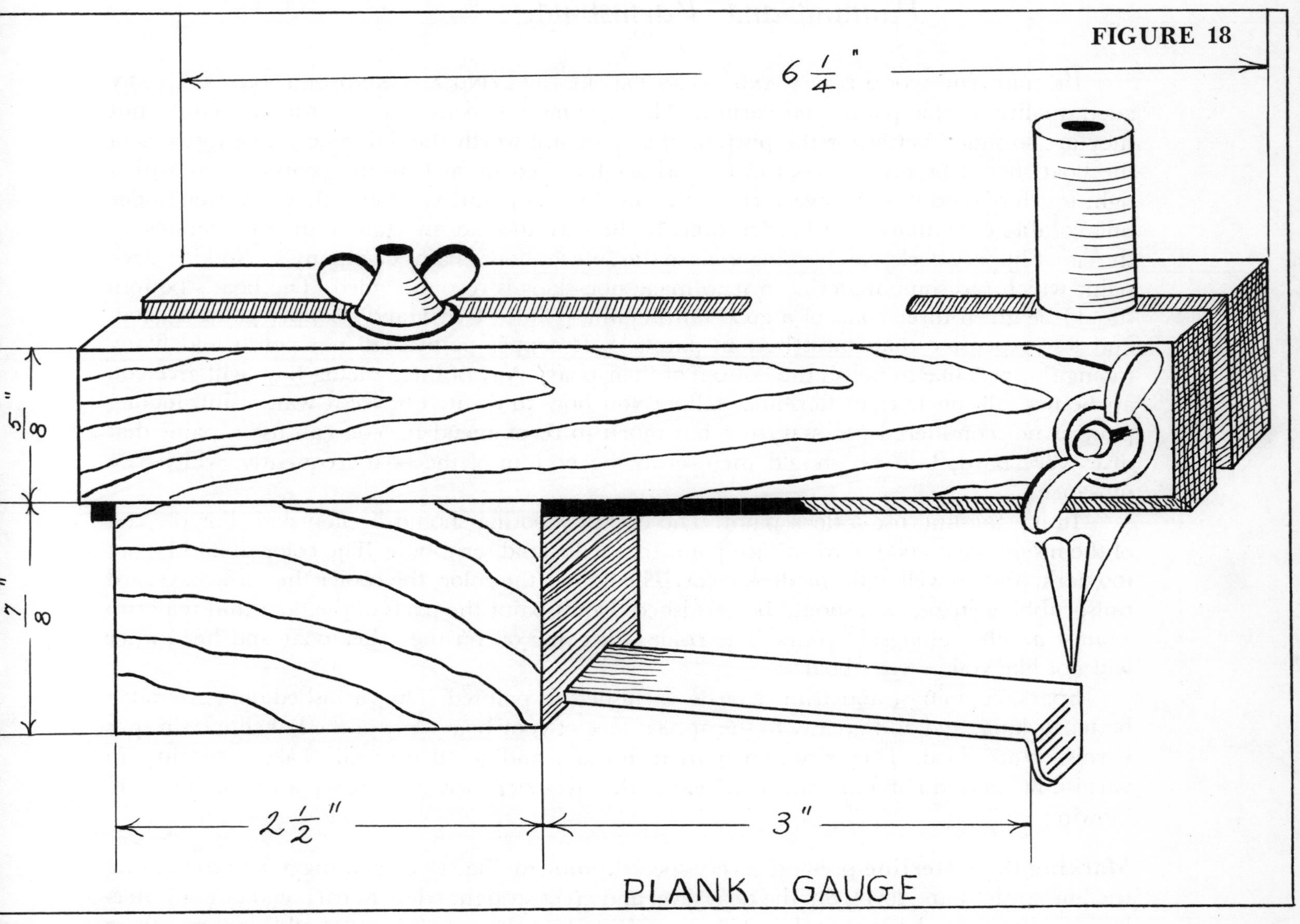

CHAPTER VII

Painting and Varnishing

BE SURE THE WOOD IS DRY AND CLEAN BEFORE APPLYING ANY KIND OF FINISH. USE ONLY good quality marine paints and varnish. They are more expensive than ordinary paints, but they are so much better for the purpose that they are worth the difference. The topsides of the boat should be given a coat of flat primer followed by at least two coats of gloss, with a light touch of sandpaper between coats. "Dulux" yacht paints are good; they dry even under unfavorable conditions, and harden quickly. Be sure to read and follow the instructions on the can. Slippery decks can be dangerous so the International Paint Company's "Noskid" deck paint which has some material in it to make non-skids is recommended. The boat's bottom should be given three coats of a good anti-fouling paint. "Red Hand" copper paint is good, and less expensive than most bottom paints. Soft copper paints will not polish and many racing skippers like to polish the bottom of their boats. Any of these racing boys will give you an hour's talk on bottom finishing, telling you how to do it. For fresh water, anti-fouling paint is not considered necessary but has much to recommend it. You can use a paint that dries very hard, but you should then scrub the bottom of the boat frequently, which is a nuisance.

Inside the hull use a deck paint. The cockpit flooring should be non-skid. For the rest of the inside use a good hard surface paint that will stand scrubbing. The color should be not too dark, and go well with the deck color. The lighter the color, the cooler the surface. Guard rails, rubbing strips, etc., should be varnished. Don't paint the parts of the boat that may rub against another alongside yours. The color will come off on the other boat and her owner will not like you or your boat.

Spars, coamings, and trim may be varnished or painted. The varnished ones are much better looking, and add greatly to the appearance of your boat. Any of the Bakelite resin spar varnishes are good. They dry and harden quickly, and stand up well. Take your time in varnishing and do it only in good warm dry weather, when there is little or no wind blowing.

Marking the waterline presents a very special problem. Fig. 19 gives a suggestion for getting the line straight and level. Set the boat level and erect straight edges at each end of the waterline, as shown in the sketch. Level the straight edges. By stretching a chalkline across these straight edges you can spot points along the waterline. A batten held or tacked along these points gives you a line to paint to. The boat may be either right side up or upside down

FIGURE 19

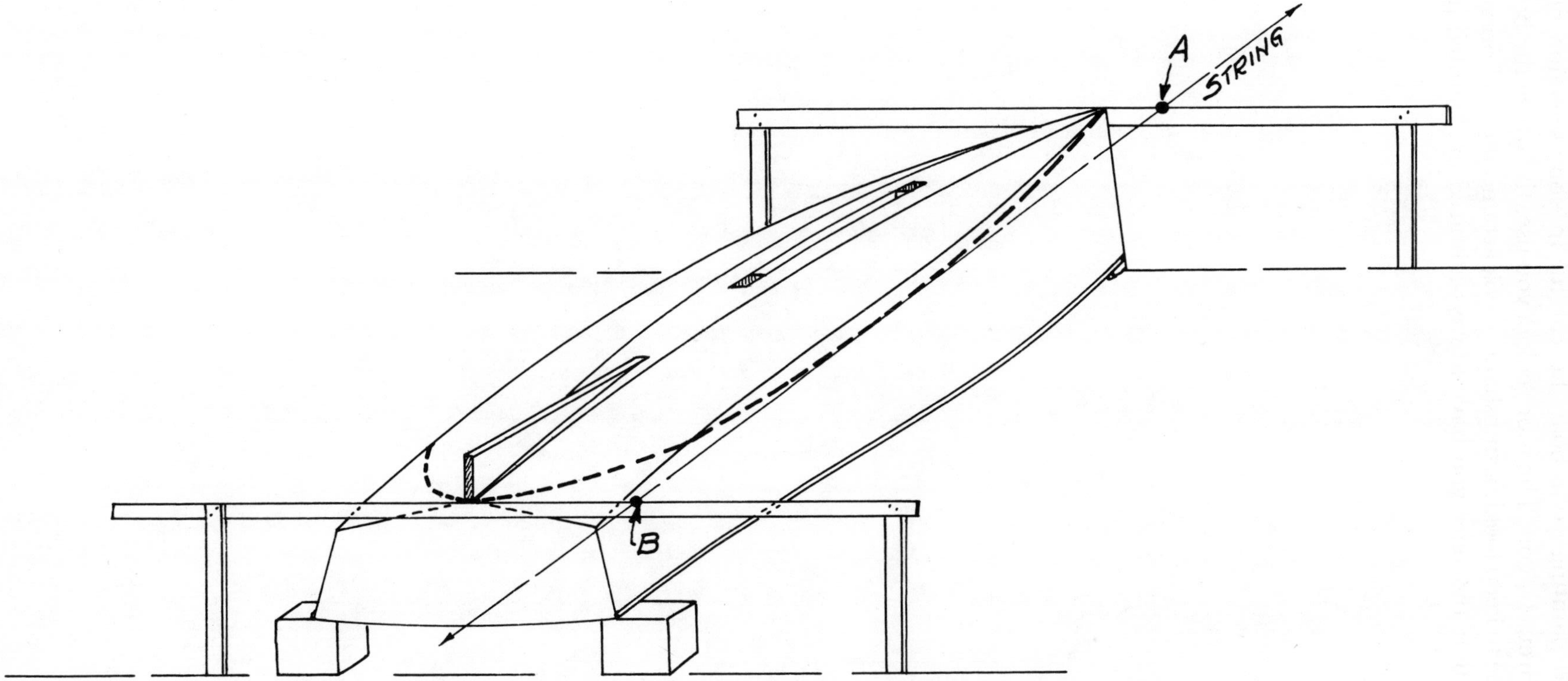

STRAIGHTEDGES SET UP FOR MARKING THE WATERLINE.

NOT TO SCALE.

E. I. SCHOCK.

when you do this. The sketch shows her upside down, with the stem head resting on the floor and the transom on boxes. Have her level both fore and aft and athwartships.

When you come to painting your boat, be careful in your selection of colors. Don't paint her to look like a circus wagon. The more colors you use, the worse the boat will appear, and the harder she will be to keep looking shipshape. Look around the anchorage at the yachts; you will probably find that the ones you have always admired are painted inconspicuously and in good taste.

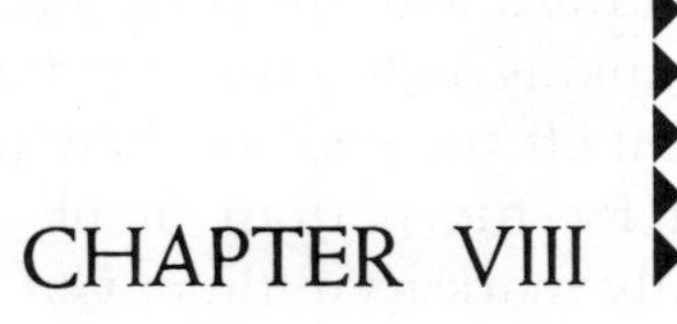

CHAPTER VIII

Twelve Boats and How To Build Them

7′4″ PLYWOOD PRAM

This boat was designed as a tender for a small yacht, where a larger tender would be too bulky or too heavy to take aboard. She rows easily and tows well. Perhaps it is an exaggeration to say that any dinghy tows well, they all give more or less trouble, but this one is no worse than the others. She has good stability, and will carry her share of the load.

Mold Loft Work

To build her, first make the mold loft drawings, as described in Chapter III, and show the construction details on these drawings. Be sure to subtract the planking thickness from the body plan before you make the frames.

Preliminary construction (Chapter IV describes this work.)

Make the bow and stern transoms.
Make the keel.
Make two chine pieces.
Make the three frames, leaving the ends long enough to reach to the floor.
Make the six knees, but do not bevel them until you have some of the framing set up, so that you can check the angles and bevels.

Framing

Build her upside down. Mark the centerline on the building floor, and measure the frame locations along this line. Draw the frame lines at right angles to the centerline. Mark the location of each transom on the floor. Plan 12, page 126, shows the general method of setting up the frame.

Bolt the transoms, keel, and frames together, and set them on the marks. Put in temporary bracing enough to keep the whole assembly reasonably rigid. Two posts under the keel will keep it bent to the proper curve until the side planks are on.

Bend the chines into place. Fit them into the notches in the frame gussets. Fasten them in place with 1¾″ No. 10 screws.

Bolt the skeg through the keel and stern knee with ¼″ bolts. Use carriage bolts with the heads outside and washers and nuts inside. It is not necessary to counterbore and plug the heads; just leave them flush.

Planking

Lay out the side planks, as described in Chapter IV, page 21, and cut them to shape. Fit the planks along the chine first, then fit the ends. Drill along the edges for screws. Use ⅝″-No. 7 screws spaced about 2½″ apart. Spread glue on the plank where it fits the chine, and on the chine where it fits the plank, and screw the plank in place, bringing the screws in until the heads are just flush with the plywood. Do not sink them in with the idea of puttying them afterward; the planking is too thin for this. Work fast before the glue sets. Fasten the ends the same way. Trim off the ends of these planks flush with the transom face.

Hold the plywood for the bottom plank against the frames, keel and transoms so it cannot shift, and carefully mark its outline. Cut to size, and fit the edge along the keel rabbet first. Next fit the chine edge, and last the ends. Since this plank has to fit all around, it is a difficult job to get it right, and mistakes cannot be corrected if you happen to make the piece too small. To avoid this possibility another system may be employed, where you first make a pattern of stiff building paper by fitting the paper to the boat, then marking the plywood from the paper pattern. The homemade gauge shown in Fig. 18 is a great help in marking the plank edges accurately.

Drill for the screws, and screw and glue the bottom planks in place, fastening the keel edge first, the chines next, and the ends last. When driving screws into oak, put soap on them; they will drive easier.

Flooring and Interior Details

When the planking is finished and the glue has set, turn the boat over and saw off the frames at the sheer line. Smooth the top edge of the side planks with a rasp and sandpaper and give the planking a coat of plywood sealer.

Fit the knees at the bow and stern, then the rubbing strips and inwales.

Make the floor boards and risings to support the thwarts.

Make reinforcing pads to go under the rowlocks and glue and screw them in place.

Painting and Finishing

Paint the boat, one coat, all over, then install the flooring, risings, thwarts and the two little posts under them.

Paint the floor boards with non-skid paint, and give the rest of the pram two more coats to match her mother ship.

Paint her name on the inside of the stern transom; it is easier to see it there than on the outside.

Put on the hardware. Davis-pattern rowlocks are recommended, because they cannot get lost. An eye bolt at each end of the boat is handy, but one in the bow is essential for towing.

The rubbing strip may be varnished, or covered with a canvas-and-rubber gunwale guard, or protected with a 1″ diameter cotton rope all around. The rubber guards are the best, and are sold by the foot at marine hardware stores. They protect both the pram and the boat she is trying to bump.

Buy her a pair of spruce oars about 6′ long. They should be short enough to stow inside the boat, but if too short they are not much good for rowing. Varnish the oars, three coats, fit leathers where they chafe in the rowlocks and put copper tips on the blade ends. It is not necessary to use copper paint on the pram's bottom, unless she is to be in the water for long periods of time.

Let her soak in water a couple of days before you use her the first time, to swell the wood.

PLAN 1

7'–4" PLYWOOD PRAM					
ITEM	LUMBER MATERIAL	NO. PIECES REQ'D	SIZE IN INCHES	LENGTH	
KEEL	OAK	1	7/8 X 2 5/16	7'–0"	
FRAMES	OAK		5/8 X 1 1/4	14 LINEAR FEET	
CHINES	OAK	2	1 X 1	7'–0"	
KNEES	APPLE	6	3/4		
FLOORS	OAK	6	3/4 X 1 1/2	10"	
SKEG	SPRUCE	1	3/4 X 4	22"	
RUBBING STRIP	OAK	2	3/4 X 1 1/4	8'–0"	
TRANSOM	W. PINE	1 1	5/8 X 12	1 PC. 3'–3" 1 PC. 1'–10"	
CLAMP	OAK	2	5/8 X 1	8'–0"	
FLOORING	SPRUCE	7	5/8 X 3	4'–3"	
SEATS	W. PINE	1 1 1	5/8 X 9 5/8 X 12 5/8 X 12	3'–6" 3'–6" 2'–6"	
PLANKING	FIR PLYWOOD	2	1/4 X 48	8'–0"	
TRANSOM FRAME	OAK		5/8 X 3/4	8 LIN. FT.	
RISINGS	SPRUCE	2	3/4 X 1 1/2	8'–0"	

PLAN 1

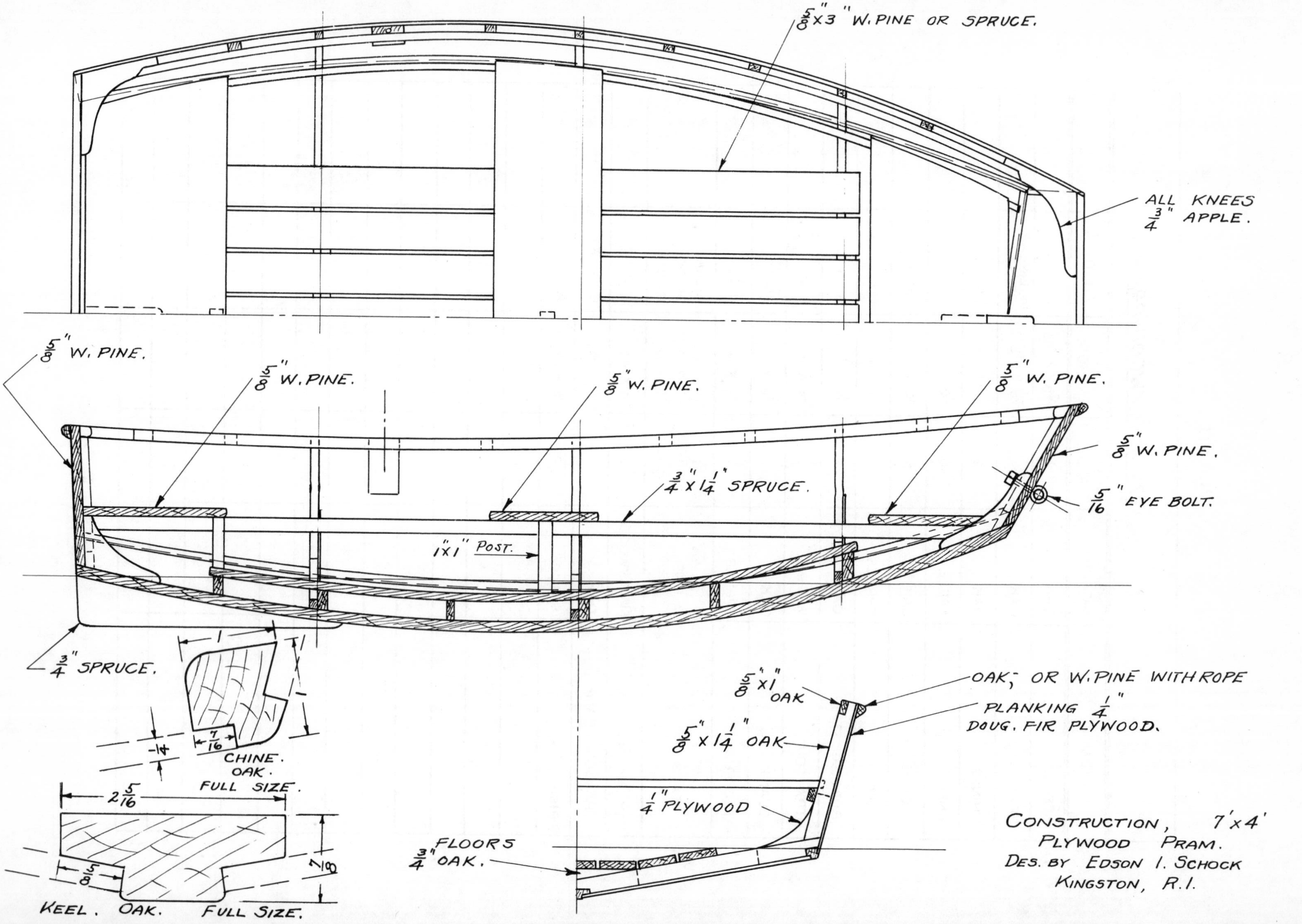
5/8" x 3" W. PINE OR SPRUCE.
ALL KNEES 3/4" APPLE.
5/8" W. PINE.
5/8" W. PINE.
5/8" W. PINE.
5/8" W. PINE.
5/8" W. PINE.
3/4" x 1 1/4" SPRUCE.
5/16" EYE BOLT.
1" x 1" POST.
3/4" SPRUCE.
CHINE. OAK. FULL SIZE.
7/16
1/4
KEEL. OAK. FULL SIZE.
2 5/16
5/8
7/8
5/8" x 1" OAK
OAK; OR W. PINE WITH ROPE
PLANKING 1/4" DOUG. FIR PLYWOOD.
5/8" x 1 1/4" OAK
1/4" PLYWOOD
3/4" FLOORS OAK.
CONSTRUCTION, 7' x 4' PLYWOOD PRAM.
DES. BY EDSON I. SCHOCK
KINGSTON, R.I.

LINES. 7' x 4'
PLYWOOD PRAM.
DES. BY EDSON I. SCHOCK,
KINGSTON, R.I.

DIMENSIONS
ARE TO
OUTSIDE OF PLANKING.

9′6″ PLYWOOD OUTBOARD SKIFF

The first boat built from these plans was a father-and-son project, and the whole construction took only a weekend. Lumber and materials were bought Saturday morning and Saturday afternoon the work was started by getting out the parts which could be made on the bench in the shop. By Sunday noon these were all finished. This sounds as though they had worked all night, but they had not. By Sunday evening the boat was finished except for a little trim. Monday father had to work, and son finished the trim and started the painting, which was completed Tuesday, and she was launched late on Tuesday.

Her name was "Half Shell." At the time of this writing she is six years old, and has never had any repairs, nor does she need any. She is a very plain boat. Sandpaper was not much in evidence during her building, and the screw holes are not puttied, but she is not too rough looking a boat either. For several years she was used as a work boat, powered with a 1¾-horsepower outboard motor. The photograph shows her with this motor, towing an experimental model of a V-bottom powerboat.

Besides being easy to build, "Half Shell" proved extremely stable and drove easily up to about six miles an hour. A larger motor did not appreciably increase her speed, so probably six miles is about as fast as she can be driven.

The building process followed this general outline:

Mold Loft Work

Paper patterns were made for the transom, the two frames, and the side planks. No other mold loft work was necessary.

Preliminary Construction

Make the transom. To do this cut the plywood to shape from the pattern, glue and screw the transom frame to the plywood, including the reinforcing motor board in the center of the transom. Leave space at the transom top for the quarter knees to fit in. Bevel the bottom and sides, using the bevels taken from the construction plan with your adjustable square.

Next make the midship thwart frame by fitting the pieces to the pattern and gluing and screwing them together. Then plane the side and bottom bevels to fit. The lazyback can be fitted later.

Now make the frame at the after end of the forward deck. Lay the pieces out on the pattern and glue and screw them together. The crown of the deck is an arc of a circle, and the small deck beam is cut and planed on top to this arc.

Make the stem following the procedure outlined in Chapter IV, page 12.

Last to be made are the side planks. See Chapter IV, page 21, for detailed instructions.

Assembly of Parts, and Finishing Operations

First glue and screw the side planks to the stem. Drill holes for No. 10-1¼″ screws in the forward edge of each side plank, where they will be fastened to the stem. Spread glue on one plank edge and one stem rabbet, and fasten the first plank to the stem. Drive the screws so that the heads are just flush, not sunk below the surface of the plywood. These screws may be spaced about 2½″ apart. Repeat the process for the second plank.

Glue and screw the transom to the after end of the first side plank, screwing into the oak transom frame. By bending planks into position as a test, make sure that the transom bevel is correct before you put on the glue. If it is wrong it is hard to take apart once the glue has set.

Screw the midship frame in place on this same plank, but do not use glue on this. The after edge of the frame goes just to the pencil line.

Screw the remaining frame to the side plank in the same manner. The assembly will now look like a big V with the transom and frames attached to one side. Lay this on the floor with the bottom edge up.

We hope that about this time some kind friends will drop in to see how your boat is coming along. While they are telling you all the things you did wrong, and criticising the design, you can relax and get a few minutes' rest. As soon as three of them are on hand, you can get them to help you bend the side planks. Put one man at the stem, one at the transom, and get the third to hold the loose end of the second side plank. You take hold of the plank which is screwed to the transom and slowly and carefully pull the two planks around the frames, until the second also touches the transom. Temporarily nail the two frames in place; glue and screw the second side plank to the transom, with the screws going into the oak transom frame. Finally screw the frames in position.

Now check to see if the two sides are alike by stretching a cord from a tack centered in the stem to one in the center of the transom, along the bottom of the boat. If the two sides are not symmetrical, push the wide one in until they are and fasten them temporarily with cross bracing.

Fit the nailing strips along the inside bottom edge of the side planks to take the bottom plank, using clamps to hold them until the gluing and fastening is completed. Since the boat is upside down, these strips will come along the upper edges of the planks. Glue and screw them in and plane their edges so that they are straight across the bottom. A long straight-edge used as a test piece across the boat from side to side will show you where to plane. This joint between sides and bottom must be a good fit, and the bottom plank must lie snugly on these strips, or the boat will leak.

The bottom plank comes next. Lay your plywood on the bottom of the boat and mark around the edge. Cut to this line or just a little outside of it. Drill the screw holes about 3″ apart, and glue and screw the bottom plank in place and plane its edges. This completes the planking.

Now screw on the rubbing strips, and the oak guard rail. In putting on the guard rail the screws go from the inside through the plywood into the oak. Hold the rail in position with clamps while drilling the holes and driving the screws.

Fit the knees at the transom. The one in the center, over the skeg, should be bolted through the skeg and transom with ¼″-diam. bolts, two bolts in each. The forward end of the skeg can be fastened from inside with screws.

The deck can be put on the same way as the bottom.

Fit the lazyback, and the thwarts.

Put an eyebolt in the stem and one in the transom for mooring lines. If you are going to use an outboard motor, you might put a cleat on the inside of the transom, just in case you want to give a sailing friend a tow some day when he is becalmed.

Paint her three coats inside and out to suit your taste, but remember to varnish the rubbing strips. See pages 38 to 40 for painting hints.

If you intend to carry oars, fit her with rowlocks as described for the 7-foot pram; if on the other hand you plan to use canoe paddles you will not, of course, need the rowlocks. Paddles will get you home if the outboard will not run but these motors are remarkably reliable, though sometimes when they get wet they will not start.

After launching let her soak a couple of days before you use her with the motor.

PLAN 2

9'–6" - PLYWOOD - OUTBOARD SKIFF					
ITEM	LUMBER MATERIAL	NO. PIECES REQ'D	SIZE IN INCHES	LENGTH	
STEM	OAK	1	2 3/8 X 2 1/2	22"	
FRAMES	SPRUCE		3/4 X 2	18 LIN. FT.	
CHINES	OAK	2	3/4 X 1 1/4	10'–0"	
KNEES	OAK	3	3/4		
SKEG	FIR	1	7/8 X 5	2'–3"	
RUBBING STRIP	OAK	2 2	5/8 X 5/8 3/4 X 1 3/4	10'–0" 10'–0"	
TRANSOM	OAK PLYWOOD OAK	1 1 1	3/4 X 1 1/4 1/2 X 17 7/8 X 12	6'–0" 44" 18"	
DECK	PLYWOOD				SCRAP FROM BOTTOM
DECK BEAMS	SPRUCE		3/4 X 3 3/4	3'–0"	
SEATS	W. PINE	1 1	3/4 X 12 3/4 X 12	4'–2" 4'–0"	
PLANKING	PLYWOOD	1 1	1/2 X 36 1/2 X 48	10'–0" 10'–0"	COULD BE 3/8" PLYWOOD

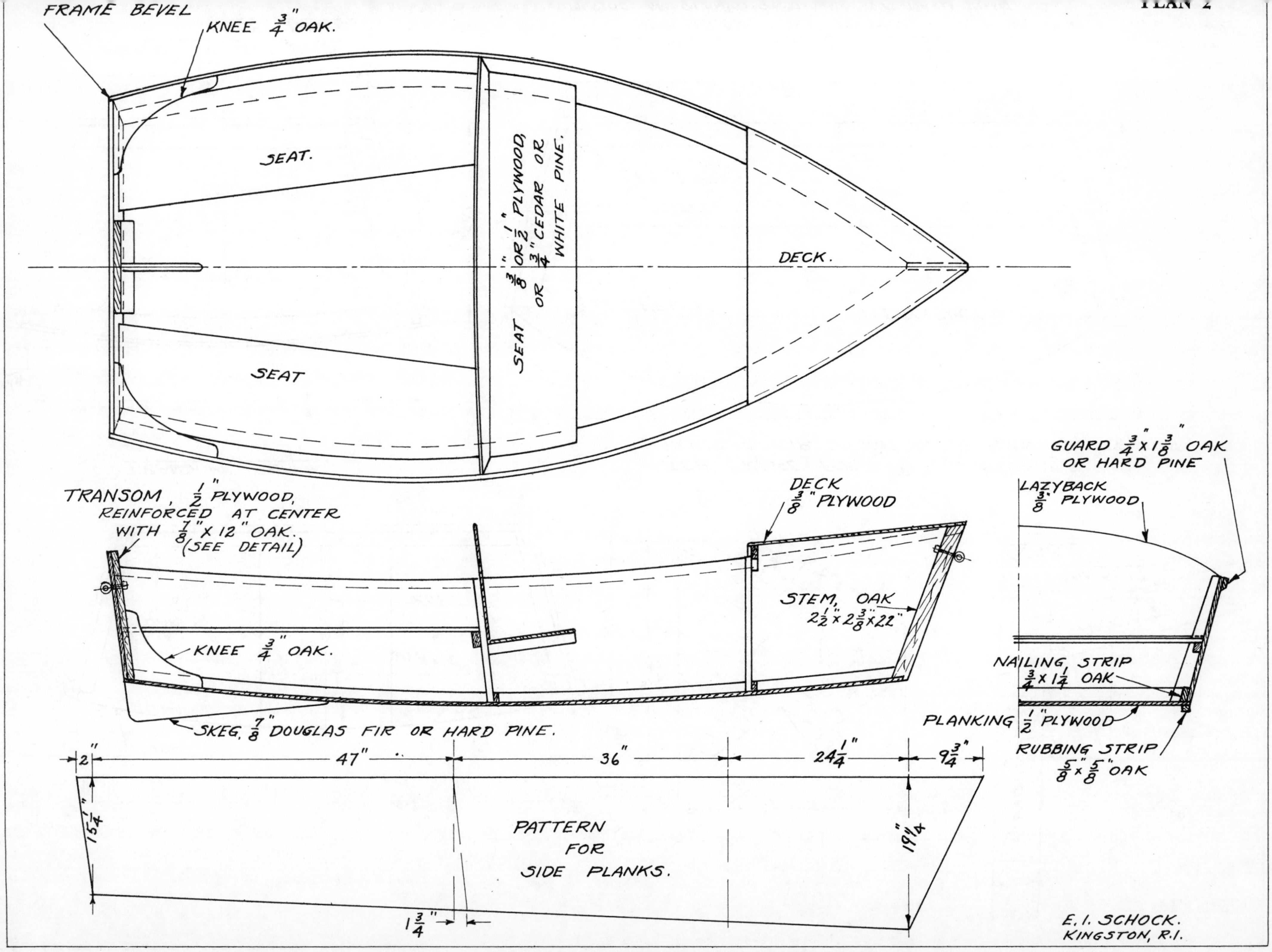

FRAME BEVEL

KNEE $\frac{3}{4}$" OAK.

SEAT.

SEAT

SEAT $\frac{3}{8}$" OR $\frac{1}{2}$" PLYWOOD, OR $\frac{3}{4}$" CEDAR OR WHITE PINE.

DECK.

TRANSOM, $\frac{1}{2}$" PLYWOOD, REINFORCED AT CENTER WITH $\frac{7}{8}$" X 12" OAK. (SEE DETAIL)

DECK $\frac{3}{8}$" PLYWOOD

STEM, OAK $2\frac{1}{2}$" x $2\frac{3}{8}$" x 22"

KNEE $\frac{3}{4}$" OAK.

SKEG, $\frac{7}{8}$" DOUGLAS FIR OR HARD PINE.

GUARD $\frac{3}{4}$" X $1\frac{3}{8}$" OAK OR HARD PINE

LAZYBACK $\frac{3}{8}$" PLYWOOD

NAILING STRIP $\frac{3}{4}$ X $1\frac{1}{4}$ OAK

PLANKING $\frac{1}{2}$" PLYWOOD

RUBBING STRIP $\frac{5}{8}$" x $\frac{5}{8}$" OAK

2" 47" 36" $24\frac{1}{4}$" $9\frac{3}{4}$"

$15\frac{1}{4}$"

PATTERN FOR SIDE PLANKS.

$19\frac{1}{4}$

$1\frac{3}{4}$"

E. I. SCHOCK.
KINGSTON, R.I.

PLAN 2

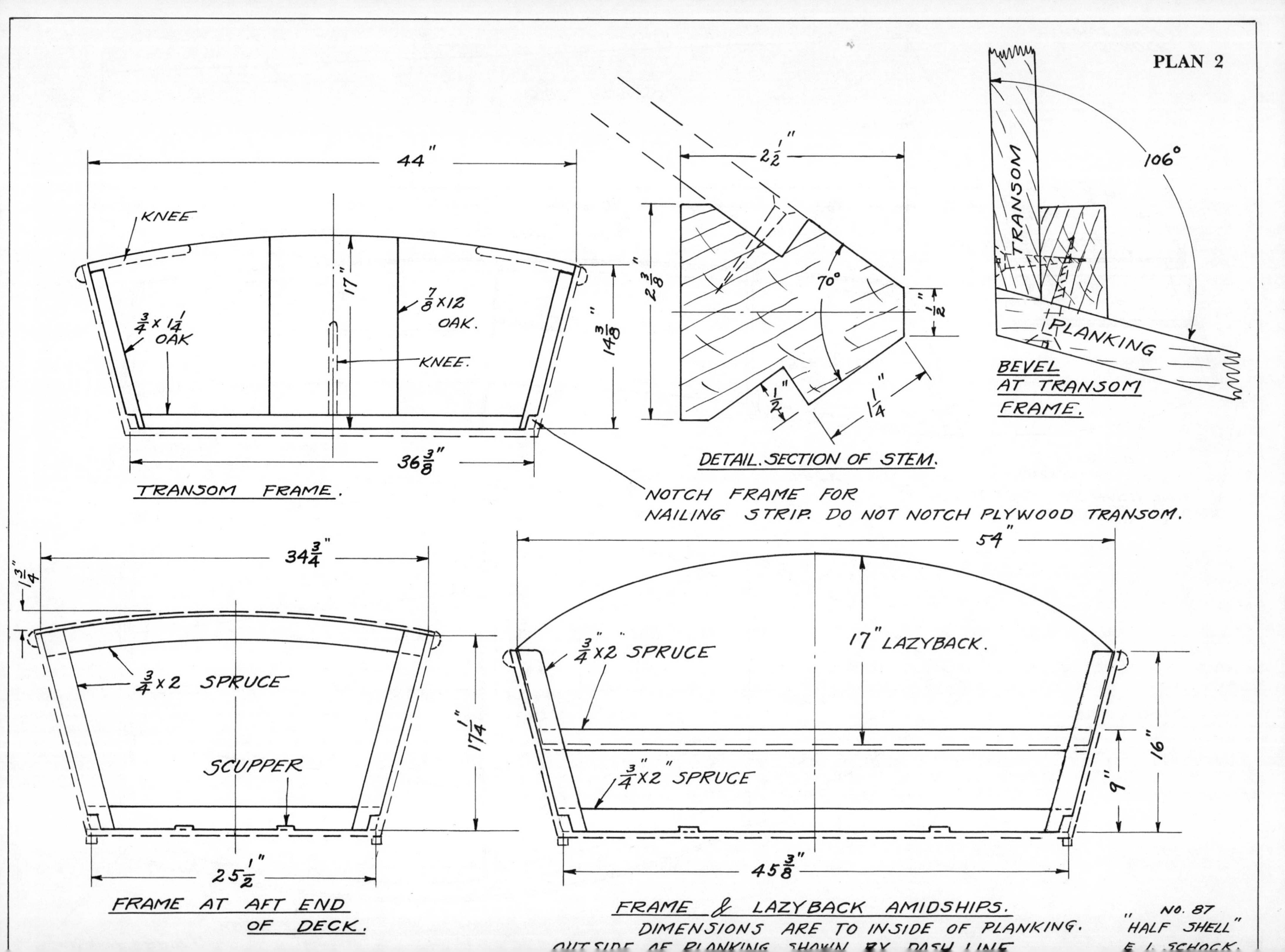

44"
KNEE
17"
7/8 X12 OAK.
3/4 X 1 1/4 OAK
KNEE.
14 3/8"
36 3/8"
TRANSOM FRAME.
2 1/2"
2 3/8"
70°
1/2"
1/2"
1 1/4"
DETAIL. SECTION OF STEM.
106°
TRANSOM
PLANKING
BEVEL AT TRANSOM FRAME.
NOTCH FRAME FOR NAILING STRIP. DO NOT NOTCH PLYWOOD TRANSOM.
34 3/4"
1 3/4"
3/4 X2 SPRUCE
17 1/4"
SCUPPER
25 1/2"
FRAME AT AFT END OF DECK.
54"
17" LAZYBACK.
3/4" X2" SPRUCE
3/4" X2" SPRUCE
9"
16"
45 3/8"
FRAME & LAZYBACK AMIDSHIPS.
DIMENSIONS ARE TO INSIDE OF PLANKING.
NO. 87
"HALF SHELL"

SKIFF "HALF SHELL" UNDER WAY

11′6″ AND 13′6″ SKIFFS

The same general method of construction as described for No. 2 may be used for both these skiffs. They were designed as good all-around boats for fishing, picnics, rides, camp utilities, or work boats. The smaller boat is well suited to an outboard motor as she is straight along the bottom and will not squat under power. The larger skiff is cut up at the stern which makes her easier to row. She also would be all right under power at slow speeds, but would not be satisfactory with a large motor, since she would squat at speed. About 2½ horsepower would be plenty.

For building these skiffs use following method:

Mold Loft Work

The full-size drawings needed would be a pattern for the side planks, and a body plan for making the molds. For the 11′6″ skiff the body plan shows the outside of the planking, so the planking thickness has to be subtracted on the mold loft drawing. For the 13′6″ skiff the actual molds are shown, the dimensions being to the inside of the planking. Details of mold loft work are given in Chapter III.

Preliminary Construction

Make the stem, transom, transom frame, and transom knee.

Make the molds, which may be of any scrap lumber, nailed together as shown in the drawing of No. 2 mold for the 13′6″ skiff. The exact method of putting them together is not important, but they should be strong and of correct dimensions as given on the plans.

Assembly of Parts

Draw a centerline on the building floor, and mark the correct location of the molds, transom and stem. Set up the molds, with the bottom side up, at right angles to the centerline, the waterline level, square and plumb. Set up the stem and transom. Brace these parts temporarily as you set them up.

Set the nailing strips in place, bending them around the molds and fastening them to the stem and transom. Do not fasten them to the molds unless necessary to keep the structure rigid while working on it.

Cut the side planks to the developed dimensions, or to your paper pattern if you have made one, leaving ¹⁄₁₆″ or more all around for final fitting and trimming.

Clamp the planks in place and be sure that they are a good fit, then drill for the screws. Take the planks off again. Spread glue on the plank where the joint is to come, and on the stem, transom and nailing strip. Put them back at once and screw them on, setting the screws up tight. One-inch No. 8 screws, spaced 2¼″ apart, will be about the right size for this job. Let the glue set overnight.

Plane the nailing strips and the bottom edge of the plywood sides level across the boat, using a straightedge as a guide, so the bottom plank will make a good joint at the sides. Take your time with this and do a careful job. If this is a poor joint, the boat will leak.

Next fit the bottom plank. Lay the plywood on the bottom of the boat and mark its outline all around. Cut it to shape, leaving a little extra for final smoothing. Be sure that the plywood rests tightly on the nailing strips, and that the joint is good all around before proceeding. Drill for screws, then glue and screw the bottom in place.

Turn the boat over. Fit the frames, or stiffeners, on each side, the knees at the bow and stern, and attach the skeg. Put on the bottom rubbing strips. Screw through the plywood into the oak whenever possible; they hold better this way.

Fit a couple of temporary braces across the gunwales to hold her in shape until the thwarts are in. Take out the molds.

Fit and fasten in the risings and the inwales. Fit the thwarts and screw them in. Fasten them securely, as people often step on them so they need to be strong.

Fit blocks for the rowlocks, install the rowlocks and the mooring eyebolt. Davis pattern rowlocks, which cannot fall overboard, are recommended.

Give her three coats of paint inside and out. If she is to be kept afloat in salt water, the bottom paint should be copper or other anti-fouling paint. Varnish the rubbing strips. Paint her name on the stern, and proceed with the launching ceremonies.

Let her soak up a little water before you use her. A couple of days is enough. It is not considered good for a boat to use her the same day she is launched.

SKIFF "SUZET" READY FOR LAUNCHING

PLAN 3

11'-6" SKIFF

ITEM	LUMBER MATERIAL	NO. PIECES REQ'D	SIZE IN INCHES	LENGTH	
STEM	OAK	1	1¾ X 2	2'–0"	
FRAMES	OAK	12	¾ X 2	1'–7"	
CHINES	OAK	2	¾ X 1½	12'–0"	
KNEES	OAK	4	1		
SKEG	OAK	1	¾ X 4	2'–7"	
RUBBING STRIP	OAK	7	¾ X 1½	12'–0"	
TRANSOM	OAK	1	1 X 17	3'-6"	
CLAMP	OAK	2	¾ X 1½	12'–0"	
SEATS	W. PINE	1 1	¾ X 16 ¾ X 11½	3'–9" 4'–3"	1-¾ X 11½, -3'-6" 1-¾ X 11½, -2'-4"
PLANKING	FIR. PLYWOOD	2	⅜ X 48	12'–0"	
RISINGS	OAK	2	¾ X 1½	12'–0"	

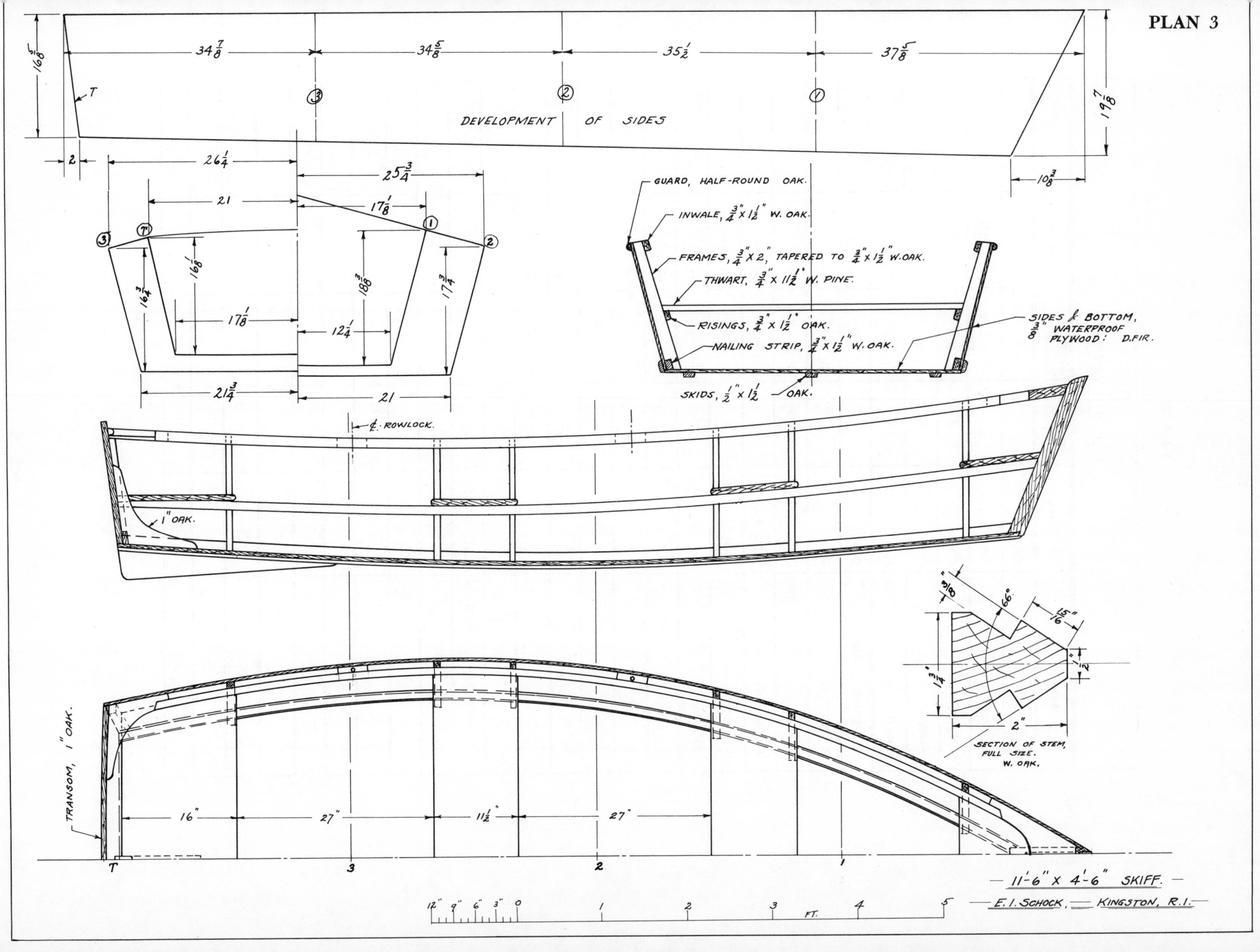

DEVELOPMENT OF SIDES
GUARD, HALF-ROUND OAK.
INWALE, 3/4" X 1 1/2" W. OAK.
FRAMES, 3/4" X 2", TAPERED TO 3/4" X 1 1/2" W. OAK.
THWART, 3/4" X 11 1/2" W. PINE.
RISINGS, 3/4" X 1 1/2" OAK.
NAILING STRIP, 3/4" X 1 1/2" W. OAK.
SIDES & BOTTOM, 3/8" WATERPROOF PLYWOOD: D. FIR.
SKIDS, 1/2" X 1 1/2 OAK.
℄ ROWLOCK.
1" OAK.
TRANSOM, 1" OAK.
SECTION OF STEM, FULL SIZE. W. OAK.
11'-6" X 4'-6" SKIFF.
E. I. SCHOCK, KINGSTON, R.I.
FT.

PLAN 4

13'-6" SKIFF					
ITEM	LUMBER MATERIAL	NO. PIECES REQ'D	SIZE IN INCHES	LENGTH	
STEM	OAK	1	1 3/4 X 2 3/16	29"	
FRAMES	OAK		3/4 X 2 1/2	16 LIN. FT.	
CHINES	OAK	2	3/4 X 1 1/2	14'–0"	
KNEES	OAK	3			
SKEG	FIR	1	7/8 X 6	3'–0"	
RUBBING STRIP	OAK	3 2	5/8 X 1 3/4 HALF RD.	14'–0" 14'–0"	
TRANSOM	FIR	1	3/4 X 18	3'–6"	
CLAMP	OAK	2	3/4 X 1 1/4	14'–0"	
PLANKING	PLYWOOD	2	3/8 X 48	14'–0"	
RISINGS	OAK	2	3/4 X 1 1/4	14'–0"	
SEATS	W. PINE	1	3/4 X 12	4'–6"	
"	"	1	3/4 X 12	4'–1"	
"	"	1	3/4 X 12	2'–3"	
"	"	1	3/4 X 12	1'–3"	
"	"	2	3/4 X 12	3'–9"	
"	"	1	3/4 X 12	2'–0"	
LUMBER FOR FORMS IS ALSO NEEDED					

PLAN 4

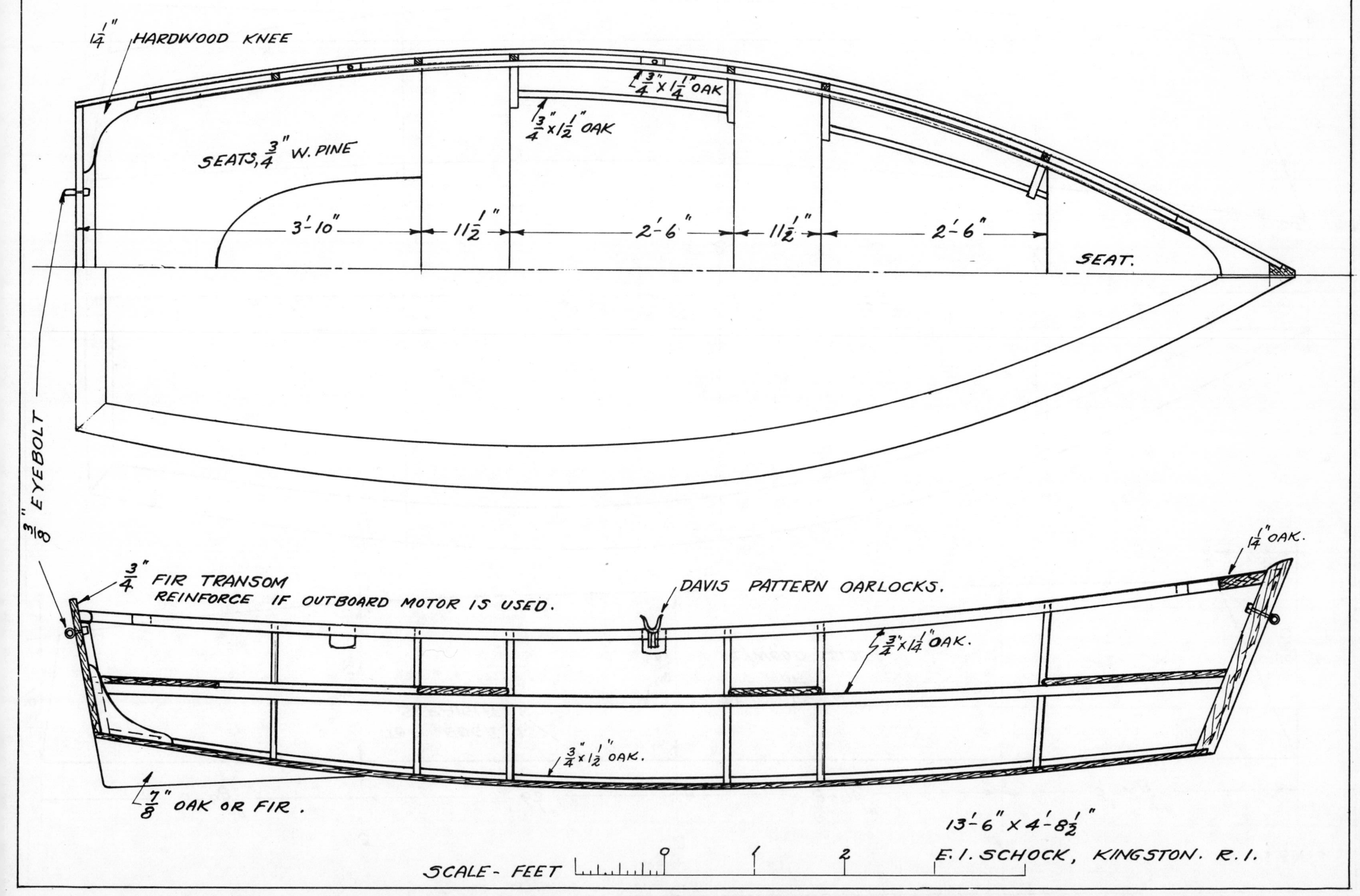

1¼" HARDWOOD KNEE
SEATS, ¾" W. PINE
¾" x 1¼" OAK
¾" x 1½" OAK
3'-10"
11½"
2'-6"
11½"
2'-6"
SEAT.
⅜" EYEBOLT
¾" FIR TRANSOM
REINFORCE IF OUTBOARD MOTOR IS USED.
DAVIS PATTERN OARLOCKS.
1¼" OAK.
¾" x 1¼" OAK.
¾" x 1½" OAK.
⅞" OAK OR FIR.
13'-6" x 4'-8½"
SCALE - FEET
0
1
2
E. I. SCHOCK, KINGSTON. R. I.

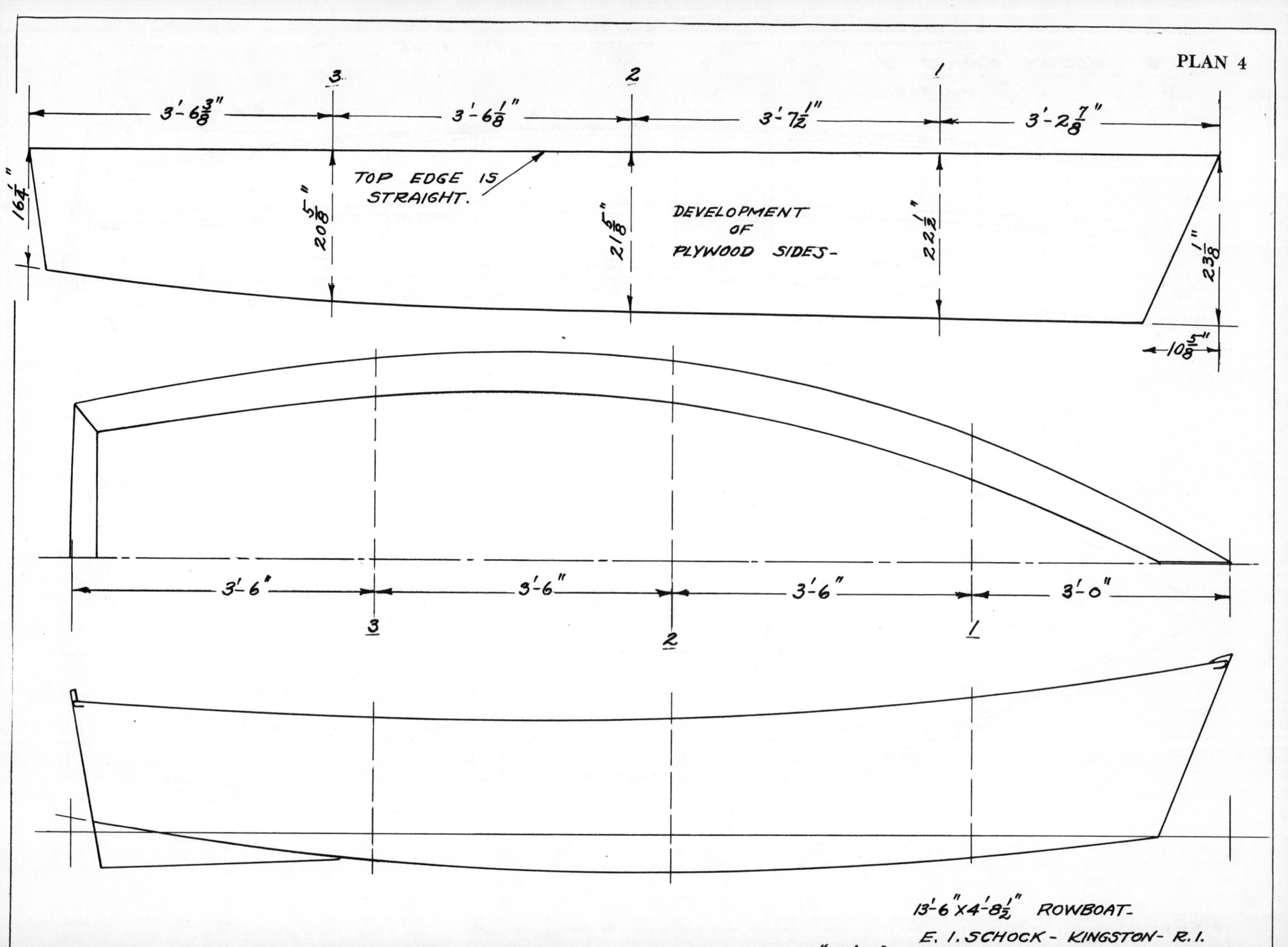
PLAN 4
3
2
1
3'-6 3/8"
3'-6 1/8"
3'-7 1/2"
3'-2 7/8"
TOP EDGE IS STRAIGHT.
DEVELOPMENT OF PLYWOOD SIDES-
16 1/4"
20 5/8"
21 5/8"
22 1/2"
23 1/8"
10 5/8"
3'-6"
3'-6"
3'-6"
3'-0"
3
2
1
13'-6" X 4'-8 1/2" ROWBOAT-
E. I. SCHOCK - KINGSTON - R. I.

SKIFF "PUDDLE DUCK" UNDER WAY

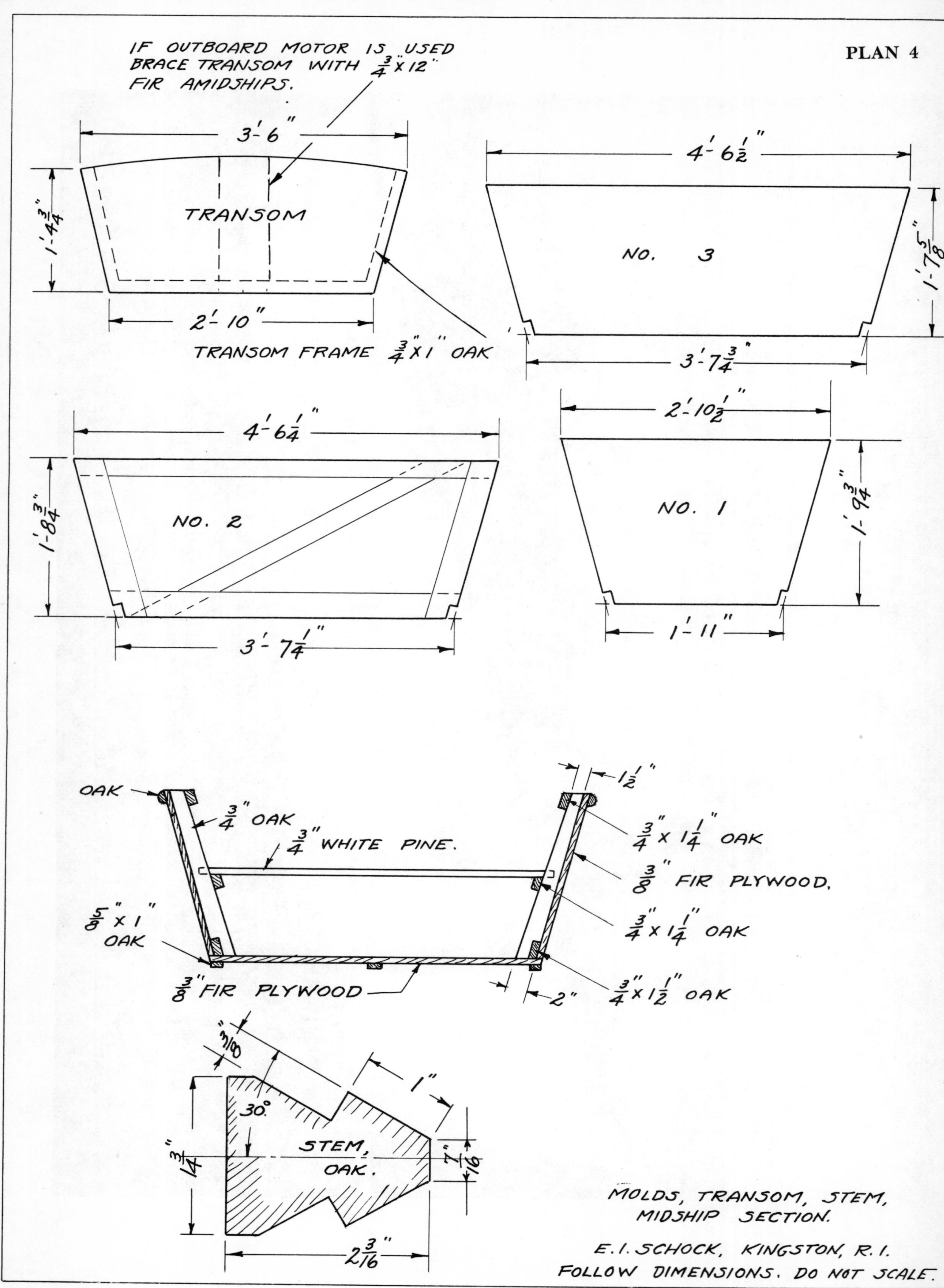
IF OUTBOARD MOTOR IS USED
BRACE TRANSOM WITH 3/4" X 12"
FIR AMIDSHIPS.
3'-6"
1'-4 3/4"
TRANSOM
2'-10"
TRANSOM FRAME 3/4" X 1" OAK
4'-6 1/2"
NO. 3
1'-7 5/8"
3'-7 3/4"
4'-6 1/4"
1'-8 3/4"
NO. 2
3'-7 1/4"
2'-10 1/2"
NO. 1
1'-9 3/4"
1'-11"
1 1/2"
OAK
3/4" OAK
3/4" WHITE PINE.
3/4" X 1 1/4" OAK
3/8" FIR PLYWOOD.
5/8" X 1"
OAK
3/4" X 1 1/4" OAK
3/8" FIR PLYWOOD
2"
3/4" X 1 1/2" OAK
3/8"
1"
30°
STEM,
OAK.
1 3/4"
7/16"
2 3/16"
MOLDS, TRANSOM, STEM,
MIDSHIP SECTION.
E. I. SCHOCK, KINGSTON, R. I.
FOLLOW DIMENSIONS. DO NOT SCALE.

12′6″ OUTBOARD RUNABOUT

This runabout was designed for a general utility, fishing, or family boat. Her carrying capacity is large, and she is steady. Around a camp she is particularly useful, serving as a towboat, grocery truck, marine hayride, or what-have-you.

She is not quite as easy to build as the type used for sailing, since the bottom planking has a sharp bend at the bow. This type of bottom, however, is better for a power boat. The bend does not require that the plywood be sprung or steamed, as the bottom is a true developable surface. (See page 21 for explanation of plywood design.) You should not have any real trouble building her.

Mold Loft Work

Lay down the complete lines, and as much of the construction as your patience will allow. Chapter III outlines loft work procedures. Detail the stem; this is shown on the construction plan drawing. You will notice it is shown in two pieces which are to be bolted together. If you can find an oak crook, you may be able to make the stem in one piece, which is easier and better. Maybe a local boatyard can sell you an oak crook or knee of suitable size, and cut it out on their bandsaw to your pattern. If only straight-grain stock is available, make the stem as shown.

Preliminary Construction

Make a paper pattern of the stem from your loft drawing and go on a stem hunt. Get your lumber dealer, or the local boatyard from whom you buy your lumber, to bandsaw the stem piece to shape. This should not cost much, and will save you a lot of hand work.

Make the keel, frames and transom, with transom frame and outboard motor board. This procedure is outlined in Chapter IV.

Framing

On the building floor lay out a centerline. Measure along this line, marking the frame locations, and at each frame station draw a cross line at right angles to the centerline. Locate the transom and stem. Build her upside down.

Set up the frames, transom and stem in their proper places, with the waterline level, frames plumb and brace everything well.

Bend in the chine pieces, and fasten them to the frames.

Planking

The side planks may now be laid out either by putting the plywood against the boat and marking it, or by first making a paper pattern. The paper pattern method is safer, since nothing of value is spoiled if you miss the fit. A piece of stiff paper or light cardboard held against the side of the boat with a few tacks can be marked and cut to exact shape, and used as a pattern for the plywood side planks. Cut out and fit the side planks. Drill the screw holes, glue and screw the planks to the stem, transom and chine pieces. Try the pattern on both sides of the boat before cutting, as the two sides may not be exactly alike. Let the glue set overnight.

Do the bottom planks the same way, using a pattern, and checking both sides. Since the bottom planks overlap the chine on this boat, you can leave the edges a little full, for planing off after they are fastened and the glue has set.

The planking should be fastened with 1″ No. 8 screws, set about 2¼″ apart along the chine and keel, stem and transom, and 5″ or 6″ apart along the frames.

Plane the edges of the bottom planks smooth and fair, and paint them with plywood sealer. Screw on the spray strips. No glue will be necessary this time as this is not a watertight joint.

Finishing and Painting

Turn the boat over, and saw off the long frame ends.

Put on the guard strips, fastening them with screws from the inside.

Fit the quarter knees at the stern, and the breast hook at the bow. Fit the inwales. Notice that these are beveled where they are notched into the knees and breast hook; this makes fitting easier. You can fit one end and screw it fast, then spring the inwale around, holding it against each frame with a clamp or a nail, and mark the length. Cut it just a bit too long to fit in. Plane a bit off the end and try it again for length; plane off another shaving. Keep this up until it fits exactly. A nice fit here looks neat and strengthens the boat.

Install the floor boards, painting the under side before they go in. Also paint the bottom of the boat on the inside, two coats, before fitting the flooring. Last come the thwarts, well fastened to tie the two sides of the hull together.

Rowlocks may be fitted and a pair of oars carried along for emergencies. Oars are handy for pushing off the beach, even if you never row with them.

Paint the flooring with non-skid paint, the sides with yacht paint, and the bottom with a good anti-fouling paint, using three coats throughout.

Finally put in a 3/8" eyebolt at both bow and stern, for mooring, and launch her. Let her swell for a day or two before using her.

PLAN 5

12'–6" OUTBOARD RUNABOUT					
ITEM	LUMBER MATERIAL	NO. PIECES REQ'D	SIZE IN INCHES	LENGTH	
STEM	OAK	1 1	2½ X 4½ 2½ X 5	26" 20"	
KEEL	OAK	1	1 X 4½	12'–0"	
FRAMES	SPRUCE		⅝ X 1¾	70 LINEAR FEET	
CHINES	OAK	2	¾ X 1¼	14'–0"	
KNEES	HACKMATACK	4	1		
FLOORS	SPRUCE	8	¾ X 3	2'–0"	
RUBBING STRIP	OAK	2 2	⅜ X 1 1⅛ HALF RD.	14'–0" 14'–0"	
TRANSOM	SPRUCE	1	¾ X 17	4'–0"	
CLAMP	SPRUCE	2	¾ 1¼	14'–0"	
FLOORING	SPRUCE	13	⅝ X 3¾	10'–6"	
SEATS	W. PINE	3	⅝ X 18	ONE 4'–3" ONE 4'–6" ONE 3'–0"	
PLANKING	FIR PLYWOOD	2	⅜ X 48	14'–0"	
MOTORBOARD (OUTBOARDS)	OAK	1	¾ X 12	17"	
GUSSETS	FIR PLYWOOD	16	⅜ SCRAP PLYWOOD		

PLAN 5

	HEIGHT FROM W. L.			HALF BREADTHS.	
	DECK	CHINE	KEEL	DECK	CHINE
0	25 1/4	10 7/8		1/4	
1	23 5/8	7 7/8	1 1/2	11 3/8	7 1/8
2	22 1/4	5 1/4	− 1 1/4	19 1/8	13 7/8
3	20 3/8	2 1/2	− 3	25 1/4	20 1/8
4	18 5/8	1 1/4	− 3 7/8	28 1/8	24
5	17 3/8	1/4	− 4 1/8	29	26 1/8
6	16 1/8	− 3/8	− 4	28 7/8	27
7	15 1/4	− 5/8	− 3 7/8	28	27 1/4
8	14 5/8	− 7/8	− 3 3/4	26 3/4	27 1/8
9	14 1/4	− 1 1/4	− 3 3/8	25 3/8	26 3/4
T	14	− 1 1/2	− 3	23 5/8	26 1/4

OFFSETS.

E. I. SCHOCK, KINGSTON, R.I.

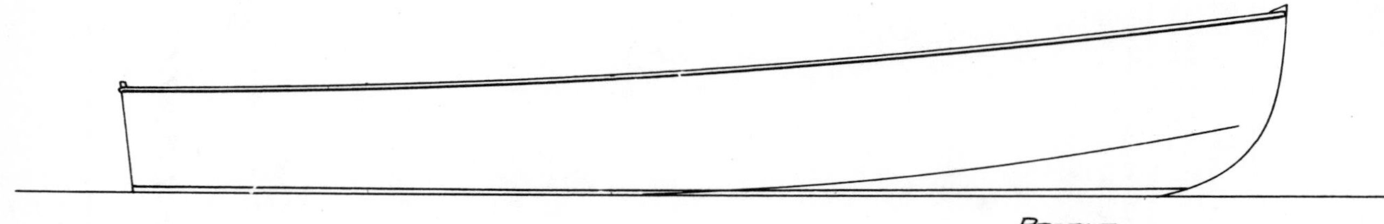

PROFILE.

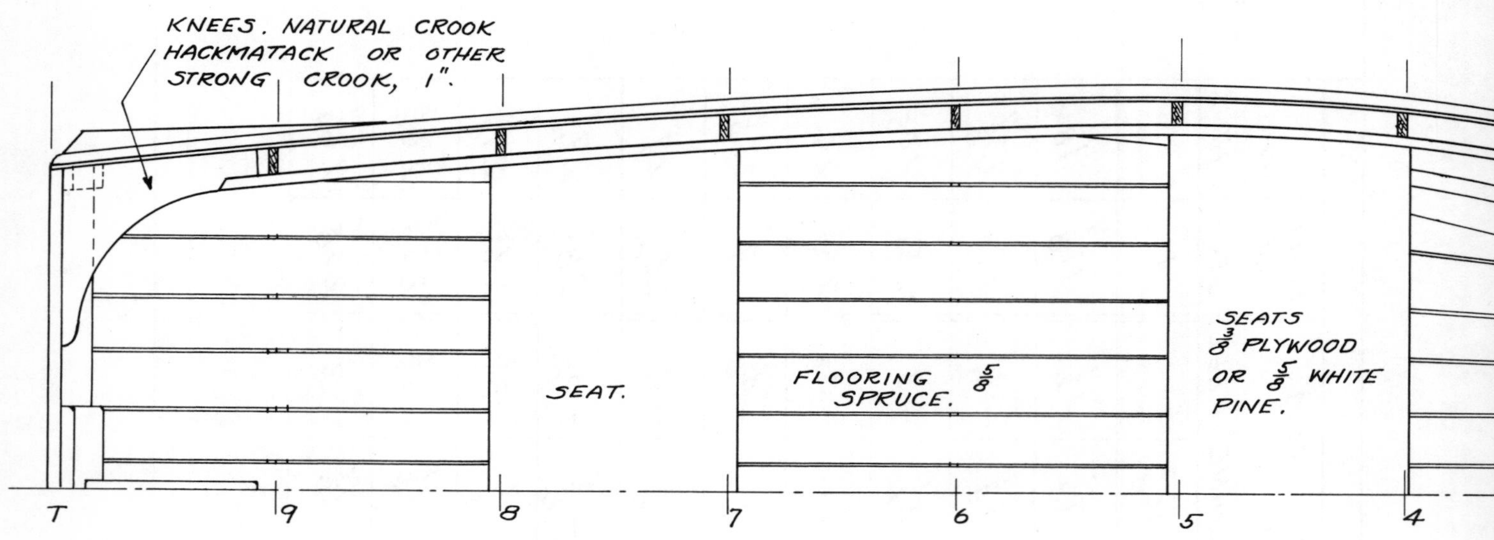
KNEES. NATURAL CROOK
HACKMATACK OR OTHER
STRONG CROOK, 1".
SEAT.
FLOORING 5/8
SPRUCE.
SEATS
3/8 PLYWOOD
OR 5/8 WHITE
PINE.
T
9
8
7
6
5
4

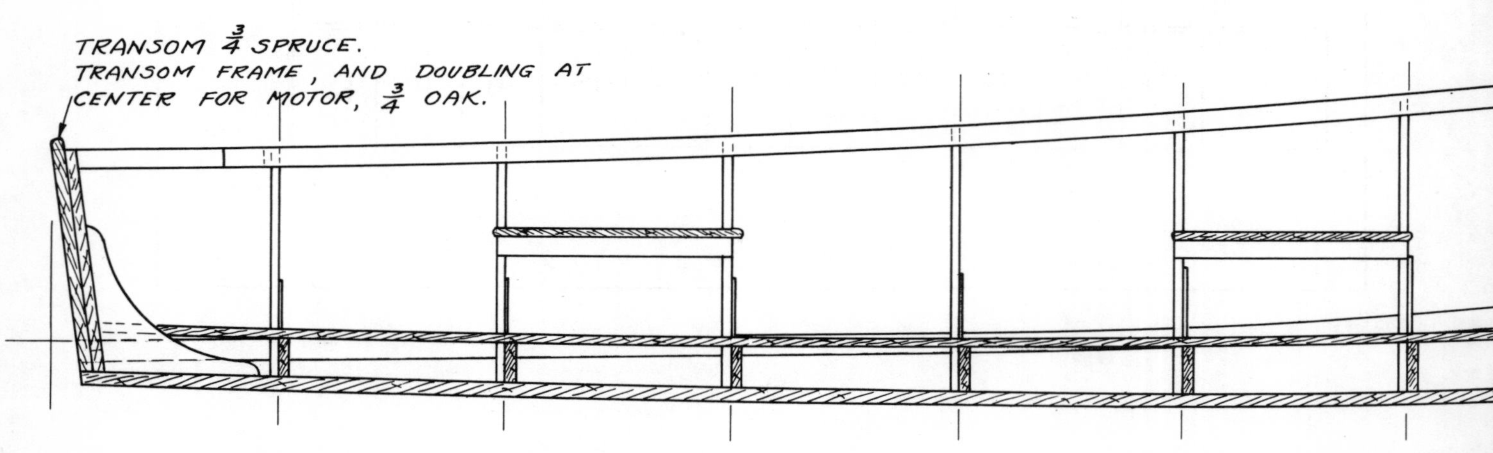
TRANSOM 3/4 SPRUCE.
TRANSOM FRAME, AND DOUBLING AT
CENTER FOR MOTOR, 3/4 OAK.

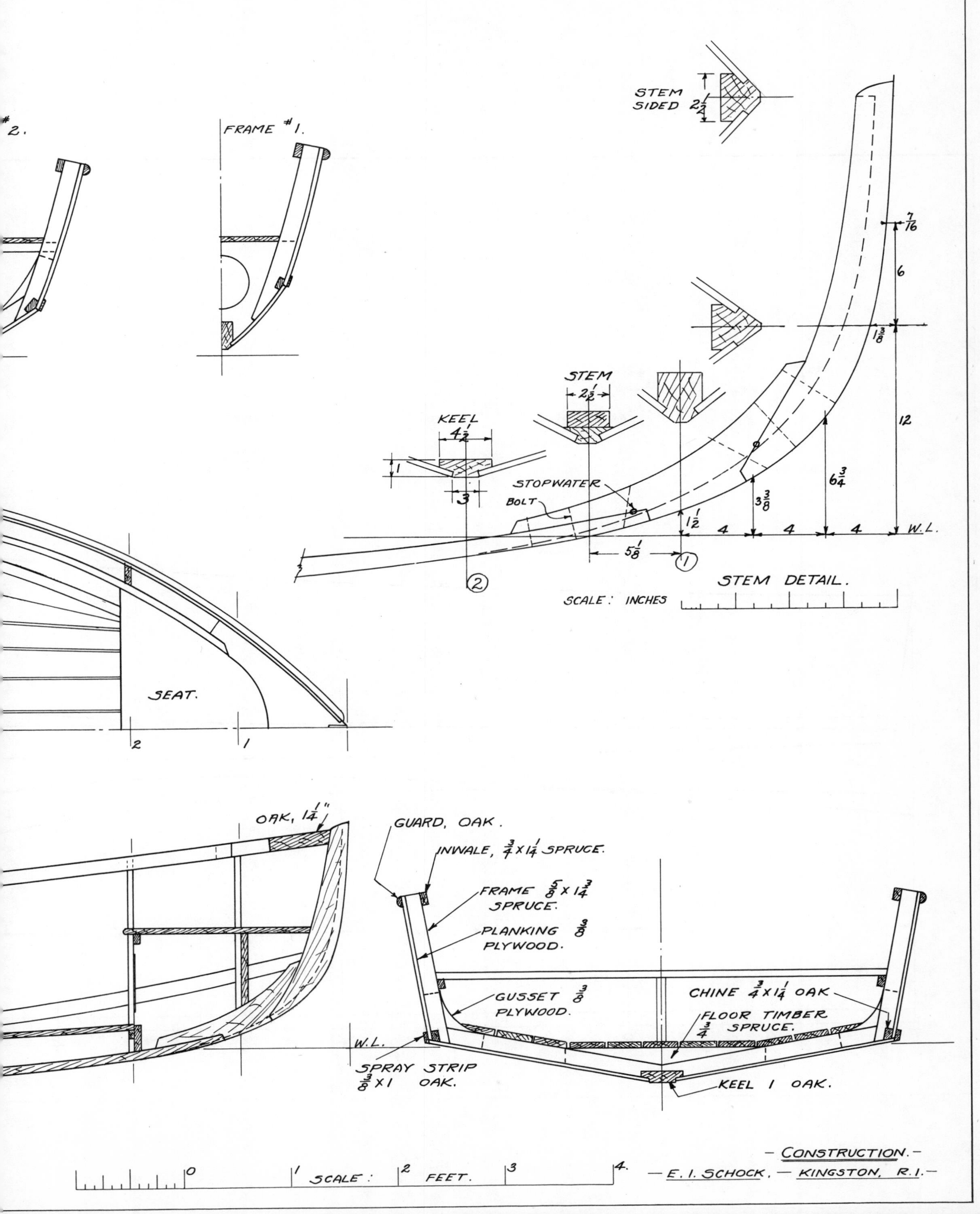

#2.
FRAME #1.
STEM SIDED $2\frac{1}{2}$
STEM $2\frac{1}{2}$
KEEL $4\frac{1}{2}$
1
3
STOPWATER
BOLT
$\frac{7}{16}$
6
$1\frac{3}{8}$
12
$6\frac{3}{4}$
$3\frac{3}{8}$
$1\frac{1}{2}$
4
4
4
W.L.
$5\frac{1}{8}$
1
2
STEM DETAIL.
SCALE: INCHES
SEAT.
2
1
OAK, $1\frac{1}{4}$"
GUARD, OAK.
INWALE, $\frac{3}{4}$ x $1\frac{1}{4}$ SPRUCE.
FRAME $\frac{5}{8}$ x $1\frac{3}{4}$ SPRUCE.
PLANKING $\frac{3}{8}$ PLYWOOD.
GUSSET $\frac{3}{8}$ PLYWOOD.
CHINE $\frac{3}{4}$ x $1\frac{1}{4}$ OAK
FLOOR TIMBER $\frac{3}{4}$ SPRUCE.
W.L.
SPRAY STRIP $\frac{3}{8}$ x 1 OAK.
KEEL 1 OAK.
0
1
SCALE:
2
FEET.
3
4.
- CONSTRUCTION. -
- E. I. SCHOCK. - KINGSTON, R.I. -

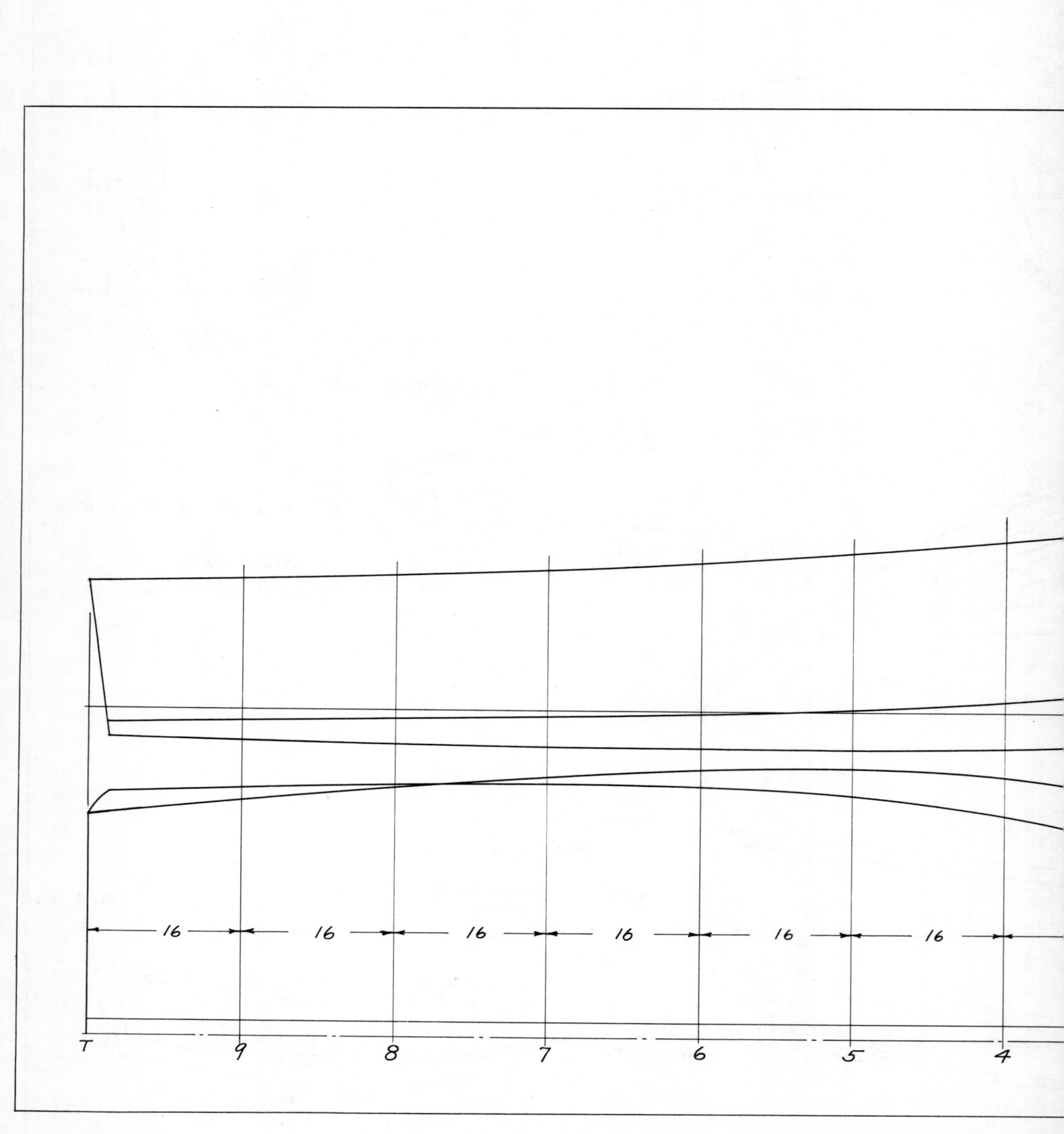

16
16
16
16
16
16
T
9
8
7
6
5
4

PLAN 5

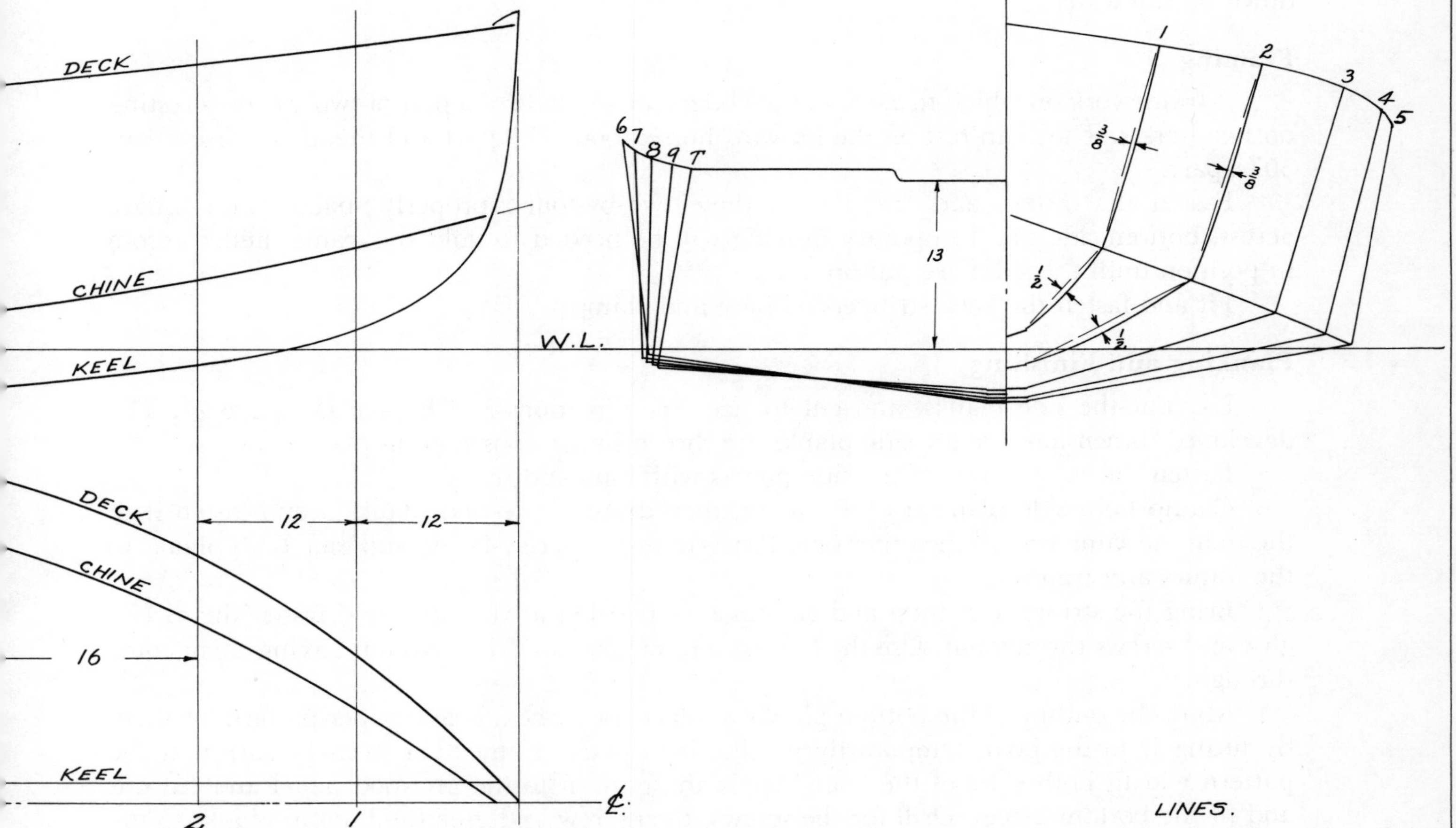

DECK

CHINE

KEEL

W.L.

13

DECK

CHINE

KEEL

12 12

16

2 1 ℄

0 SCALE: 1 2 FEET. 3 4

LINES.

E. I. SCHOCK.
KINGSTON, R.I.

10′6″ RACING OUTBOARD

This little skimmer is a simple construction job, and should be built without any real difficulty. But a boat of this type needs to be rugged, which means good workmanship throughout, and careful fitting, yet it is important that she be kept light, so do not add any unnecessary weight in her construction. The lighter she is the faster she will go.

Mold Loft Work

Lay down the complete lines full size, as described in Chapter III. Note that the bottom of the keel on the lines is shown to the outside of the planking, so take off the planking thickness along the keel bottom the same as you do for the frames.

Preliminary Construction

The transom and stem are made as described in Chapter IV.

The frames are a little different construction. Each frame consists of a bottom piece extending right across the boat, deck beams at the top, and two plywood webs with stiffeners, for side pieces.

Cut out the pieces: one bottom piece, two side webs, one deck beam, and the stiffeners for the side webs. Glue and screw the bottom frame to the side webs. If you prefer, rivets may be substituted for screws. Glue and screw (or rivet) the deck beam to the side webs. Fit the stiffeners to each side web, and glue them on. Notch the bottom of the completed frame to take the longitudinal stringers. These fore and aft stringers help to distribute the stress on the bottom when she bounces on a wave. These little boats hit hard when they come down on the water.

Framing

A framework on which to assemble the boat can be made of a pair of two-by-fours resting on two horses. They can rest on the forward horse about 9″ apart and the after horse about 30″ apart.

Fasten the frames and transom to these two-by-fours, properly spaced, and square across, bottom side up. Temporary bracing will be needed to hold the frames and transom in position until the sides are put on.

Fit and fasten the keel, stringers, chines, and clamps.

Planking and Finishing

Lay out the side planks, and cut to size. See directions in Chapter IV, page 21. The developed dimensions for the side planks are shown in the construction plan.

Fasten the stem to one of the side planks with glue and screws.

Clamp both side planks to the frames, then draw the second plank in and fasten it to the stem the same way as the other one. Proceed next to screw-fasten and glue both planks to the frames and transom.

Bring the stringers, chines, and clamps into position at the bow, and fasten them. Use glue and screws throughout. Use the longest screws you can drive without having them come through.

Mark the outline of the bottom planks in place, or make a heavy paper pattern for them by fitting it to the boat, temporarily tacking it in place. Remember to make sure that the pattern will fit both sides of the boat. Apply the pattern to the plywood panel and cut out and fit the bottom pieces. Drill for the screws, then screw and glue the bottom planks to the chines, frames, stringers and transom.

Trim off excess from the edges of the bottom planks. Sandpaper the bottom and sides, and give them a coat of plywood sealer.

Turn the boat over. Remove the two-by-fours. They should be slid out endways, toward the stern. Give the interior a coat of plywood sealer.

Fit and screw down the flooring before putting on the deck, and do any painting that needs to be done up forward under the deck.

Mark the deck planks by fitting them to the boat, cut them out, and glue and screw them in place. Trim edges and apply a coat of plywood sealer.

Fit the backing for the coaming, and the coaming itself.

This boat can be painted fancy colors on the outside if you like. These little skimmers look all right in fancy dresses. The flooring should be painted with non-skid deck paint. Remember to fit a cleat or ring so you can tie her up to a dock.

The first time you start the motor be careful not to run into anything. She starts all-of-a-sudden.

PLAN 6

10'-6" RACING OUTBOARD

ITEM	LUMBER MATERIAL	NO. PIECES REQ'D	SIZE IN INCHES	LENGTH	
STEM	OAK	1	2 1/8 X 2 1/8	6"	
KEEL	OAK	1	7/8 X 3	10'-6"	
FRAMES	SPRUCE	7 14	3/4 X 4 1/2 1/4 PLYWOOD	4'-0"	
CHINES	OAK	2	3/4 X 1 1/4	12'-0"	
KNEES	OAK	1	1 1/4		
TRANSOM	SPRUCE	1	3/4 X 16	3'-7"	
CLAMP	SPRUCE	2	3/4 X 1 1/4	12'-0"	
DECK	FIR PLYWOOD	1	1/4 X 48	12'-0"	
DECK BEAMS	SPRUCE	1	5/8 X 6	14'-0"	
FLOORING	SPRUCE	3	5/8 X 8	7'-0"	
COAMING	OAK	2	1/2 X 2	6'-0"	
PLANKING	PLYWOOD (FIR)	2	1/4 X 48	12'-0"	
MOTOR BOARD (OUTBOARDS)	OAK	1	3/4 X 14	14"	
STRINGERS	OAK	4	5/8 X 1	12'-0"	

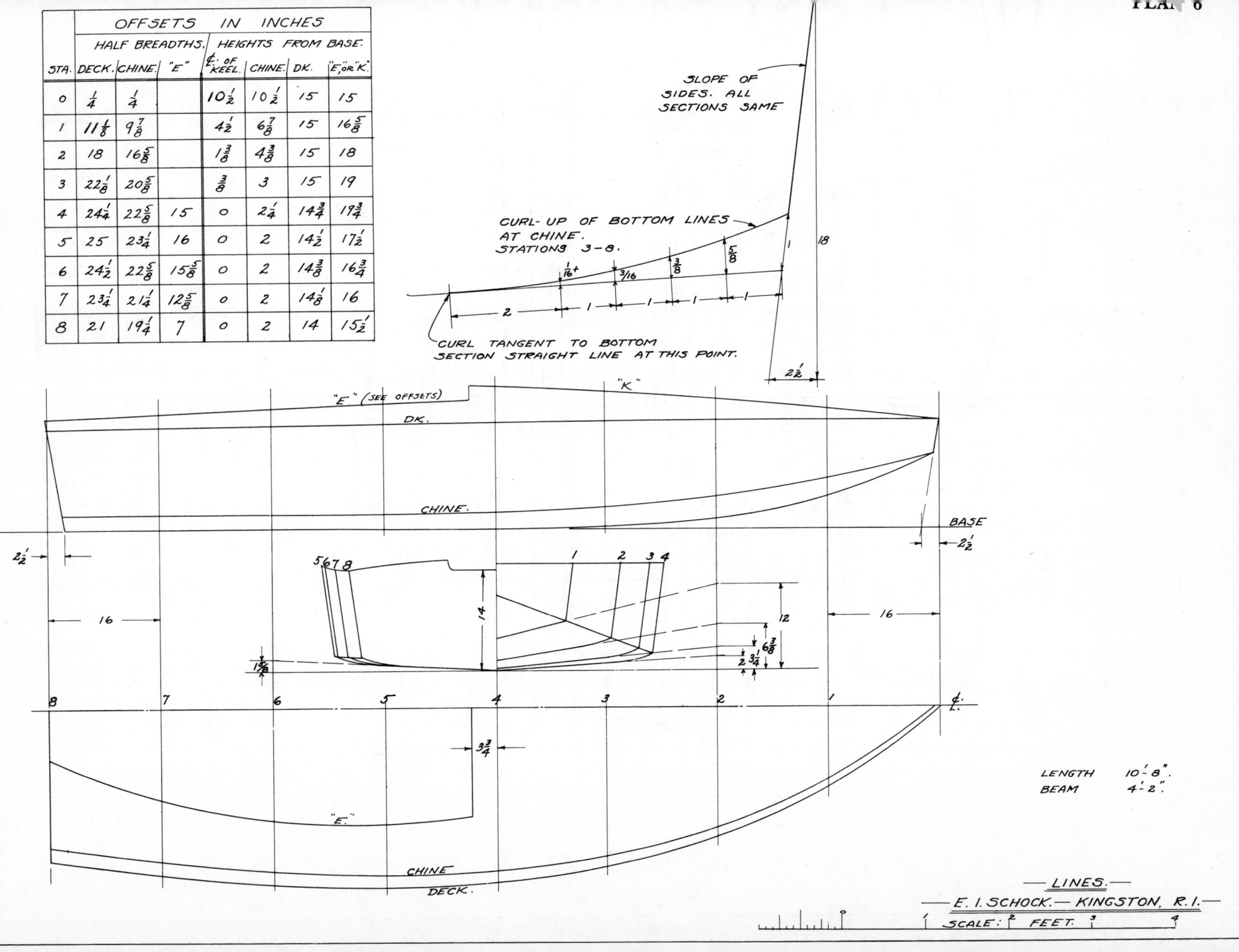

	OFFSETS IN INCHES						
	HALF BREADTHS.			HEIGHTS FROM BASE.			
STA.	DECK.	CHINE.	"E"	℄ OF KEEL.	CHINE.	DK.	"E" OR "K".
0	1/4	1/4		10 1/2	10 1/2	15	15
1	11 1/8	9 7/8		4 1/2	6 7/8	15	16 5/8
2	18	16 5/8		1 3/8	4 3/8	15	18
3	22 1/8	20 5/8		3/8	3	15	19
4	24 1/4	22 5/8	15	0	2 1/4	14 3/4	19 3/4
5	25	23 1/4	16	0	2	14 1/2	17 1/2
6	24 1/2	22 5/8	15 5/8	0	2	14 3/8	16 3/4
7	23 1/4	21 1/4	12 5/8	0	2	14 1/8	16
8	21	19 1/4	7	0	2	14	15 1/2

—LINES.—

—E. I. SCHOCK.—KINGSTON, R.I.—

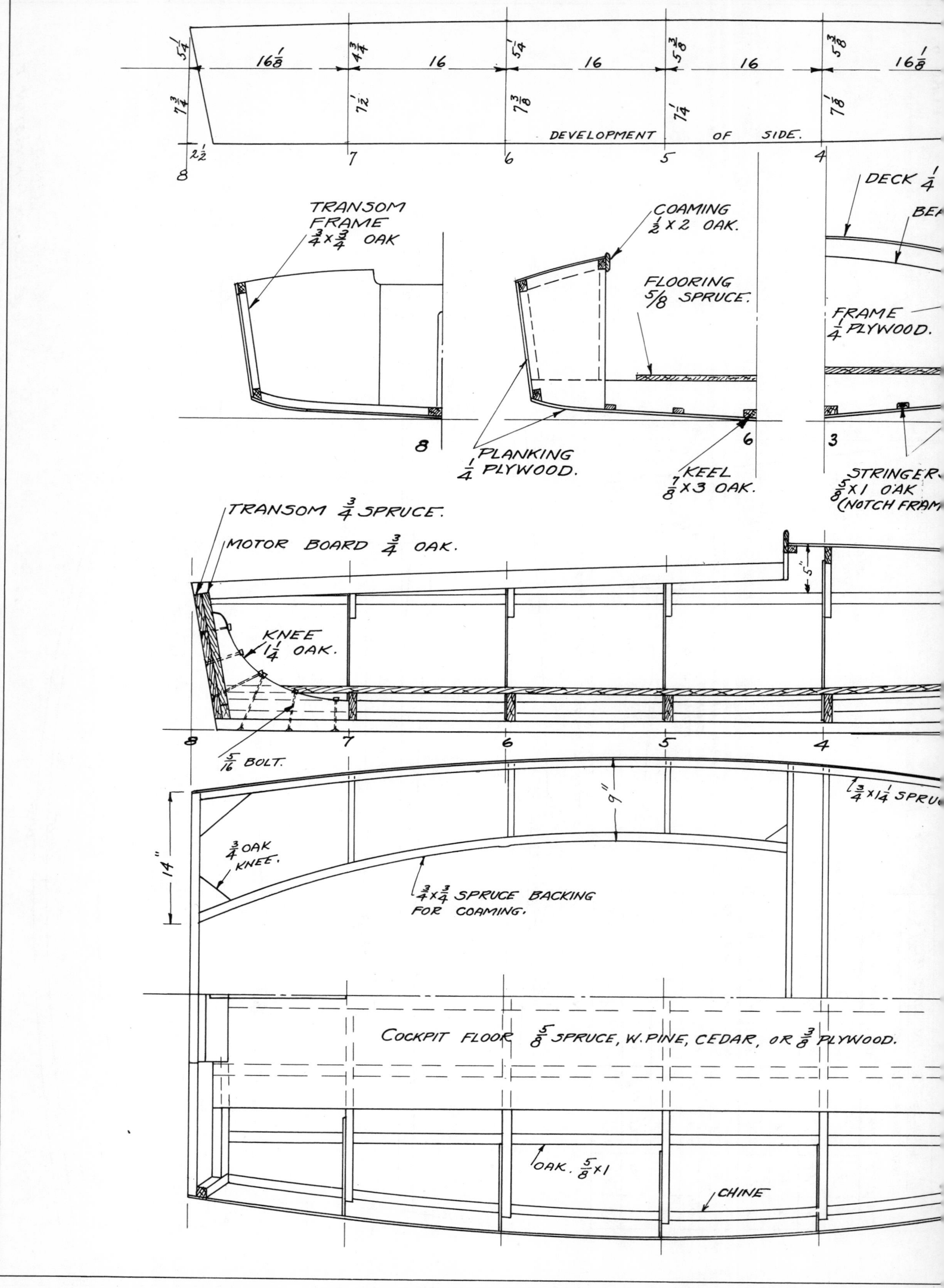

DEVELOPMENT OF SIDE.
TRANSOM FRAME 3/4 X 3/4 OAK
COAMING 1/2 X 2 OAK.
FLOORING 5/8 SPRUCE.
DECK 1/4
FRAME 1/4 PLYWOOD.
PLANKING 1/4 PLYWOOD.
KEEL 7/8 X 3 OAK.
STRINGERS 5/8 X 1 OAK (NOTCH FRAM
TRANSOM 3/4 SPRUCE.
MOTOR BOARD 3/4 OAK.
KNEE 1 1/4 OAK.
5/16 BOLT.
3/4 OAK KNEE.
3/4 X 3/4 SPRUCE BACKING FOR COAMING.
3/4 X 1 1/4 SPRU
COCKPIT FLOOR 5/8 SPRUCE, W. PINE, CEDAR, OR 3/8 PLYWOOD.
OAK. 5/8 X 1
CHINE

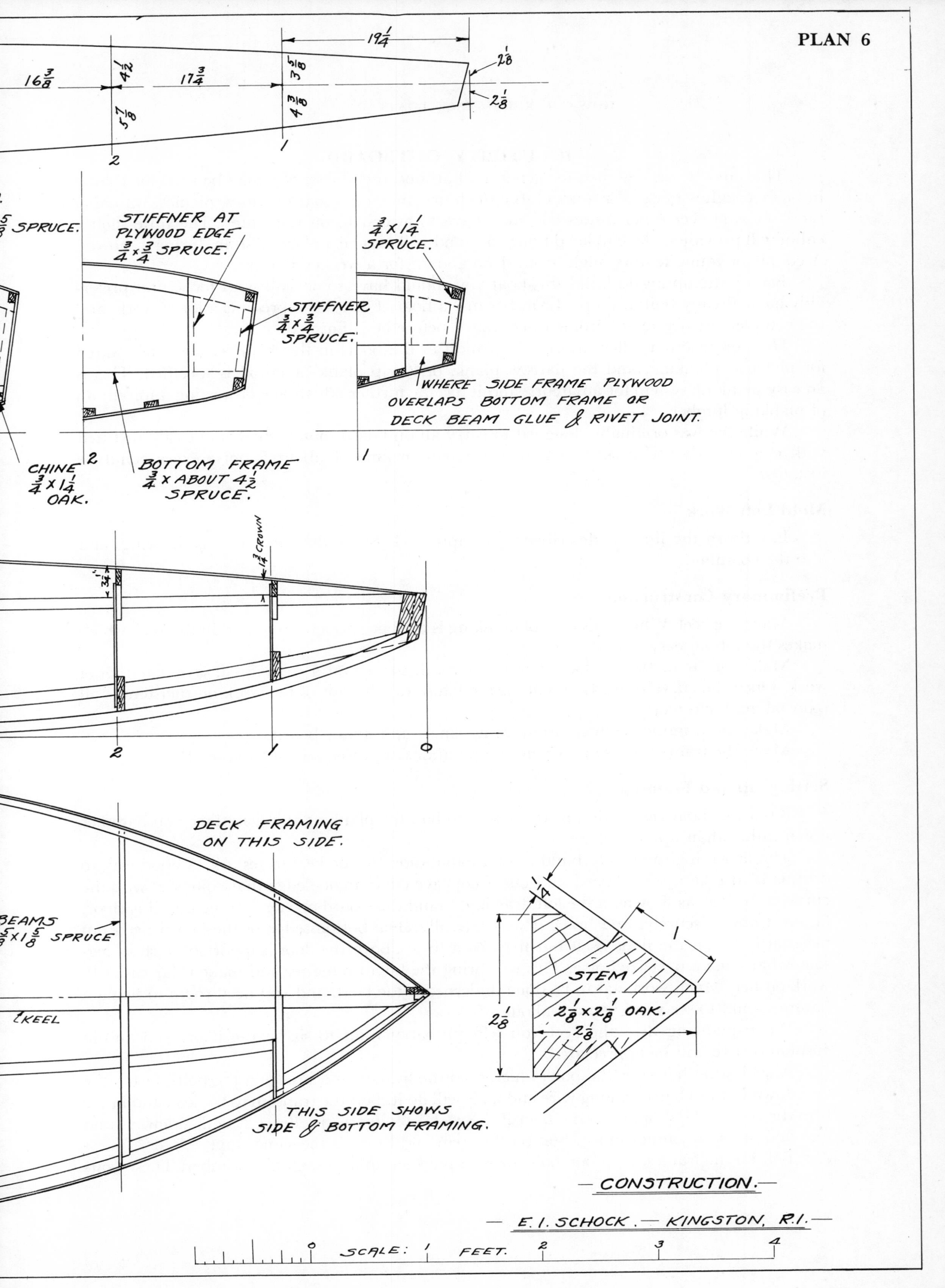

19 1/4
2 1/8
16 3/8
4 1/2
17 3/4
3 5/8
2 1/8
5 7/8
4 3/8
2
1
5/8 SPRUCE.
STIFFNER AT PLYWOOD EDGE 3/4 x 3/4 SPRUCE.
STIFFNER 3/4 x 3/4 SPRUCE.
3/4 x 1 1/4 SPRUCE.
WHERE SIDE FRAME PLYWOOD OVERLAPS BOTTOM FRAME OR DECK BEAM GLUE & RIVET JOINT.
CHINE 3/4 x 1 1/4 OAK.
BOTTOM FRAME 3/4 x ABOUT 4 1/2 SPRUCE.
1 3/4 CROWN
3 1/4
0
DECK FRAMING ON THIS SIDE.
BEAMS 5/8 x 1 5/8 SPRUCE
KEEL
THIS SIDE SHOWS SIDE & BOTTOM FRAMING.
1/4
1
STEM
2 1/8 x 2 1/8 OAK.
2 1/8
— CONSTRUCTION. —
— E. I. SCHOCK. — KINGSTON, R.I. —
SCALE: 1 FEET. 2 3 4

16′ UTILITY OUTBOARD

This launch was designed for general all-around usefulness. She may be used for fishing in fairly rough waters, as a small club launch, a family day-boat for rides, picnics, watching races, or whatever other duties you may have to attend to on the water. The little shelter cabin will provide a place to keep things dry and will also be a place to sit in during a shower. A couple of young fellows might even sleep aboard for a weekend cruise.

Before attempting to build this boat you should have some skill with tools, and preferably have already built a simple boat, because a boat of this size represents a lot of work, and the complete novice may become discouraged before he is finished.

Her construction differs from that of most of the boats in this book as she is not suited for plywood planking, and the narrow plank, or "strip plank" method is specified. This is an easy planking system for amateurs, and it has the further advantage of wasting a minimum of planking lumber.

While she was originally designed to carry an outboard motor, she could easily be fitted with engine beds and a skeg so that an inboard engine of about 5 horsepower could be installed.

Mold Loft Work

Lay down the lines as described in Chapter III. Show the stem on this drawing, and also the coaming.

Preliminary Construction

Make the keel. Where this type of planking is used no rabbet is required in the keel, which makes the job an easy one.

Make the stem. If your local boatbuilder will make you a stem it will save you a lot of work. Once the curves have been cut on the bandsaw, the rest of the work on the stem is all painstaking hand work.

Make the transom, with transom frame, knee, and motor board.

Make the frames. These preliminary operations are discussed in Chapter IV.

Setting-up and Framing

Build this boat right side up. It is easier to nail the planking this way since you hammer down rather than up.

The first thing to do is to build a solid foundation for the keel to rest on. A good way to do this is to take a wide board and cut a concave curve in one edge that coincides with the curve of the keel as shown on the loft drawing. Stand this board on edge on the building floor, fasten it down securely, and brace it well laterally. The bottom edge of the board need not necessarily be on the floor itself but may be a little above the floor, supported on short legs somewhat like an oversize horse. This will bring the boat up higher and make it far easier to work on her. Much work has to be done underneath the boat, and you need room to swing a hammer, and to see what you are about.

When planking near the keel you will probably want to sit on the floor, and an old cushion or two will be appreciated.

After boring holes for the bolts which hold the frames, and inserting the bolts, fasten the keel down to this board; bailing wire and nails will do it. Bolt the transom to the keel and brace it to the roof of the shop, or to the floor if the roof is too far away. Brace it both sideways and fore and aft, so it cannot move. Bolt on the stem and brace it the same way.

Bolt on the frames, with one bolt through the keel up into each floor timber. These bolts will have been put through the keel before it is fastened to the keel foundation, as mentioned above. Set the frames square across the keel, with the waterline marks exactly level crosswise.

Brace the frames as necessary to hold them firm.

Check the waterline. It should be marked on each frame, and also on the stem and transom. This is important, as you have to measure from it, and it is hard to measure from a line that isn't there.

Fit the clamps, and fasten them with ¼″ galvanized carriage bolts through the frames. Put in the breast hook which shows as an oak block away up in the bow of the boat, under the deck.

Fit the chines and screw them to the frames with 1½″ bronze (Everdur) screws, one screw per frame, and one each at the stem and transom. Plane the bevel on the bottom edge of the chines after fastening.

Planking

Have the cedar for the planking ripped to 1³⁄₁₆″ wide, and planed to ⅝″ thickness. The edges do not need to be planed at the mill as each one has to be hand planed later, to make a good fit.

Sometimes, on this type of planking, the garboard (the plank next to the keel) is made wide amidships, and tapered down to a sharp point at each end. This is not necessary, however, and the only advantage of this method is that it permits the planking of a round bottom boat to be laid parallel to the sheer line. Thus the side planks do not end in feather edges at the sheer as they do where a narrow garboard is put on first and the planking done from the bottom up.

Much the easiest method is to start at the keel with one of the long narrow strips, and bevel its edge to a nice fit along the entire length of the keel, finishing at the stem by fitting it into the stem rabbet. You also have to plane the other edge of the plank before you nail it on, because once it is on you can't plane it. Commence fastening at the bow and work aft, nailing through the plank into the keel, edgewise, with nails about 4″ apart. The exact spacing of these nails can best be determined on the job. They must be close enough to assure a watertight joint between the plank and the keel, but if you use too many you add unnecessary weight to the boat.

The nailing should be done this way: first, nail the planks together edgewise, then nail them to the frames. To prevent splitting the planks it is advisable to drill small diameter holes (No. 42 drill) for the nails. This also makes it easier to drive them straight. Do not nail each plank to each frame. This would split the frames, as the nails would be too close together. About every third plank should be fastened to the frame, alternating from plank to plank as you go along. The nails should be galvanized-finish nails, or a rough-sided bronze or Monel nail, like "Anchorfast" or "Stronghold." Do not use smooth copper or bronze nails as they will pull out, the boat will leak, and you never can get her tight no matter how you try. For planks 1⅛″ wide, the nails should be not less than 2″ long, preferably longer. Eightpenny, hot-dipped galvanized, finishing nails are the old standby for this job, but they have the disadvantage of any iron fastening; they may rust-stain the boat after a few years. Bronze or Monel nails will never do this. When hammering in the nails make the last blow a good one, to set the head of the nail a little below the surface of the plank edge; if the head stands above the surface of the plank it will cause a leak. Nails may also be driven in a little way by using a nail set.

Some builders put glue on each edge of each plank as they plank the boat. This makes a very strong structure, but it is likely to be a messy job, as both you and your tools may get covered with glue, and it is advisable to have a wet towel handy to wipe your hands and the hammer handle. Other builders use only nails for fastenings. This makes a good boat, provided the plank edges are well fitted, and is easier than the glue method. If you want an extra fine job, however, the glue-in-each-seam construction is recommended.

To get back to our planking: make the joint between the stem rabbet and the end of the garboard planks an extra good one. This is one of the places to look for poor workmanship when you inspect a boat. If this joint is well made usually you are looking at a well-built boat. Edge nail, working along from bow to stern. This process goes on, plank after plank, first a plank to starboard, then one to port, until she is planked about half way from the keel to the chine. Leave the outer half of the bottom until the part above the chine is planked.

With the topside planking, start at the chine and plank both sides, alternating as before, all the way up to the sheer, completing the sides. Then go back and finish the bottom. The reason for this is so the last bottom plank will overlap the first side plank at the chine, as shown on the midship section drawing. The lowest plank on each side will be nailed to the chine and its lower face must be planed fair with the corresponding face of the chine.

If the planks do not stay in place while you are nailing, clamp each one in turn to the last one you put on, using "C" clamps. A clamp with two small pieces of wood under its grips will hold everything flush and smooth. This takes a little extra time now, but saves more time later on. Space the clamps about two feet, or less, apart, removing them as you nail along. This not only will hold the planks from falling off while you are busy nailing, but it also will help to keep the outer surface of the planking smooth. It is an awful job to plane the planking smooth once it gets away from you.

The planks MUST fit all along the faying edges as this type of boat is not caulked. Consequently she must be tight in every seam when she is launched.

Finishing

Once planked the worst is over. The planking was a long job, we admit, but it is finished, so now get out the deck beam stock and fit the deck beams. Lay the deck of plywood or of white pine planks, but do not use boards that are too wide since wide lumber on the deck will surely warp. About 4″ is wide enough, with no plank over 5″. The deck is a straightforward job, and you should not run into any complications. Fit the coamings, fasten them well, and then put in the flooring. Keep painting as you go along, so that no space is forgotten and covered up, unpainted.

The shelter cabin offers an opportunity to show how good a cabinetmaker you are. Mortise and tenon joints are in order here, and everything should be fitted to the queen's taste. Fasten the house sides down through the coaming with long rods, threaded on each end and set up with nuts and washers, top and bottom. If the house is not strongly built the first sea that hits it will probably knock it to pieces.

The cabin roof may be covered with canvas if you want a really tight roof that looks neat and shipshape. The canvas should be stretched very taut. To do this, paint the cabin roof with any of the good compounds made for cementing down canvas, or with white lead and boiled linseed oil mixed to a paste consistency. Stretch the canvas as tight as you can get it, and tack it with 5⁄8″ copper tacks closely spaced (about 1″) all around. Then take a stiff scrubbing brush, very wet with water, and scrub the canvas down onto the plywood roof. The canvas should be damp when you finish this, but not dripping wet. Paint it at once, while still wet, with flat white. It should stay tight and not wrinkle.

The windshield may be either glass or plastic. Glass is more satisfactory, but quite heavy. Plastic scratches easily, but it is light. Glass should be 1⁄4″ shatterproof. Don't use thin, cheap glass as it may break. Lucite or Plexiglas make the best plastic windows.

Seats in the open cockpit, and in the shelter cabin can be arranged to suit the owner's fancy.

Cleats, chocks, chock rails, and other trimmings complete the job. Finally paint the cabin roof a light color; it will make it cooler inside.

The house sides may be varnished the same as the rubbing strips and other trim. Paint the topsides with yacht paint, and the bottom with a good grade of anti-fouling paint, using three coats all around.

After launching give her three or four nights to soak up before using her under power.

PLAN 7

16'-0" UTILITY OUTBOARD

ITEM	LUMBER MATERIAL	NO. PIECES REQ'D	SIZE IN INCHES	LENGTH	
STEM	OAK	3	2 1/2	LAY OUT ON LOFT	
KEEL	OAK	1	7/8 X 4	14'-0"	
FRAMES	OAK		3/4 X 1 3/4	80 LINEAR FEET	
CHINES	OAK	2	3/4 X 2 1/4	18'-0"	
KNEES	OAK	1	7/8		
FLOORS	OAK	10	7/8 X 4	22"	
RUBBING STRIP	MAHOGANY	2	1 1/4 HALF ROUND	18'-0"	
TRANSOM	W. PINE	1	3/4 X 19	4'-4"	
CLAMP	SPRUCE	2	3/4 X 1 1/4	18'-0"	
DECK	W. PINE		3/4	LAY OUT ON LOFT	
DECK BEAMS	SPRUCE		3/4 X 2 1/2	12 LINEAR FEET	
FLOORING	W. PINE	3 4	3/4 X 6	14'-0" 8'-0"	
COAMING	MAHOGANY	2	3/4 X 12	14'-0"	
SEATS	W. PINE	6	3/4 X 6	4'-4"	
PLANKING	W. CEDAR	40 40	5/8 X 1 1/8 5/8 X 1 1/8	16'-0" 18'-0"	
MOTOR BOARD (OUTBOARDS)	OAK	1	3/4 X 19	14"	

NO. 110 OFFSETS. PLAN 7

FRAME	HEIGHT FROM W.L.				HALF BREADTH				DIAGONALS		
	KEEL	B-1	CHINE	SHEER	KEEL	W.L.	CHINE	DECK	1	2	3
0				27 7/8	3/8			3/8			
1	-5 1/8	4 7/8	6	25 1/2	1/2	2 3/4	6 7/8	12 1/4	9 3/4	5	2 5/8
2	-8 1/2	-2 7/8	3 3/4	23 1/4	1	8 7/8	13 1/4	20 3/4	17 5/8	9 7/8	6 1/4
3	-9 1/4	-6 3/8	1 3/4	21 1/4	1 1/2	15 5/8	18 1/8	26 1/4	23 1/4	13 1/8	8 3/4
4	-9 5/8		1/8	19 5/8	1 7/8		21 3/4	29 1/2		45° WITH W.L.	45° WITH W.L.
5	-9 7/8		-7/8	18 1/4	2		24	31 1/4			
6	-9 5/8		-1 5/8	17 1/8	2		25 1/2	31 7/8			
7	-9 1/8		-1 7/8	16 1/2	2		26	32			
8	-8 1/8		-1 3/4	16 1/8	2		26	31 5/8			
9	-6 3/4		-1 1/4	16 1/8	1 3/4		25 1/4	30 7/8			
10	-5 1/8		-1/2	16 3/8	1 5/8		24	29 5/8	29 1/8		
11	-3 1/4		1/2	17 1/8	1 3/8		22 3/8	28	27 5/8		
12	-1 1/8		1 3/4	18 1/4	1 1/8		20 1/2	25 7/8	25 3/8		

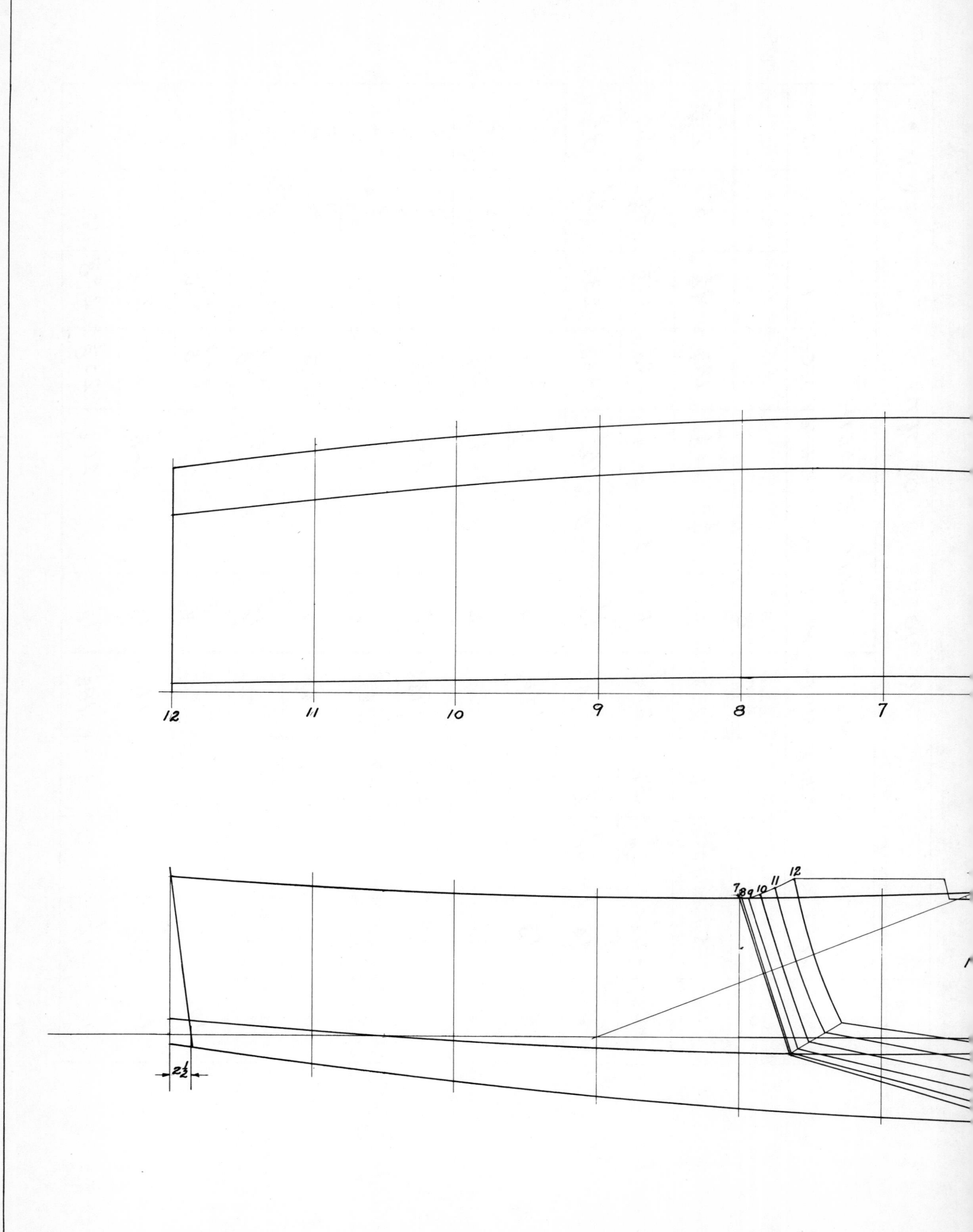

12
11
10
9
8
7
7
8
9
10
11
12
2½

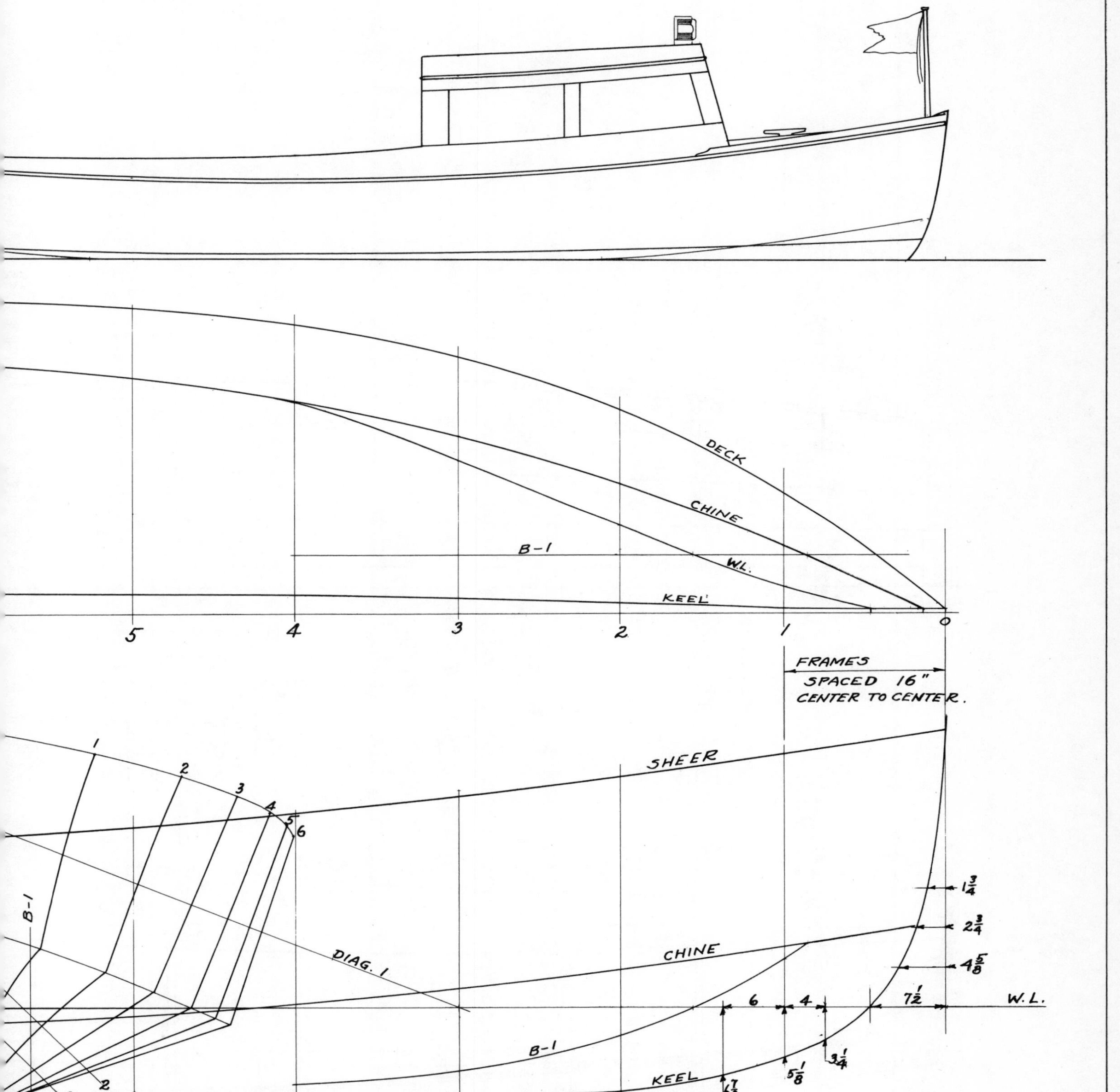

DECK
CHINE
B-1
W.L.
KEEL
5 4 3 2 1 0
FRAMES
SPACED 16"
CENTER TO CENTER.
SHEER
1 2 3 4 5 6
B-1
DIAG. 1
CHINE
W.L.
B-1
KEEL
$1\frac{3}{4}$
$2\frac{3}{4}$
$4\frac{5}{8}$
6 4 $7\frac{1}{2}$
$6\frac{7}{8}$ $5\frac{1}{8}$ $3\frac{1}{4}$
3 2

NO. 110.
LINES.
E. I. SCHOCK. KINGSTON, R. I.
0 1 2 3 4
SCALE FEET

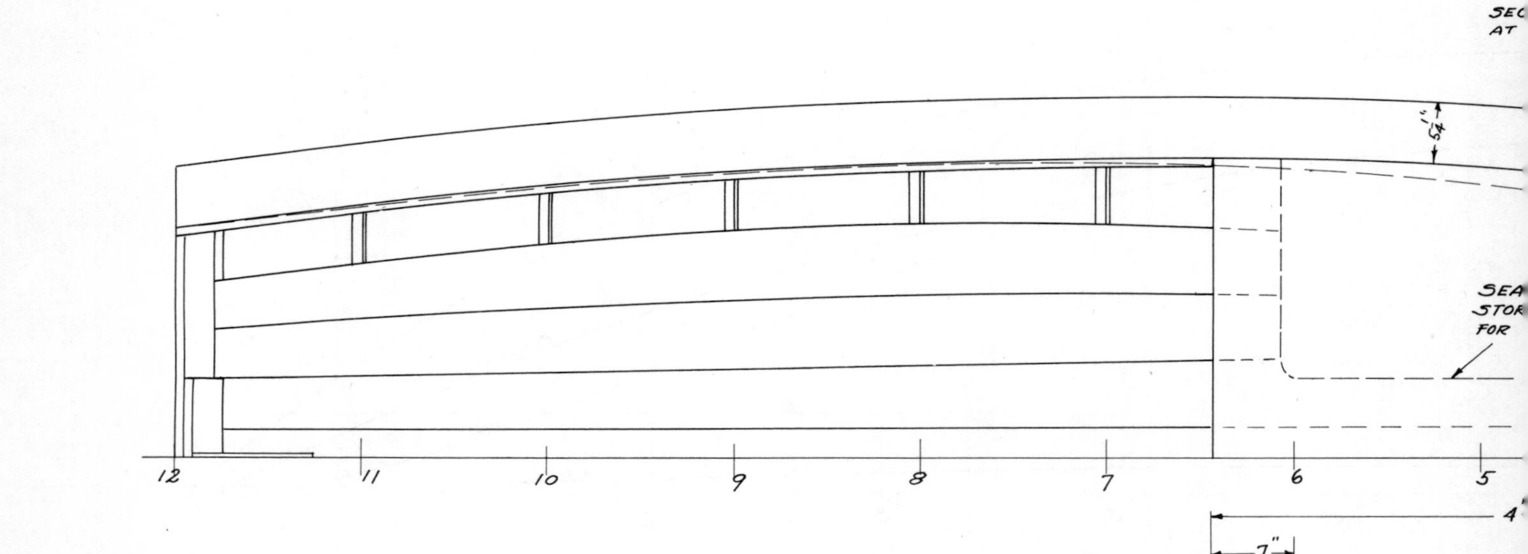

SEC
AT

SEA
STOR
FOR

12 11 10 9 8 7 6 5

4"

7"

CROWN OF ROOF

$4\frac{1}{4}$

$2\frac{1}{2}$

5

$11\frac{1}{2}$

MOTOR REINFORCING $\frac{3}{4}$ OAK, OR HARD PINE.

3 $3\frac{1}{2}$ $4\frac{1}{8}$ $4\frac{5}{8}$ $5\frac{1}{2}$ 6 10

TRANSOM $\frac{3}{4}$ WHITE PINE

BOLT

$\frac{7}{8}$ OAK KNEE.

CLAMP.

PLAN 7

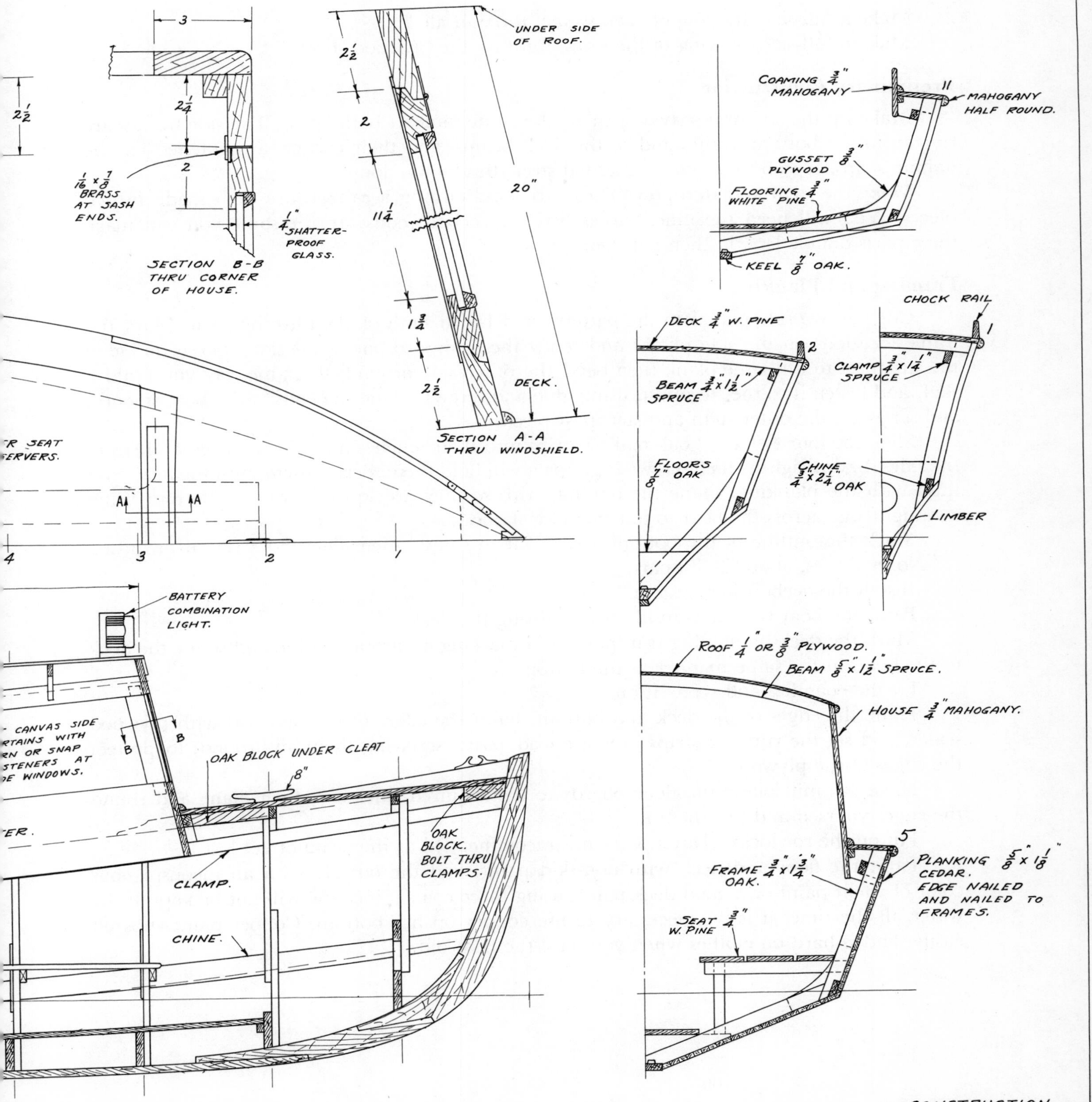

3
2 1/2
2 1/4
2
1/16 x 7/8 BRASS AT SASH ENDS.
1/4" SHATTER-PROOF GLASS.
SECTION B-B THRU CORNER OF HOUSE.
UNDER SIDE OF ROOF.
2 1/2
2
20"
11 1/4
1 3/4
2 1/2
DECK.
SECTION A-A THRU WINDSHIELD.
COAMING 3/4" MAHOGANY
11
MAHOGANY HALF ROUND.
GUSSET 3/8" PLYWOOD
FLOORING 3/4" WHITE PINE
KEEL 7/8" OAK.
CHOCK RAIL
DECK 3/4" W. PINE
2
1
BEAM 3/4" x 1 1/2" SPRUCE
CLAMP 3/4" x 1 1/4" SPRUCE
FLOORS 7/8" OAK
CHINE 3/4" x 2 1/4" OAK
LIMBER
R SEAT SERVERS.
A
A
4
3
2
1
BATTERY COMBINATION LIGHT.
CANVAS SIDE RTAINS WITH RN OR SNAP STENERS AT DE WINDOWS.
B
B
OAK BLOCK UNDER CLEAT
8"
OAK BLOCK. BOLT THRU CLAMPS.
TER.
CLAMP.
CHINE.
ROOF 1/4" OR 3/8" PLYWOOD.
BEAM 5/8" x 1 1/2" SPRUCE.
HOUSE 3/4" MAHOGANY.
5
FRAME 3/4" x 1 3/4" OAK.
PLANKING 5/8" x 1 1/8" CEDAR. EDGE NAILED AND NAILED TO FRAMES.
SEAT 3/4" W. PINE

— CONSTRUCTION. —

— E. I. SCHOCK, — KINGSTON, R.I. —

SCALE OF FEET 0 1 2 3 4

11′3″ DUCK BOAT

Assuming that the owner of this craft will be more interested in duck shooting than in boatbuilding, she has been designed to be as simple as possible to build, yet to produce a boat that will have good stability and will row reasonably well.

Mold Loft Work

Make a full-size drawing of each frame, three in all.

Make a full-size drawing of the sides, right on the plywood sheet.

Preliminary Construction

Make up the six frames, two of each (she is the same at both ends). The side frames are riveted to the bottom frames and to the deck beams, and their corners are notched for the nailing strips, top and bottom. For added strength glue the joints.

Make the stem and sternpost. These, to avoid cutting a rabbet, are each made in two pieces. You will need the inner pieces first. Since both ends are the same you can make these parts double length, then cut them in two.

Framing and Planking

Cut the two side planks to the pattern, and fasten both of them to the stem. Mark the frame locations on the side planks and screw the frames to one of the sides. Screw and glue the sternpost to the same plank then bend the other side around, the same way you build a skiff, and fasten it to the sternpost, using glue and screws. Plane the ends of the boat smooth, and screw on the outer stem and sternpost pieces.

Slide the four ¾″ x ¾″ oak nailing strips into their notches and glue and screw them to the sides. Seven-eighths-inch screws 2¼″ apart will hold them. Screw them until the heads are flush with the planking. Plane the nailing strips so they are square across the bottom, using a straightedge across the boat to test them for flatness.

Mark the outline of the bottom and cut it to shape, then glue and screw it on, using ⅞″ No. 8 screws, about 2¼″ apart.

Install the eyebolt in the stem.

Paint the boat two coats inside before fitting the deck.

Mark the deck by holding it in place and marking all around. Glue and screw the deck to the boat, in the same manner as the bottom.

Fit the coaming and screw it on.

Plane the edges of the deck and bottom. Paint the edges of the plywood with plywood sealer, and set the rubbing strips in white lead paste, screwing them all around, to protect the edges of the plywood.

Have the mill plane the floor boards to the required thickness, then plane and round the edges yourself and put them in.

Put on the rowlocks. (Davis pattern is recommended as they cannot get lost.)

Paint the floor and deck with non-skid paint, and the outside with an inconspicuous color of yacht paint or a good deck paint, using three coats. Since she will not be kept in the water all the time, it is not necessary to use copper on her bottom. Copper paint rubs off easily, and is hard on clothes when you haul the boat out.

PLAN 8

11'-3" DUCKBOAT

ITEM	LUMBER MATERIAL	NO PIECES REQ'D	SIZE IN INCHES	LENGTH	
STEM	OAK	1 1	2 X 4 1 X 2	19" 19"	
FRAMES	SPRUCE		5/8 X 1 1/2 5/8 X 5 5/8 X 8	20 LIN. FT. 4'-0" 7'-0"	
CHINES	OAK	2	3/4 X 3/4	12'-0"	
RUBBING STRIP	OAK	5 2	1/2 X 1 1/2 X 1	12'-0" 10'-0"	
DECK	PLYWOOD	1	3/8 X 48	12'-0"	
DECK BEAMS	SPRUCE		5/8 X 4	16 LIN. FT.	
FLOORING	SPRUCE	7	5/8 X 4	4'-6"	
COAMING	1/4 PLYWOOD W. PINE	2 2	1/4 X 10 5/8 X 9	4'-6" 2'-0"	
PLANKING	PLYWOOD	2 1	3/8 X 8 3/8 3/8 X 48	12'-0" 12'-0"	

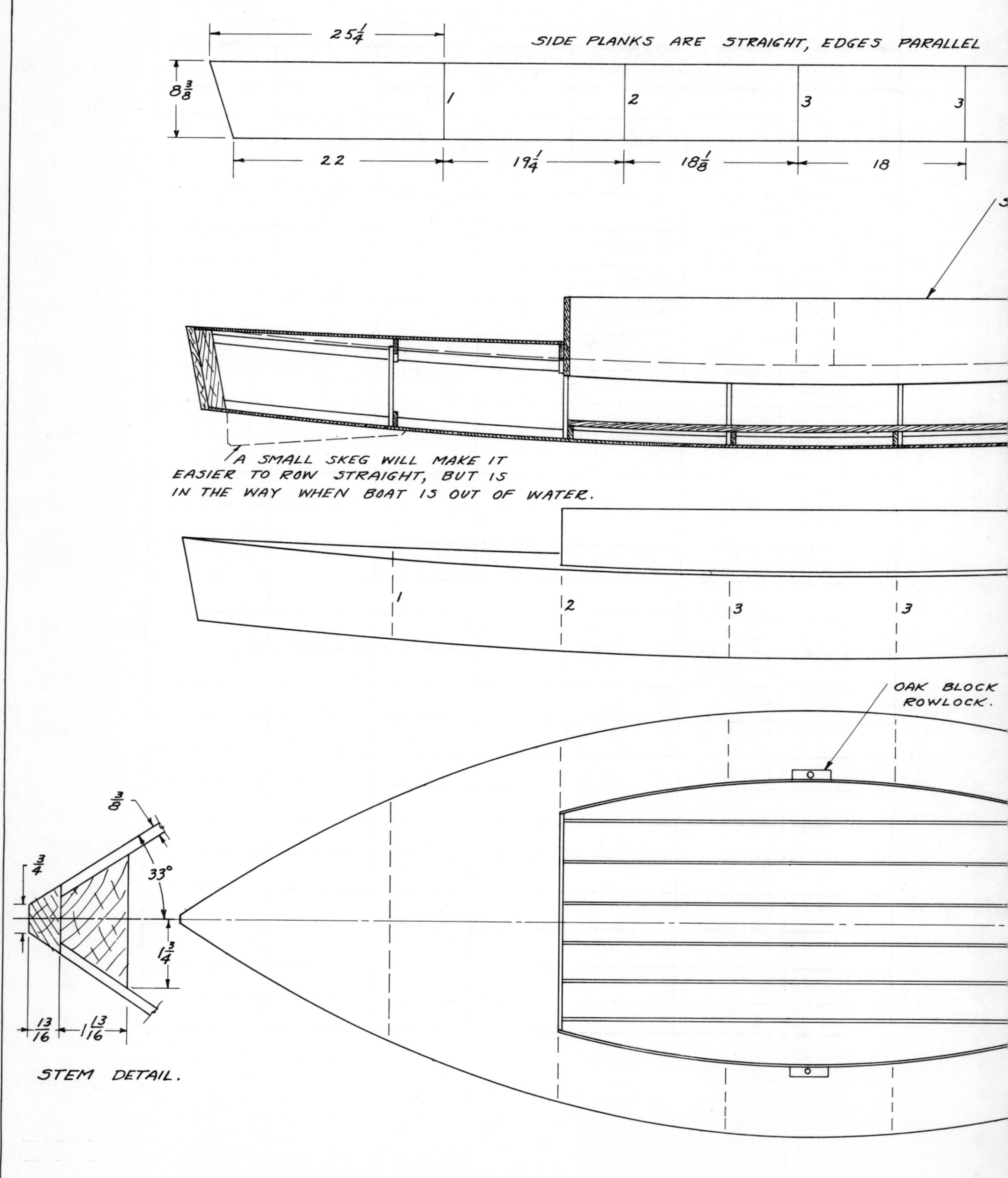

25 1/4
SIDE PLANKS ARE STRAIGHT, EDGES PARALLEL
8 3/8
1
2
3
3
22
19 1/4
18 1/8
18
A SMALL SKEG WILL MAKE IT EASIER TO ROW STRAIGHT, BUT IS IN THE WAY WHEN BOAT IS OUT OF WATER.
1
2
3
3
OAK BLOCK ROWLOCK.
3/8
3/4
33°
1 3/4
13/16
1 13/16
STEM DETAIL.

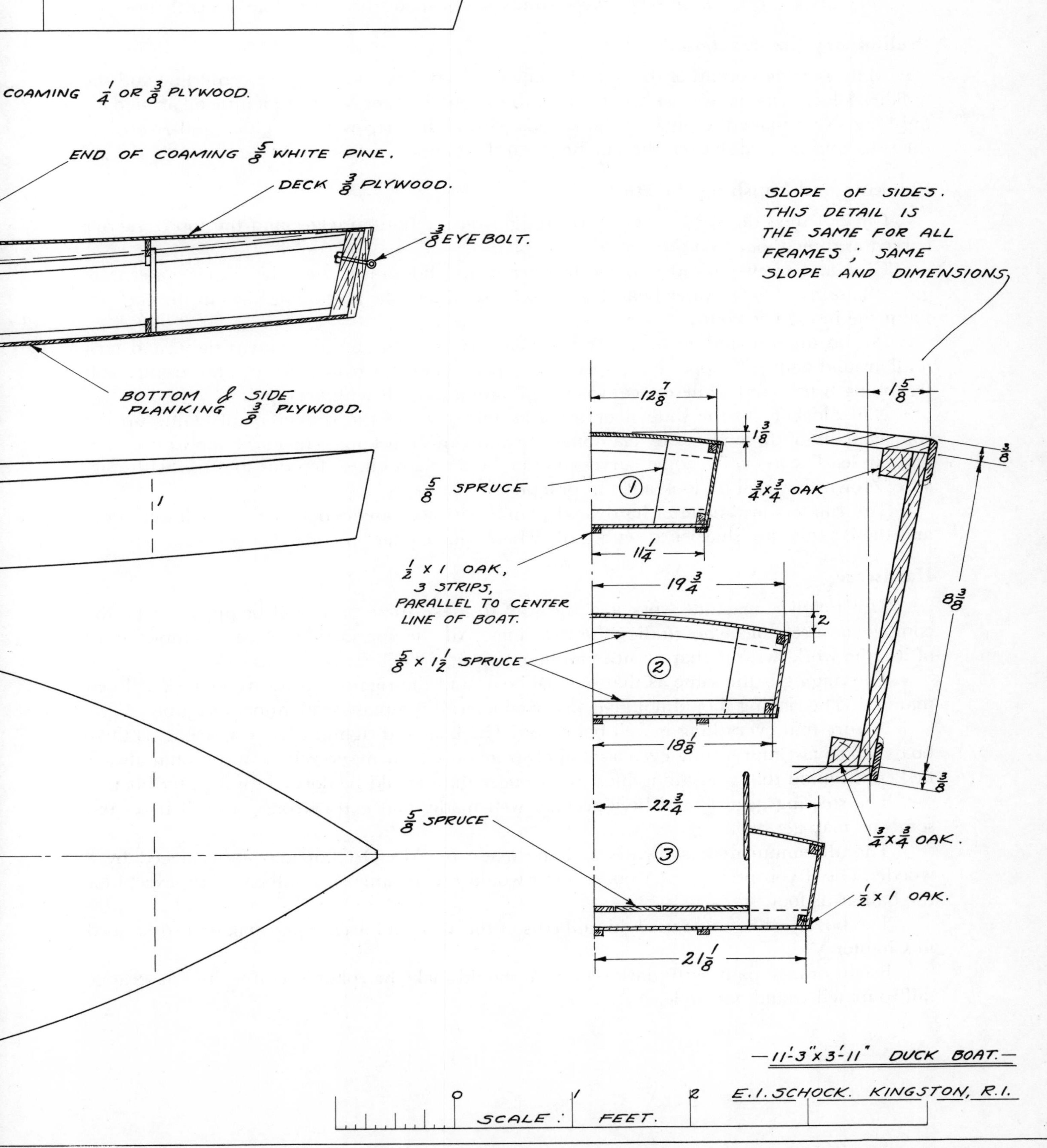
2
1
COAMING 1/4 OR 3/8 PLYWOOD.
END OF COAMING 5/8 WHITE PINE.
DECK 3/8 PLYWOOD.
3/8 EYE BOLT.
BOTTOM & SIDE PLANKING 3/8 PLYWOOD.
1
SLOPE OF SIDES. THIS DETAIL IS THE SAME FOR ALL FRAMES ; SAME SLOPE AND DIMENSIONS.
12 7/8
1 3/8
5/8 SPRUCE
1
11 1/4
1/2 X 1 OAK, 3 STRIPS, PARALLEL TO CENTER LINE OF BOAT.
19 3/4
2
5/8 X 1 1/2 SPRUCE
2
18 1/8
22 3/4
5/8 SPRUCE
3
21 1/8
1 5/8
3/8
3/4 X 3/4 OAK
8 3/8
3/8
3/4 X 3/4 OAK.
1/2 X 1 OAK.
— 11'-3" X 3'-11" DUCK BOAT. —
E. I. SCHOCK. KINGSTON, R.I.
0
1
2
SCALE : FEET.

75-SQUARE-FOOT ICE BOAT

This small ice yacht was designed to fit the 75 square-foot racing class. While the woodwork on her is very simple, there is quite a bit of machine work to be done, and the prospective builder should be able to do this, or have facilities available to do it for him.

Mold Loft Work

No real loft work is necessary, since layouts can be made directly on the pieces themselves.

Preliminary Construction

Mark out the bottom of the hull on your plywood sheet, showing the centerline and the bulkhead locations, as well as the main outline. Cut to shape, allowing a little all around for finishing. Next make the plywood bulkheads with nailing strips of oak glued and riveted to the sides and bottom. Fasten the bulkheads to the bottom.

Planking and Finishing the Hull

Cut out the side planks. These are straight on the bottom edges and the top edges are curved as dimensioned on the construction plan.

Glue and screw the sides to the bulkheads and bottom to the sides, using waterproof glue, the same as for a water boat. Fit the mast step, and the four angle clips in the cockpit. Paint the inside two coats.

Put on the fore-and-aft battens for the canvas deck. Stretch the canvas tight, and tack it all around with ⅝″ copper tacks spaced 1″ apart. Paint the canvas with water, using a stiff scrubbing brush, and while the canvas is still damp, paint it with deck paint.

Nail blocking to the shop floor to make the curve of the runner plank. Glue up the runner plank of three pieces by clamping it against this blocking. The curve shown is an arc of a circle. Theoretically, some curves may be better than others for this job, but with only 4″ of crown they will all look alike in practice.

The runners are made of hardwood planks with steel angles bolted to their lower edges and these angles are sharpened with a file where they contact the ice.

Hardware

This involves machine work and the way to make these parts will be apparent to any competent mechanic who studies the drawings. All the special hardware is simple, most of it lathe work, with perhaps a little milling.

The rigging is the same as that of a sailboat, and the rigging hardware is stock sailboat material. The rigging should not give any trouble, as it is a plain straightforward job.

Be sure that everything is well bolted on. The boat and rig must be very strong as these boats sail so fast that hitting even a small obstruction jars them severely, and it should always be kept in mind that everything must be stronger than would be normal for a water boat.

The steering gear should be especially well made, and extra strong, since if it breaks, someone may get hurt.

The aluminum mast shown is a shape made by ALCOA but may be replaced by a wooden one if you prefer it. A wooden mast would be the same as a sailboat mast, except for the ball at its foot.

The boom is like those used on sailboats of the same sail area. Spar making is described in Chapter V.

Bright orange paint with dark blue trim should make her plainly visible, and an orange sail to match would add style.

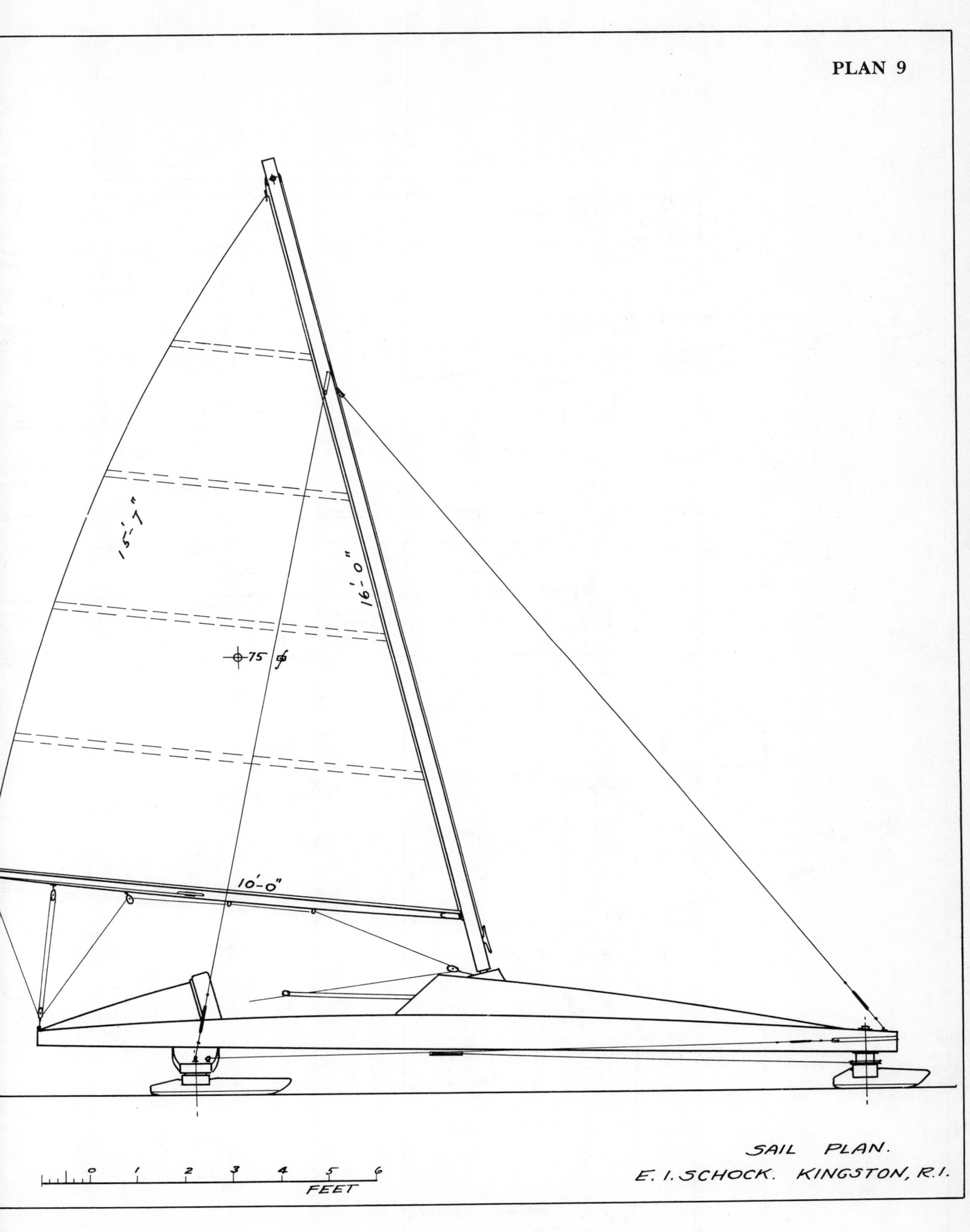
15'-7"
16'-0"
75
10'-0"
0 1 2 3 4 5 6
FEET
SAIL PLAN.
E. I. SCHOCK. KINGSTON, R.I.

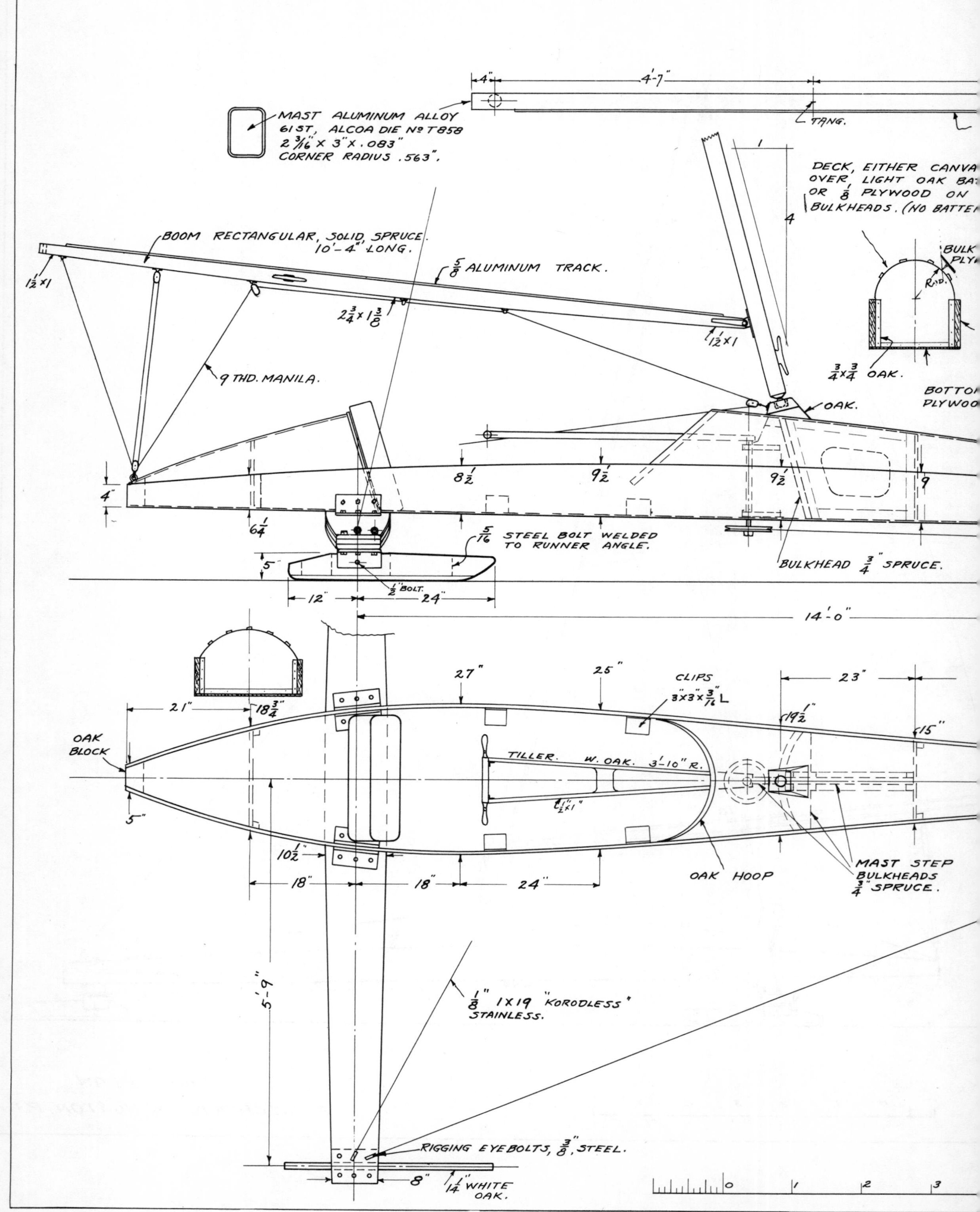
4"
4'-7"
TANG.
MAST ALUMINUM ALLOY
61 ST, ALCOA DIE Nº T858
2 3/16" X 3" X .083"
CORNER RADIUS .563".
DECK, EITHER CANVA
OVER LIGHT OAK BA
OR 1/8 PLYWOOD ON
BULKHEADS. (NO BATTE
BOOM RECTANGULAR, SOLID, SPRUCE.
10'-4" LONG.
5/8 ALUMINUM TRACK.
1 1/2 X 1
2 3/4 X 1 3/8
1 1/2 X 1
BULK
PLY
3/4 X 3/4 OAK.
BOTTO
PLYWOO
9 THD. MANILA.
OAK.
8 1/2
9 1/2
9 1/2
9
4"
6 1/4
5/16 STEEL BOLT WELDED
TO RUNNER ANGLE.
5"
1/2" BOLT.
12"
24"
BULKHEAD 3/4" SPRUCE.
14'-0"
27"
25"
CLIPS
3X3X3/16 L
23"
21"
18 3/4"
19 1/2"
15"
OAK
BLOCK
TILLER. W. OAK. 3'-10" R.
1 1/2" X 1"
5"
10 1/2"
18"
18"
24"
OAK HOOP
MAST STEP
BULKHEADS
3/4" SPRUCE.
5'-9"
1/8" 1X19 "KORODLESS"
STAINLESS.
RIGGING EYEBOLTS, 3/8", STEEL.
8"
1 1/4" WHITE
OAK.
0
1
2
3

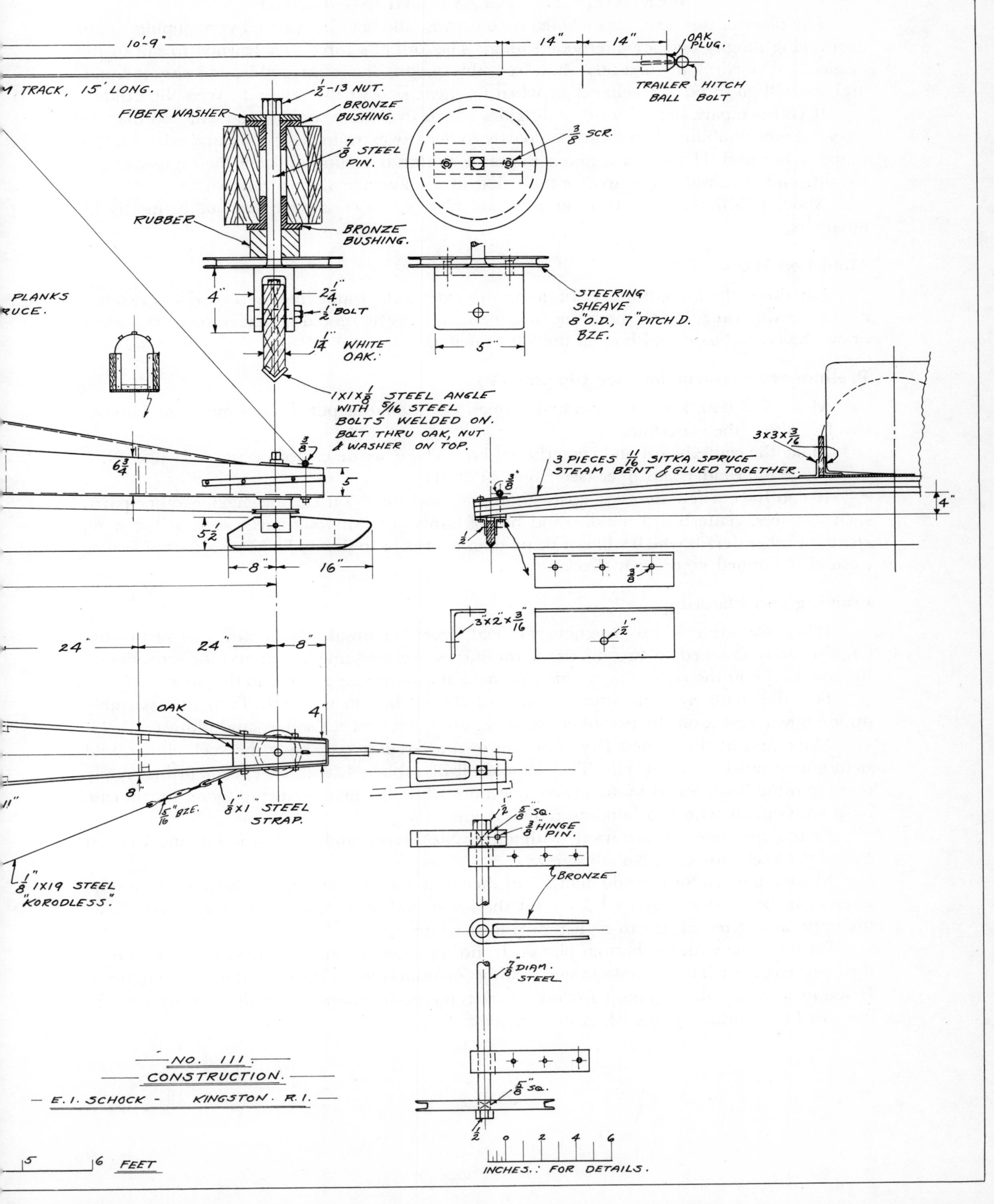
10'-9"
14"
14"
OAK PLUG.
TRAILER HITCH BALL BOLT
M TRACK, 15' LONG.
1/2-13 NUT.
FIBER WASHER
BRONZE BUSHING.
7/8 STEEL PIN.
3/8 SCR.
RUBBER
BRONZE BUSHING.
PLANKS
RUCE.
4"
2 1/4"
1/2" BOLT
1 1/4" WHITE OAK.
STEERING SHEAVE 8" O.D., 7" PITCH D. BZE.
5"
1X1X1/8 STEEL ANGLE WITH 5/16 STEEL BOLTS WELDED ON. BOLT THRU OAK, NUT & WASHER ON TOP.
3/8
6 3/4
5
5 1/2
8"
16"
3x3x3/16
3 PIECES 11/16 SITKA SPRUCE STEAM BENT & GLUED TOGETHER.
3/8"
1/2
4"
3/8"
3"x2"x3/16
1/2"
24"
24"
8"
OAK
4"
8"
11"
5/16" BZE.
1/8"x1" STEEL STRAP.
1/8" 1X19 STEEL "KORODLESS".
1/2
5/8" SQ.
3/8" HINGE PIN.
BRONZE
7/8" DIAM. STEEL
5/8" SQ.
1/2
NO. 111.
CONSTRUCTION.
E. I. SCHOCK - KINGSTON. R. I.
0 2 4 6
INCHES.: FOR DETAILS.
5
6 FEET

"WEE NIP," 11′6″ CLASS SAILING DINGHY

The plans of this boat are included here because the boat has proved very popular, both as a racing dinghy and for afternoon sailing. The author's three sons learned to sail in the original "Wee Nip," the first boat built from this design. She is fast, stable, and easy to build, and she will go through a cellar door when finished; at least the original "Wee Nip" did.

If you compare her with other dinghies which look quite similar, you will find that she has a lot more stability than most, due partly to her few extra inches beam, and partly to the shape of her hull. Her speed is about the same as that of sailing dinks of the same size and weight, and is considerably greater than that of the average 12-foot sailboat.

About two hundred to two hundred and fifty of this class have been built, mostly by amateurs.

Mold Loft Work

Lay down the lines, full size. In doing this extend the frame lines to a base line two feet above the waterline. When the frames are made, a cross tie should be nailed on at this level. Show the centerboard and box on the loft drawing.

Preliminary Construction (see Chapter IV)

Make the stem, keel, transom and frames. On the latter put the ties mentioned above, two feet above the waterline.

Make the centerboard and centerboard box. These are described on pages 17 and 19.

Make the rudder and tiller (see pages 20 to 21).

If you have a few minutes' spare time now and then you can be making other parts, such as knees, centerboard handle, and bits of hardware. Any oak parts, such as the stem, cleats, or other details which will not be used for a week or so should be given a coat of shellac as soon as finished, to prevent checking.

Framing and Planking

When you are ready to assemble the boat, erect her upside down on a pair of two-by-fours securely fastened to two horses. If the horses are the same height and the cross ties on the frames are in the right places, this will make the waterline parallel to the floor.

Bolt the stem, transom, frames and centerboard box to the keel. Turn this assembly upside down, rest it on the two-by-fours, and fasten and brace it square and plumb.

Make and fit the chines. If you do not own a circular saw, have the keel, chines, and stem gotten out by a local mill. They should all be rabbeted, and, except for fitting, ready to go into the boat. Stand by to answer questions while the man is sawing them, just in case he is not familiar with boatbuilding requirements.

Fasten the chines to each frame with a long No. 7 screw and to the transom and forward end of the keel with short No. 10 screws.

Make a pattern for the side planks, cut them out and glue and screw them in place. The screws can be 1″ No. 8, spaced 2¼″. Fit the lower and forward edges to the rabbets first; the upper and after edges can be trimmed to size later.

Do the same with the bottom planks. In fitting these, do the edge next to the keel first, the chine edge last. These planks fit into a rabbet on both edges, so be careful to get them right. If you make a mistake you spoil a plank; there is no second chance. (See drawing on page 37 for a tool for marking plank edges to fit rabbets.)

Finishing the Hull

When the glue has set, turn the boat over, cut off the excess length from each frame, and fair the top edge of the planks. Paint the exposed edges with plywood sealer.

Make and install the inwales, the knees at the stern and the breast hook at the bow. Note that the inwale is beveled slightly where it butts against the knees. This bevel makes it easier to fit than if it were cut square across. Screw the inwale to knees and frames.

Fit the mast step and its bracing.

Put in the midship thwart. This is one of the strength members of the boat, and should be fastened to the risings and to the centerboard box, and braced with knees as shown on the construction plan. Being an open boat she will collect rain water even if she never leaks, and these knees prevent the sides of the boat from breaking when she is rolled up on her side on the float to dump the water out.

Put in the mast partners, with their flat-ended pipe braces.

Paint the bottom inside three coats.

Put in the floor boards after they also have been painted. Fasten them with screws so that they may be easily removed.

Install the centerboard and rudder.

Put the cap on the centerboard box. This should be a good tight joint, with a muslin gasket and white lead, like the joint between the centerboard box and the keel. (See Chapter IV, page 17.)

Screw on the guard rails.

Install the hardware, such as rowlocks, towing eye, main halyard lead block, centerboard lever, rigging screws and rope traveler.

Spars, Rigging and Sails

Make the mast and the boom according to the method described in Chapter IV, pages 23 to 25.

Attach the hardware to the spars. In fastening the tangs for the shrouds to the mast, step the mast with the tangs held in place by a clamp. See if the shrouds are the right length; if they are not, unstep the mast and try again. They should come right the second time, and you can then fasten them permanently.

Finish the painting, using two or three coats of non-skid for the floor boards, gloss yacht enamel for the topsides, and racing copper for the bottom. Put four coats of varnish on the trim, spars, rudder and tiller. Rub each coat lightly, except the last, with fine wet-or-dry sandpaper, used wet.

The sail for the original boat was home-made from the best-grade bed sheeting, and it turned out well. But one made by a good sailmaker would doubtless be much better, and a professionally made sail is strongly recommended. If you are going to race the boat you should have a really good sail. Ratsey and Lapthorn, at City Island, New York, make very fine ones. Local yachtsmen can probably tell you of a good sailmaker in your own neighborhood.

She will need a sponge to keep her dry and clean. The Cellulose ones are best, as they will not sink if you drop them overboard. A natural sponge sinks when wet and if you drop it overboard you lose it.

When she is overboard, let her soak for a couple of days before you sail her and never step into a dinghy forward of the mast as she may roll over.

PLAN 10

WEENIP 11'-6" CLASS SAILING DINGHY

ITEM	LUMBER MATERIAL	NO. PIECES REQ'D	SIZE IN INCHES	LENGTH	
STEM	OAK	1	2 1/4 X 1 3/4	2'-0"	
KEEL	OAK	1	1 X 5 5/8	12'-0"	
FRAMES	OAK		9/16 X 1 3/4	50 LINEAR FEET	
CHINES	OAK	2	1 1/4 X 1 5/8	12'-0"	
KNEES	HACKMATACK OAK OR APPLE	4	3/4		
FLOORS	OAK	7	5/8 X 2 1/2	14"	
RUBBING STRIP	OAK	2	3/4 X 1 3/8	12'-0"	
CENTERBOARD	PHILIPPINE MAHOGANY	1	7/8 X 13 1/2	3'-7"	
C'BOARD BOX SIDES	W. PINE	2	3/4 X 13	4'-1"	
" " LEDGES	OAK	2	1 1/16 X 2 1/2	ONE - 14" ONE - 10"	
" " BED LOG	OAK	2	3/4 X 2 1/2	4'-1"	
MAST STEP	OAK	1	7/8 X 5 3/4	2'-8"	
RUDDER	PHILIPPINE MAHOGANY	1	7/8 X 10	3'-0"	
TILLER	OAK	1	1 X 2	2'-6"	
TRANSOM	PHILIPPINE MAHOGANY	1	5/8 X 16	3'-8"	
CLAMP	OAK	2	3/4 X 1 1/4	12'-0"	
FLOORING	SPRUCE	10	1/2 X 8	7'-2"	
SEATS	W. PINE	1	3/4 X 8 3/4	5'-0"	
PLANKING	FIR PLYWOOD	2	5/16 X 48	12'-0"	
MAST	SITKA SPRUCE	2 2	1/2 X 2 5/8 1/2 X 1 1/8	19'-2" 19'-2"	1 PC. 1 1/8 X 1 5/8 X 4'-0"
BOOM	SPRUCE	1	1 7/8 X 1 7/8	10'-0"	
MAST PARTNER	SPRUCE	1	3/4 X 11 1/2	3'-2"	

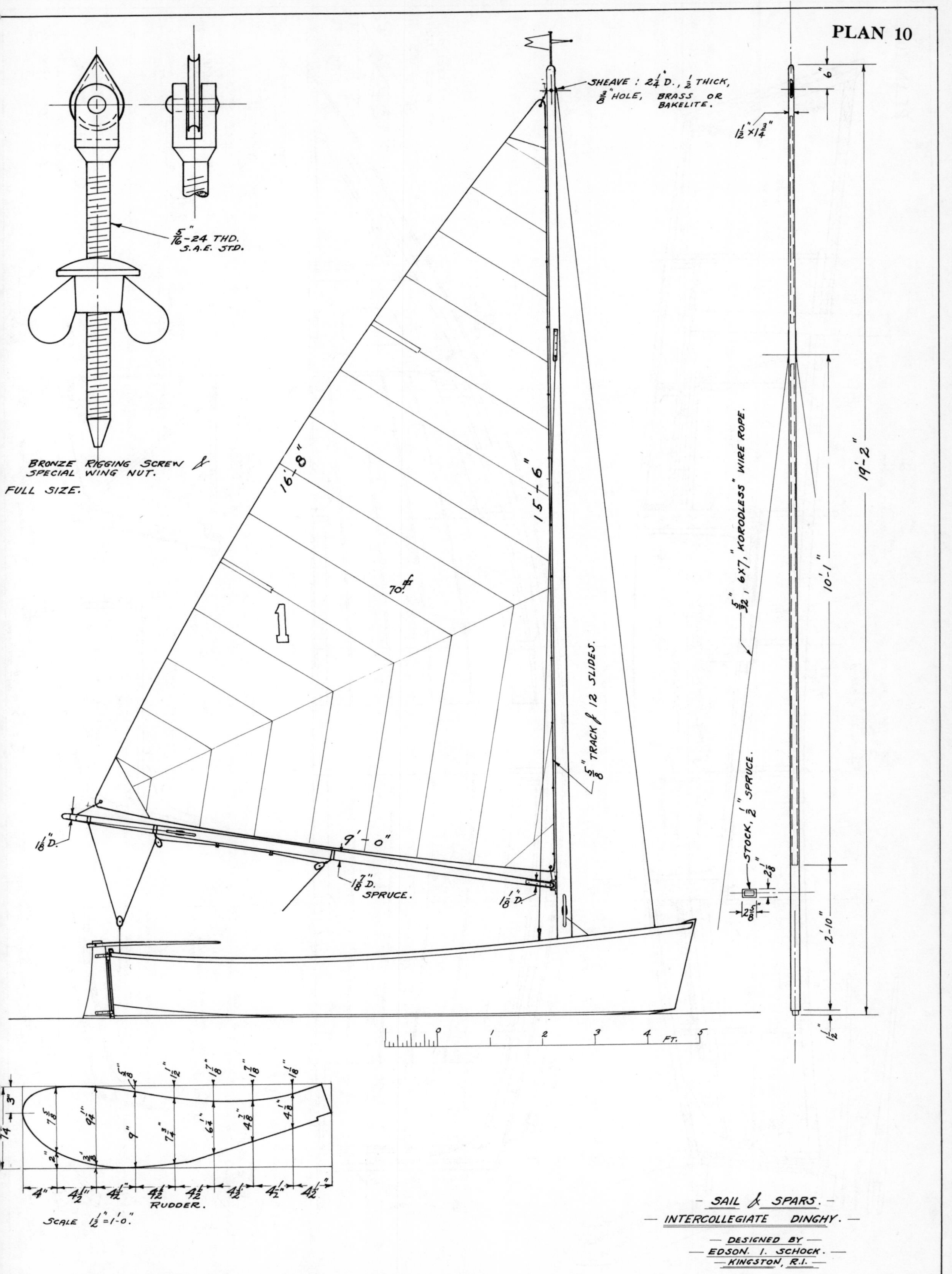

SHEAVE : 2¼" D., ½" THICK, ⅜" HOLE, BRASS OR BAKELITE.
1½" × 1¾"
6"
5/16"-24 THD. S.A.E. STD.
BRONZE RIGGING SCREW & SPECIAL WING NUT.
FULL SIZE.
16'-8"
15'-6"
70 ☐ FT
1
5/32", 6X7, "KORODLESS" WIRE ROPE.
19'-2"
10'-1"
⅝" TRACK & 12 SLIDES.
STOCK, ½" SPRUCE.
2⅛"
2⅜"
2'-10"
1⅛" D.
9'-0"
1⅞" D. SPRUCE.
1⅛" D.
1½"
0 1 2 3 4 FT. 5
3"
14"
7⅝"
9¼"
9"
7¾"
6¼"
4⅞"
4⅛"
2"
3⅜"
⅝"
½"
1⅞"
1⅞"
1⅛"
4"
4½"
4½"
4½"
4½"
4½"
4½"
4½"
RUDDER.
SCALE 1½" = 1'-0".
- SAIL & SPARS. -
- INTERCOLLEGIATE DINGHY. -
- DESIGNED BY -
- EDSON. I. SCHOCK. -
- KINGSTON, R.I. -

PLAN 10

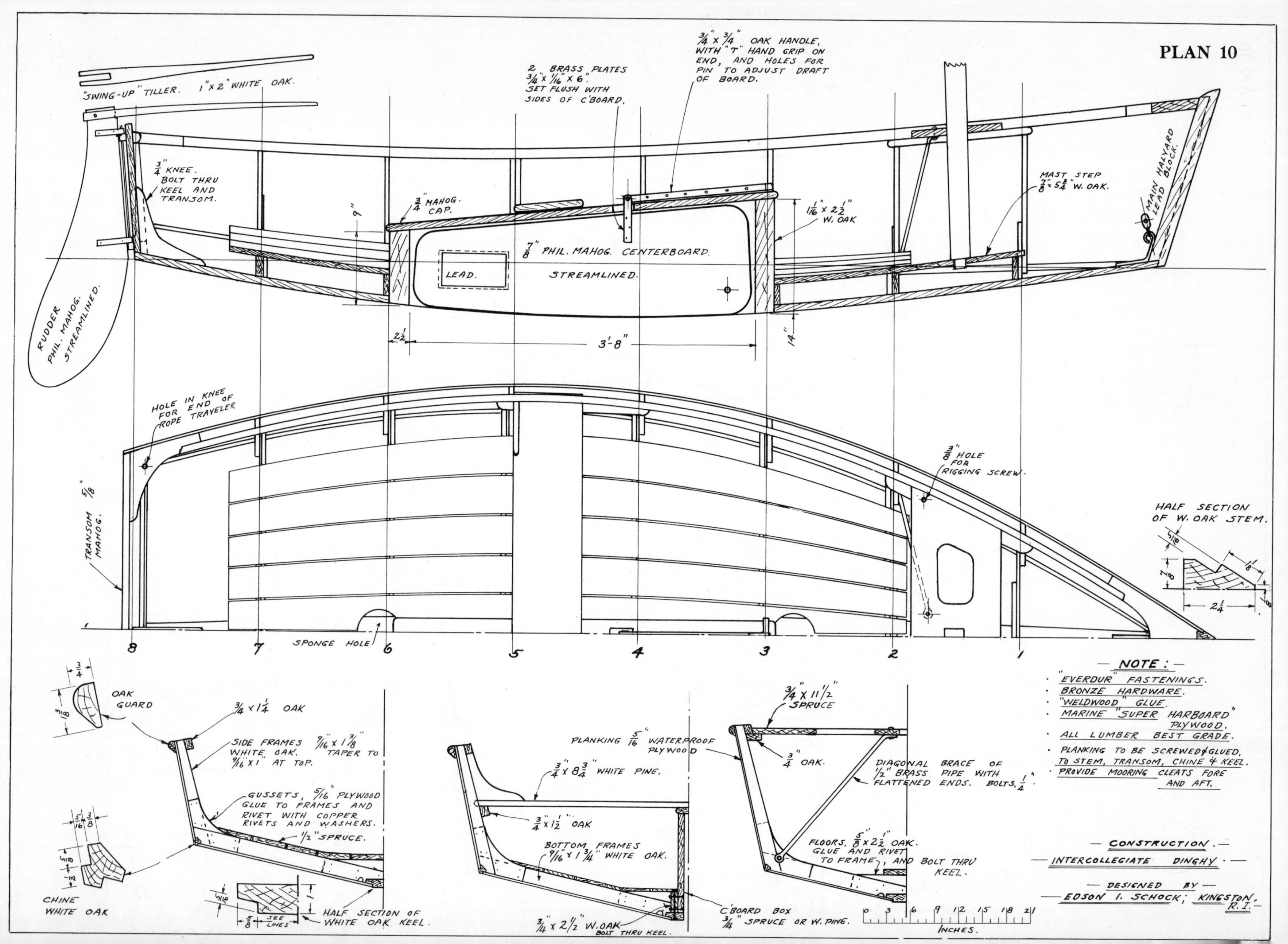
"SWING-UP" TILLER. 1" x 2" WHITE OAK.
2 BRASS PLATES 3/4" x 1/16" x 6". SET FLUSH WITH SIDES OF C'BOARD.
3/4" x 3/4" OAK HANDLE, WITH "T" HAND GRIP ON END, AND HOLES FOR PIN TO ADJUST DRAFT OF BOARD.
3/4" KNEE. BOLT THRU KEEL AND TRANSOM.
3/4" MAHOG. CAP.
7/8" PHIL. MAHOG. CENTERBOARD.
STREAMLINED.
LEAD.
1 1/16" x 2 1/2" W. OAK
MAST STEP 7/8" x 5 3/4" W. OAK.
MAIN HALYARD LEAD BLOCK.
RUDDER PHIL. MAHOG. STREAMLINED.
9"
2 1/2"
3'-8"
14"
HOLE IN KNEE FOR END OF ROPE TRAVELER
3/8" HOLE FOR RIGGING SCREW.
TRANSOM 5/8" MAHOG.
SPONGE HOLE
8 7 6 5 4 3 2 1
HALF SECTION OF W. OAK STEM.
5/16
7/8
1/8
2 1/4
1/8
OAK GUARD
3/4
3/8
3/4 x 1 1/4 OAK
SIDE FRAMES 9/16" x 1 3/8" WHITE OAK. TAPER TO 9/16" x 1" AT TOP.
GUSSETS, 5/16" PLYWOOD GLUE TO FRAMES AND RIVET WITH COPPER RIVETS AND WASHERS.
1/2" SPRUCE.
5/16 3/8
5/8
1/2
CHINE WHITE OAK
5/16
1
3/8 SEE LINES
HALF SECTION OF WHITE OAK KEEL.
PLANKING 5/16" WATERPROOF PLYWOOD
3/4" x 8 3/4" WHITE PINE.
3/4" x 1 1/2" OAK
BOTTOM FRAMES 9/16" x 1 3/4" WHITE OAK.
3/4" x 2 1/2" W. OAK BOLT THRU KEEL.
C'BOARD BOX 3/4" SPRUCE OR W. PINE.
3/4" x 11 1/2" SPRUCE
3/4" OAK.
DIAGONAL BRACE OF 1/2" BRASS PIPE WITH FLATTENED ENDS. BOLTS, 1/4".
FLOORS, 5/8" x 2 1/2" OAK. GLUE AND RIVET TO FRAME, AND BOLT THRU KEEL.
0 3 6 9 12 15 18 21
INCHES.
— NOTE: —
· "EVERDUR" FASTENINGS.
· BRONZE HARDWARE.
· "WELDWOOD" GLUE.
· MARINE "SUPER HARBOARD" PLYWOOD.
· ALL LUMBER BEST GRADE.
· PLANKING TO BE SCREWED & GLUED, TO STEM, TRANSOM, CHINE & KEEL.
· PROVIDE MOORING CLEATS FORE AND AFT.
— CONSTRUCTION. —
— INTERCOLLEGIATE DINGHY. —
— DESIGNED BY —
— EDSON I. SCHOCK, KINGSTON, R.I. —

ELEVEN FOOT DINGHY AT BUILDER'S YARD

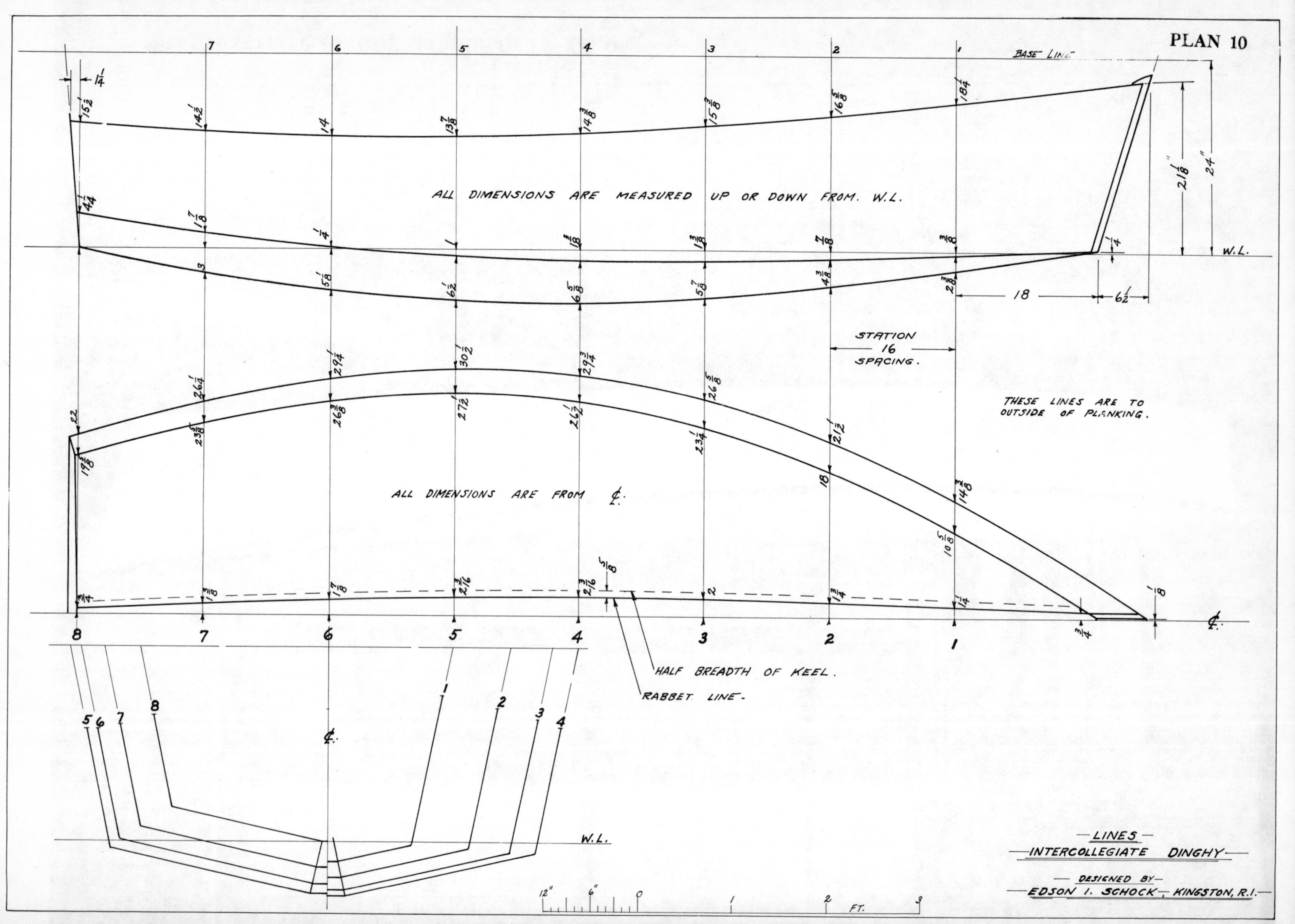

PLAN 10
BASE LINE
W.L.
ALL DIMENSIONS ARE MEASURED UP OR DOWN FROM. W.L.
STATION 16 SPACING.
THESE LINES ARE TO OUTSIDE OF PLANKING.
ALL DIMENSIONS ARE FROM ℄.
HALF BREADTH OF KEEL.
RABBET LINE.
FT.
LINES
INTERCOLLEGIATE DINGHY
DESIGNED BY
EDSON I. SCHOCK, KINGSTON, R.I.

12′6″ CATBOAT

This is an ideal boat for children. She is about as safe as a small sailing boat can be, yet is well balanced and reasonably fast, in competent hands. She will carry four people comfortably in her roomy cockpit, and there is space under the deck for lunch, sweaters, and life-preservers.

Construction has been made simple to keep her well within the ability of the average amateur to build. She should always have a good re-sale value, if well built, as boats of this type are always in demand.

The Point Judith (Rhode Island) Yacht Club is using these boats as their junior one-design class for racing and for sailing instruction.

Mold Loft Work

Lay down the lines full size, as explained in Chapter III.

Show the stem, keel, mast step, floor timbers, centerboard and centerboard box, rudder, skeg, and transom knee on the mold loft drawing. Also show the special construction of frames 1 and 2, noting that the mast step is recessed into the floor timbers.

Preliminary Construction

Make the stem, keel, and chines. These three can all be made for you at the mill where you buy your oak lumber. They should be cut out and rabbeted on a circular saw. If you have a power saw you can do it yourself, but it is a hard job to do by hand. The procedure for making these parts is given in Chapter IV.

Lay out each frame and build it as described in Chapter IV. Also make the transom, centerboard box, centerboard, rudder and tiller and the side planks.

Cut out the piece for the skeg as shown on the construction plan. Also get out the stock for the clamps, and plane them on four sides.

Framing and Planking

Bolt the centerboard box to the keel.

Next, bolt on the transom, the transom knee, and the skeg. The bolts go through the skeg and transom knee. If no long bolts are to be had for this job, make your own by threading the ends of a long bronze (not brass) rod and screwing a nut over a washer on each end. Or rivet the outside end over a washer and use a nut and washer on the inside end. Quarter-inch diameter rod is heavy enough. Brass dealers carry a kind of bronze rod known as "free cutting"; this is easy to thread and work, and is recommended. Everdur bronze is stronger, but is harder to work, while the free-cutting bronze is stronger than you really need.

The stem is fastened to the keel with a long wood screw through the keel up into the end of the stem. This holds it in place while you are planking; once the sides are planked, the planking screws will hold the stem securely. The bronze clip, or angle, holding the stem to the keel can be made of the same material as the chainplates, 1/8″ x 1″ Everdur. Screw it on with 1″, round head, bronze wood screws.

Bolt frames 10, 9, 8, 4, 3, 2, and 1 to the keel, each with a 1/4″ bronze carriage bolt through the floor timbers. Have the head of the bolt on the outside, and a nut and washer on the inside. If the bolts are too long, cut off the ends and file them smooth so that no rough edges can scratch you. If there are rough threads anywhere you will be liable to scratch your hands when sponging out the bilge.

Now set up the framework as shown in Plan 12, page 126. Mark the centerline on the floor and lay out the frame stations at right angles to it. Also mark the location of the stem and the transom. Set up the keel, frames, transom and stem, upside down. Fasten them in place and put in what bracing is necessary to hold the framework rigid. Have the center of the keel directly over the centerline, the frames all square across and plumb.

Fasten on the chines, using one long screw in each frame and one at each end. The forward screw goes into the keel, and the after one into the transom frame.

Cut out the side planks and fit them to the chine and stem. Make good fits here, as these joints have to be watertight. While doing this, the planks may be held in place with clamps or a few screws driven part way in. When you are satisfied with the fit, take off the planks, apply glue to plank and rabbet, and screw them to the framework, beginning at the stem. Use 1″ flathead No. 8 screws, spaced about 2½″.

Next fit frames 5, 6, and 7 alongside the centerboard box. Fasten the floors to the bed logs of the box with a small block of oak screwed and glued to each, or, better still, with a bronze angle on each side of the floor timber, riveted to the latter and screwed to the bed log.

Do each operation first on one side of the boat and then on the other. Do not complete one side before you start the other. Check occasionally to make sure that both sides are alike.

To plank the bottom, first fit the plywood to the rabbet along the keel. Fasten this joint temporarily and then mark the outline of the chine edge. Cut and fit this edge. Do not make a mistake here: if you cut this piece too small you will have spoiled a big sheet of plywood. Drill for the bottom planking screws, and glue and screw the bottom to the boat, using the same size screws as for the sides.

While the boat is still fastened down to the floor, sandpaper the planking and give it a coat of plywood sealer and a priming coat of paint.

Now turn the boat over and saw off the excess frame ends. Paint the top edge of the side planks with plywood sealer and give the inside of the planking a priming coat of flat white.

Fit the clamps, bolting them through the frames with ¼″-diameter galvanized flat-head bolts, with washers and nuts on the inside, and have the bolt heads flush on the outside. Fit the deck beams by bolting or screwing them to the frames. Fit and fasten the blocks between the frames along the upper edge of the side planks. These are to receive deck edge fastenings.

Bolt in the mast step with four ¼″-diameter galvanized carriage bolts from outside the keel. Finish and paint the step before putting it in. To locate the hole in the step for the heel of the mast, and the corresponding hole in the deck above it, measure along the deck and along the mast step plank from the forward edge of the centerboard box, using the distance shown on your mold loft drawing.

Decking and Finishing

Fair the deck beams by laying a batten across from beam to beam and plane off any high spots. Square the ends of the short beams where they butt against the coaming. Fit the oak block for the mast partner. This block should measure 16″ athwartships, 1¼″ thick and wide enough to be a close fit between deck beams Nos. 1½ and 2, to which it is securely fastened, in a fore-and-aft direction, by means of a ¼″-diameter galvanized rod on either side of the mast hole. The rods will be threaded at both ends and have washers and nuts. Fit oak blocks under the deck between beams, where cleats are to be located. Fit the chainplate frames and chainplates as shown on the construction plan. Put the mooring eye in the stem. Fit the oak breast hook between the clamps just behind the stem, for the forward end of the deck plank to rest on.

Clean out all the shavings and sawdust and paint the inside of the hull where the deck will cover it.

Mark its outline and fit the deck, glue and screw it in place.

Make the toe rail for the bow, and screw it on.

Screw on the guard rails.

Make the cockpit coaming, fit it carefully, and screw and glue it in place.

Fit the cap on the centerboard box.

Put in the flooring, and seats if you want them, after giving them two coats of paint or varnish.

Bolt on the deck hardware and the rudder fittings.

Install the rudder and tiller, wire rope traveler, centerboard pennant, headstay chainplate, mooring eye, and the boom crutch strap.

Finish the painting, applying a total of at least three coats.

Rigging

Make the mast and the boom as described in Chapter IV, pages 23 to 25. Fit the hardware to these spars.

To locate the tangs in exactly the right place, clamp them to the mast, with the shrouds attached, where you think they should be. Open the turnbuckles all the way. Step the mast in the boat and see that the turnbuckle-ends just reach the chainplates. If they are not the right length, try again. When the exact location has been determined, screw them on permanently. Follow the same procedure with the headstay.

Just before you launch her, put on the last coat of copper bottom paint. Be careful not to rub off the wet paint as you put her in the water.

Before going sailing you should let her lie quietly in the water for two days to soak up. During this time you can finish all the little odds and ends. Splice the running rigging neatly, and get everything shipshape for the season. Sailing a dry boat may get her out of shape or do her some other harm, but you can sit in her and wish you were out sailing.

PLAN 11

12'-6" CATBOAT					
ITEM	LUMBER MATERIAL	NO. PIECES REQ'D	SIZE IN INCHES	LENGTH	
STEM	OAK	1	1 7/8 X 2 1/4	2'-6"	
KEEL	OAK	1	1 X 7 3/8	12'-8"	
FRAMES	SPRUCE		3/4 X 1 3/4	ABOUT 80 LINEAR FT.	
CHINES	OAK	2	1 1/2 X 1 7/8	14'-0"	
KNEES	OAK	1	3/4		
FLOORS	OAK	10	7/8 X 3	2'-0"	
SKEG	OAK OR HARD PINE	1	1 X 10	3'-8"	
RUBBING STRIP	OAK	2	7/8 X 1 1/4	14'-0"	
CENTERBOARD	OAK	8	7/8 X 4	3'-4"	
C'BOARD BOX SIDES	W. PINE	2	3/4 X 16	4'-0"	
" " LEDGES	OAK	1 1	1 1/8 X 2 1/2 1 1/8 X 3 1/2	2'-2" 1'-9"	
" " BED LOG	OAK	2	1 3/4 X 9	4'-0"	
MAST STEP	OAK	1	1 X 7	1'-4"	
RUDDER	OAK	5	7/8 X 4	2'-6"	
TILLER	ASH	1	7/8 X 3 1/2	4'-9"	
TRANSOM	W. PINE	1	3/4 X 18	4'-6"	
CLAMP	SPRUCE	2	7/8 X 1 3/8	14'-0"	
DECK	FIR PLYWOOD	1	3/8 X 72	14'-0"	MAY BE BUILT OF SMALL PIECES
DECK BEAMS	SPRUCE		3/4 X 3	ABOUT 20 LINEAR FT.	
FLOORING	W. PINE	15	5/8 X 3 3/4	8'-0"	
COAMING	W. PINE	2 1	3/4 X 3 3/4 X 8	8'-0" 6'-0"	
PLANKING	FIR PLYWOOD	2	3/8 X 48	14'-0"	
MAST	SITKA SPRUCE	2 2	5/8 X 2 7/8 5/8 X 1 1/8	21'-0" 21'-0"	1 PC.-1 X 1 5/8 X 4'-0"
BOOM	SPRUCE	1	1 3/8 X 2 5/8		
TOE RAIL	OAK	2	1 1/4 X 1 1/4	3'-3"	
GUSSETS	PLY. SCRAP	18	3/8"		

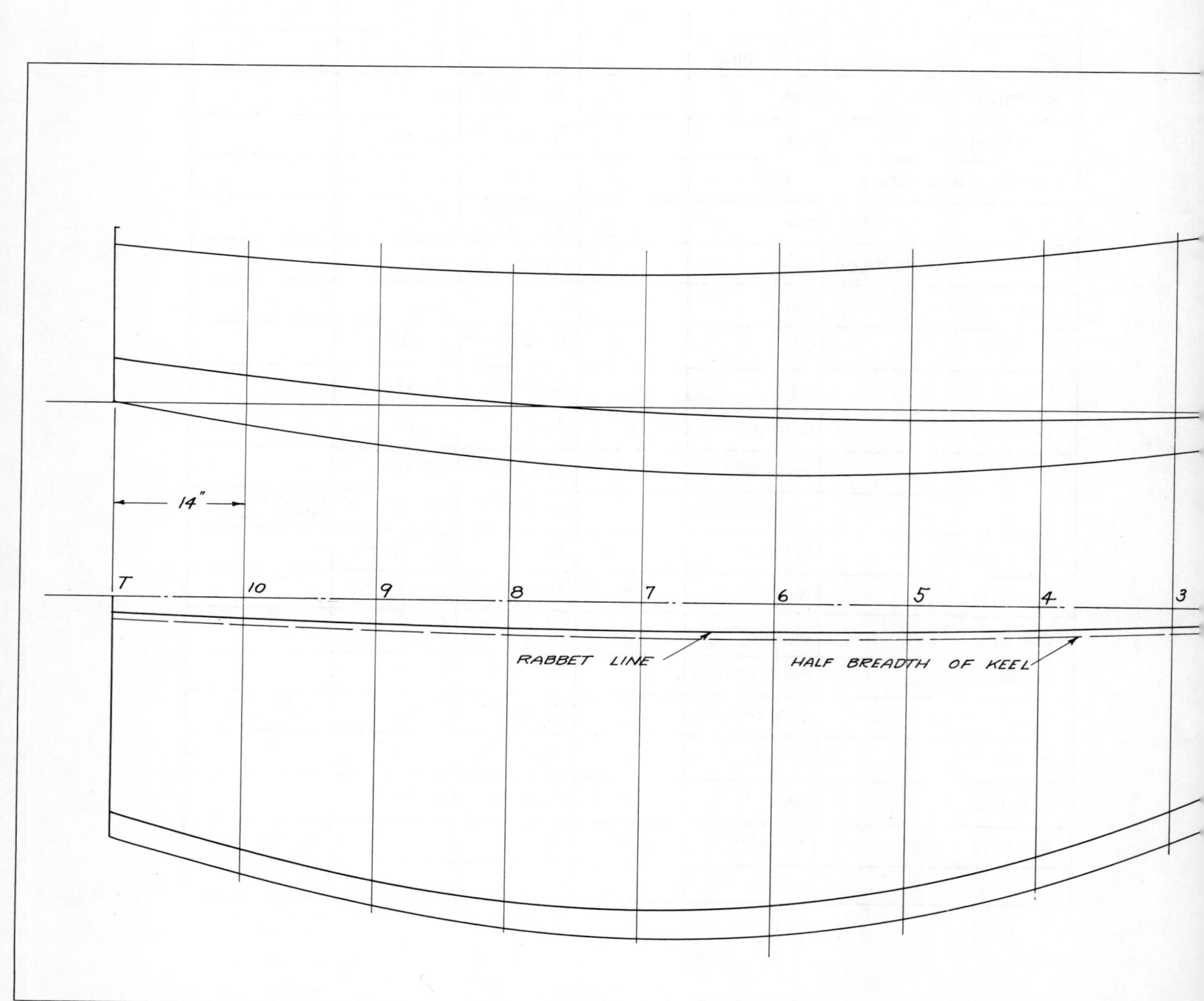

14"
T
10
9
8
7
6
5
4
3
RABBET LINE
HALF BREADTH OF KEEL

PLAN 11

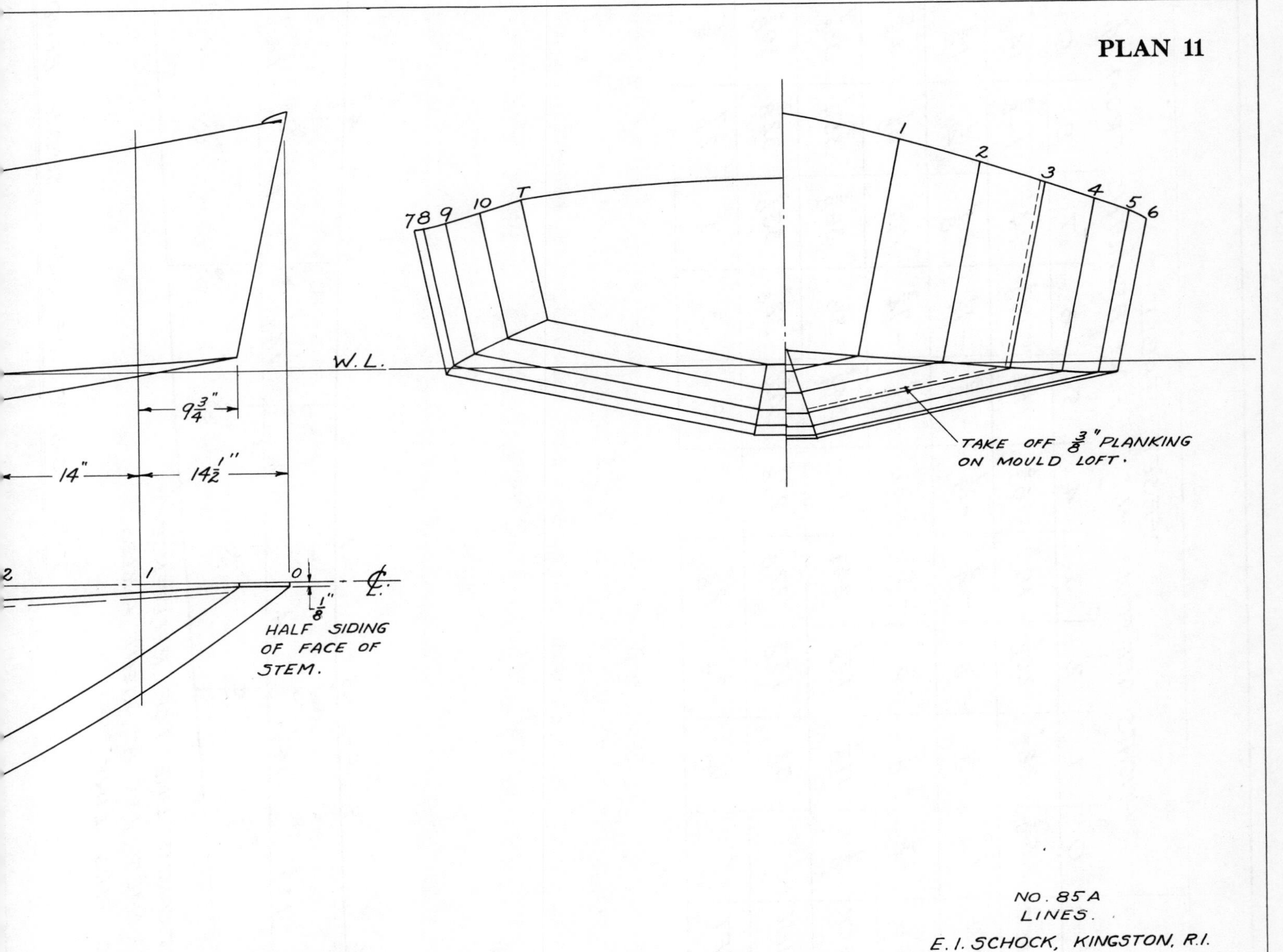

1
2
3
4
5
6
7
8
9
10
T
W. L.
9 3/4"
14"
14 1/2"
2
1
0
1/8"
HALF SIDING OF FACE OF STEM.
TAKE OFF 3/8" PLANKING ON MOULD LOFT.
NO. 85 A
LINES.
E. I. SCHOCK, KINGSTON, R.I.
SCALE- FEET
0
1
2
3

OFFSET TABLE.

HEIGHTS ARE FROM W.L., HALF BREADTHS FROM ℄, IN INCHES.

FRAME →	0	1	2	3	4	5	6	7	8	9	10	T
HEIGHT SHEER	25 5/8	22 7/8	20 1/2	18 3/8	16 5/8	15 1/4	14 3/8	14 1/8	14 3/8	14 7/8	15 3/4	17
" CHINE	1 3/8	5/8	- 1/8	- 3/4	-1 1/4	-1 3/8	-1 1/4	- 5/8	1/4	1 3/8	3	4 7/8
" KEEL	1 3/8	- 5/8	-3	-5	-6 1/2	-7 3/8	-7 3/4	-7 1/4	-6 1/8	-4 5/8	-2 1/2	0
HALF BR. DECK	1/8	11 5/8	19 7/8	26 1/4	31	34 1/4	36	36 3/8	35 1/4	33 1/8	30	26 1/8
" CHINE		7 1/8	15 5/8	22 3/8	27 3/8	30 3/4	32 7/8	33 3/8	32 3/8	30 3/8	27 3/8	23 5/8
" RABBET		1 1/4	2 1/4	2 7/8	3	3	3	3	2 7/8	2 5/8	1 7/8	7/8

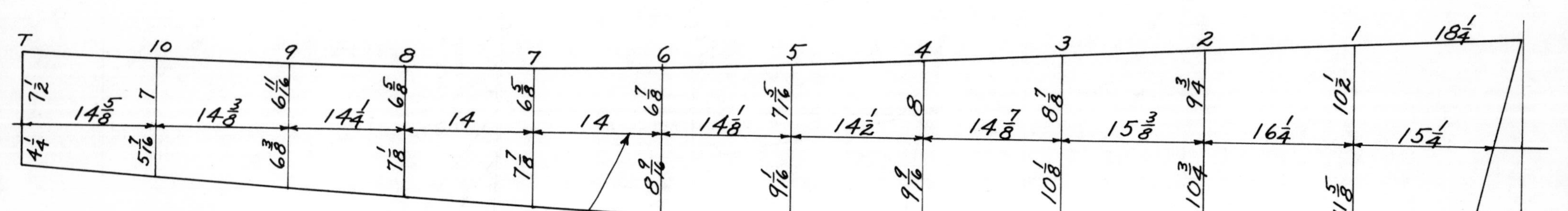

TRUE SHAPE OF SIDES BEFORE BENDING.

E. I. SCHOCK, KINGSTON, R. I.

TWELVE FOOT CAT IN FRAME

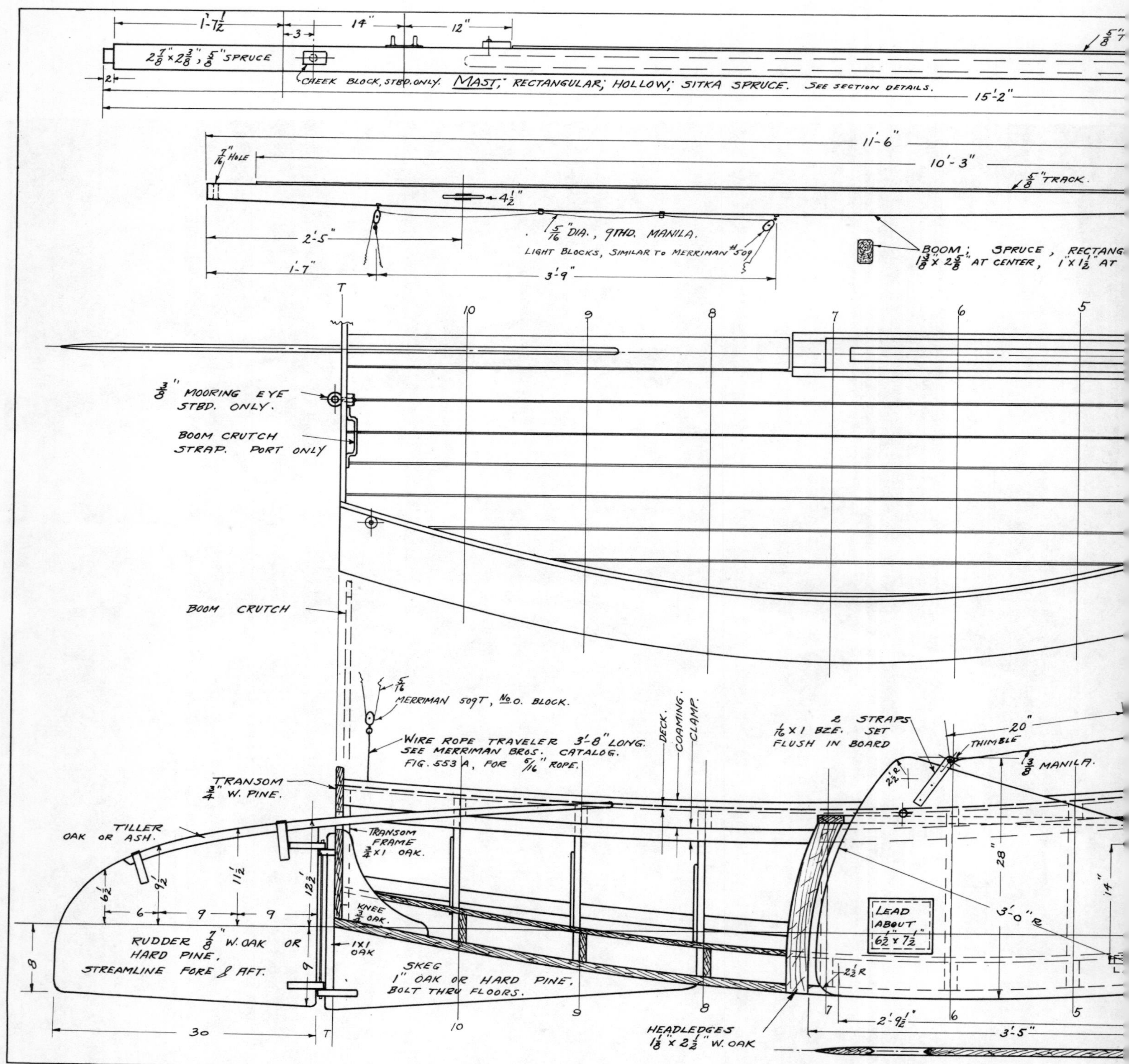

MAST; RECTANGULAR; HOLLOW; SITKA SPRUCE. SEE SECTION DETAILS.
CHEEK BLOCK, STBD. ONLY.
BOOM; SPRUCE, RECTANG
LIGHT BLOCKS, SIMILAR TO MERRIMAN #509
MOORING EYE STBD. ONLY.
BOOM CRUTCH STRAP. PORT ONLY
BOOM CRUTCH
MERRIMAN 509T, No. 0. BLOCK.
WIRE ROPE TRAVELER 3'-8" LONG. SEE MERRIMAN BROS. CATALOG. FIG. 553 A, FOR 5/16" ROPE.
TRANSOM 3/4" W. PINE.
TRANSOM FRAME 3/4 x 1 OAK.
TILLER OAK OR ASH.
DECK.
COAMING.
CLAMP.
2 STRAPS 1/16 x 1 BZE. SET FLUSH IN BOARD
THIMBLE
MANILA.
LEAD ABOUT 6 1/2" x 7 1/2"
KNEE 3/4 OAK.
RUDDER 7/8" W. OAK OR HARD PINE. STREAMLINE FORE & AFT.
SKEG 1" OAK OR HARD PINE. BOLT THRU FLOORS.
HEADLEDGES 1 1/8" x 2 1/2" W. OAK

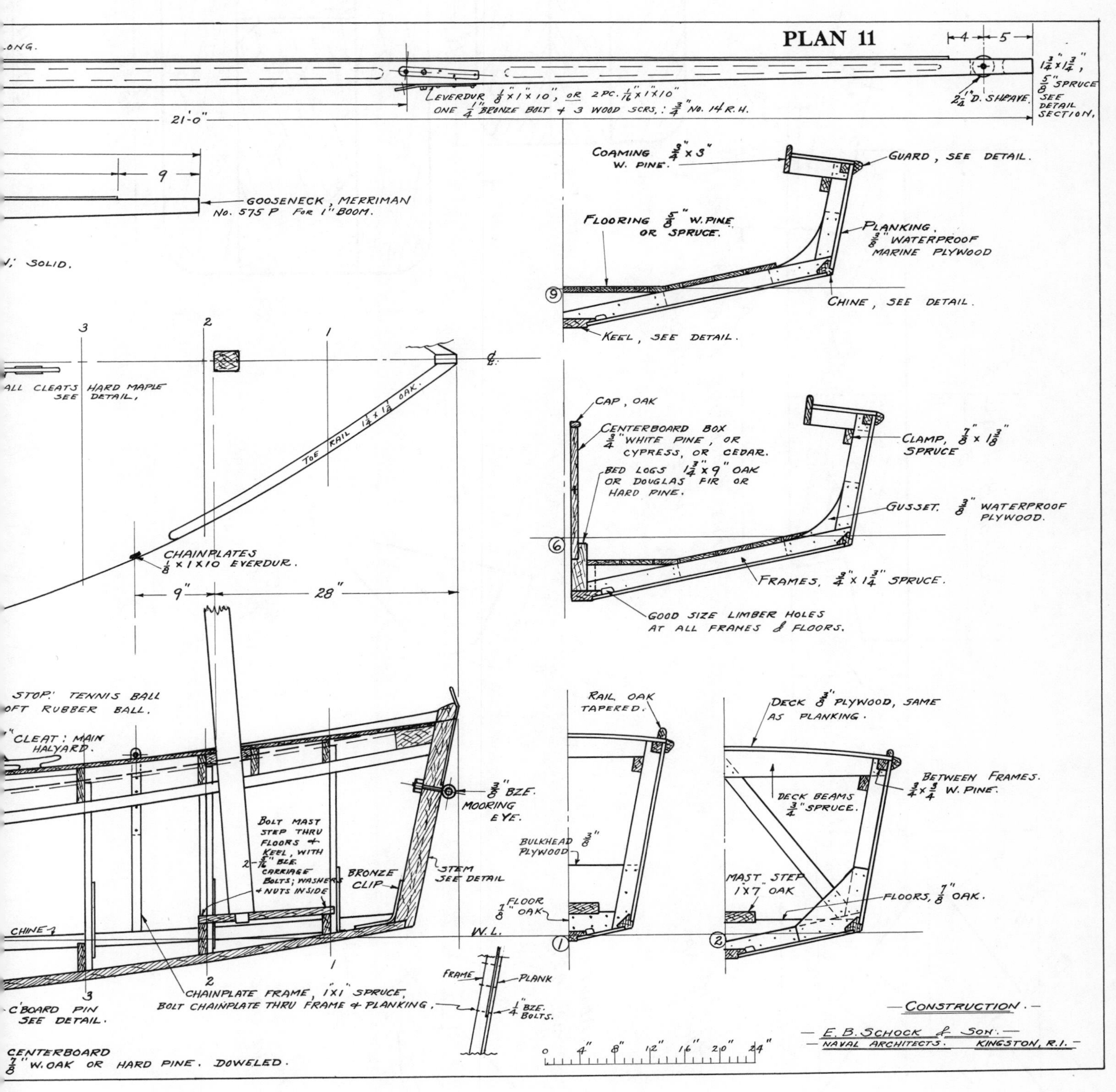

PLAN 11
LONG.
LEVERDUR 1/8"x1"x10", OR 2 PC. 1/16"x1"x10"
ONE 1/4" BRONZE BOLT + 3 WOOD SCRS.: 3/4" NO. 14 R.H.
21'-0"
1 3/4"x1 3/4", 5/8" SPRUCE
2 1/4" D. SHEAVE.
SEE DETAIL SECTION.
GOOSENECK, MERRIMAN No. 575 P FOR 1" BOOM.
SOLID.
ALL CLEATS HARD MAPLE SEE DETAIL,
TOE RAIL 1 1/4 x 1 1/2 OAK.
CHAINPLATES 1/8 x 1 x 10 EVERDUR.
9"
28"
COAMING 3/4" x 3" W. PINE.
GUARD, SEE DETAIL.
FLOORING 5/8" W. PINE OR SPRUCE.
PLANKING. 3/8" WATERPROOF MARINE PLYWOOD
CHINE, SEE DETAIL.
KEEL, SEE DETAIL.
CAP, OAK
CENTERBOARD BOX 3/4" WHITE PINE, OR CYPRESS, OR CEDAR.
BED LOGS 1 3/4" x 9" OAK OR DOUGLAS FIR OR HARD PINE.
CLAMP, 7/8" x 1 3/8" SPRUCE
GUSSET. 3/8" WATERPROOF PLYWOOD.
FRAMES, 3/4" x 1 3/4" SPRUCE.
GOOD SIZE LIMBER HOLES AT ALL FRAMES & FLOORS.
STOP: TENNIS BALL OFT RUBBER BALL.
CLEAT: MAIN HALYARD.
3/8" BZE. MOORING EYE.
BOLT MAST STEP THRU FLOORS + KEEL, WITH 2-5/16" BZE. CARRIAGE BOLTS; WASHERS + NUTS INSIDE
BRONZE CLIP
STEM SEE DETAIL
CHINE
W.L.
CHAINPLATE FRAME, 1"x1" SPRUCE, BOLT CHAINPLATE THRU FRAME & PLANKING.
C'BOARD PIN SEE DETAIL.
FRAME
PLANK
1/4" BZE. BOLTS.
CENTERBOARD 7/8" W. OAK OR HARD PINE. DOWELED.
RAIL OAK TAPERED.
BULKHEAD 3/8" PLYWOOD
7/8" FLOOR OAK
DECK 3/8" PLYWOOD, SAME AS PLANKING.
DECK BEAMS 3/4" SPRUCE.
BETWEEN FRAMES. 3/4 x 3/4 W. PINE.
MAST STEP 1x7 OAK
FLOORS, 7/8" OAK.
0 4" 8" 12" 16" 20" 24"
CONSTRUCTION.
E. B. SCHOCK & SON.
NAVAL ARCHITECTS. KINGSTON, R.I.

PLAN 11

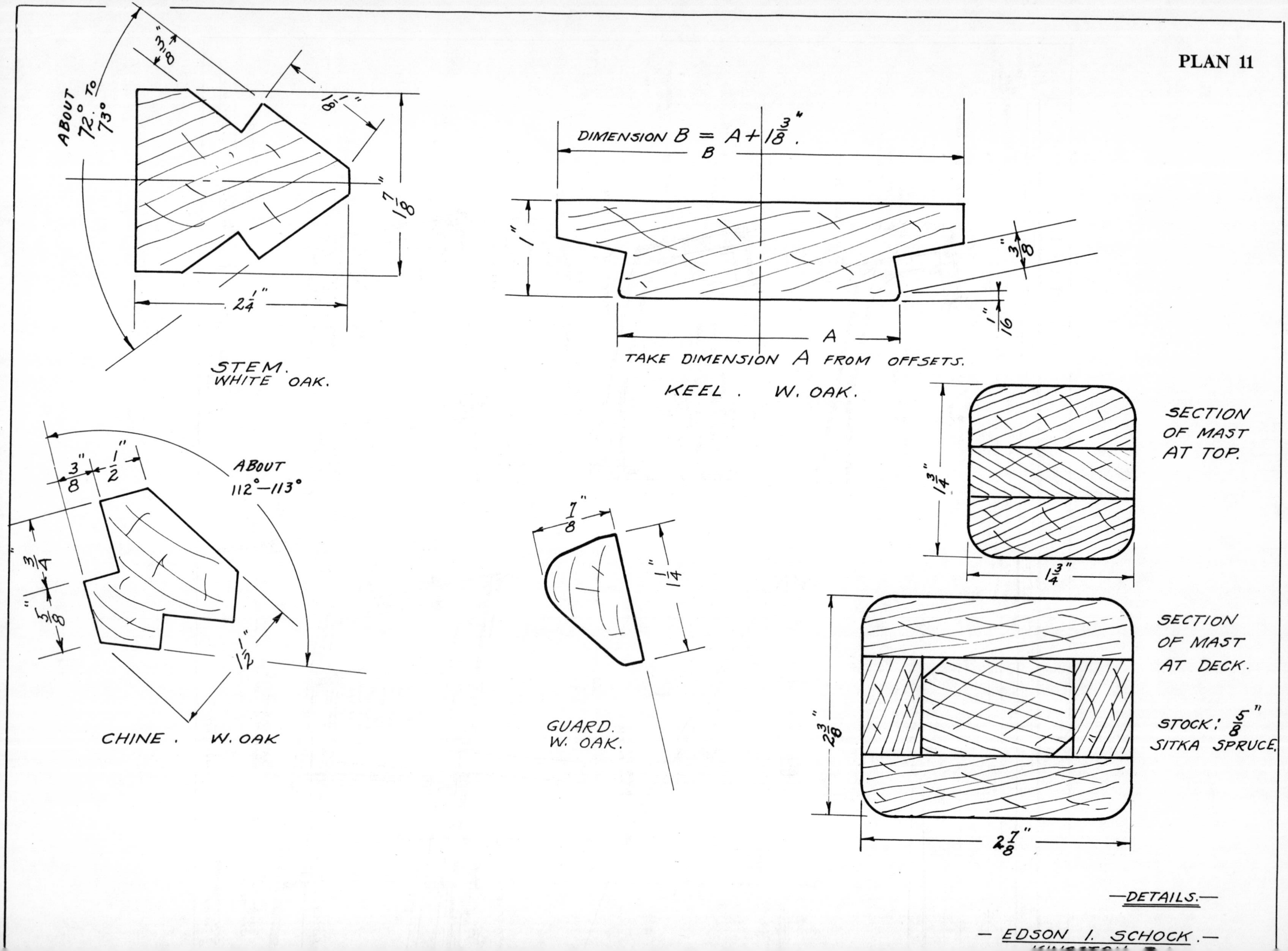

ABOUT 72° TO 73°

$\frac{3}{8}$"

$1\frac{1}{8}$"

$1\frac{7}{8}$"

$2\frac{1}{4}$"

STEM.
WHITE OAK.

DIMENSION B = A + $1\frac{3}{8}$".

B

1"

$\frac{3}{8}$"

$\frac{1}{16}$"

A

TAKE DIMENSION A FROM OFFSETS.

KEEL. W. OAK.

SECTION
OF MAST
AT TOP.

$1\frac{3}{4}$"

$1\frac{3}{4}$"

$\frac{3}{8}$" $\frac{1}{2}$"

ABOUT
112°–113°

$\frac{3}{4}$"

$\frac{5}{8}$"

$1\frac{1}{2}$"

CHINE. W. OAK

$\frac{7}{8}$"

$1\frac{1}{4}$"

GUARD.
W. OAK.

SECTION
OF MAST
AT DECK.

STOCK: $\frac{5}{8}$"
SITKA SPRUCE.

$2\frac{3}{8}$"

$2\frac{7}{8}$"

—DETAILS.—

— EDSON I. SCHOCK. —

TWELVE FOOT CAT AT THE DOCK

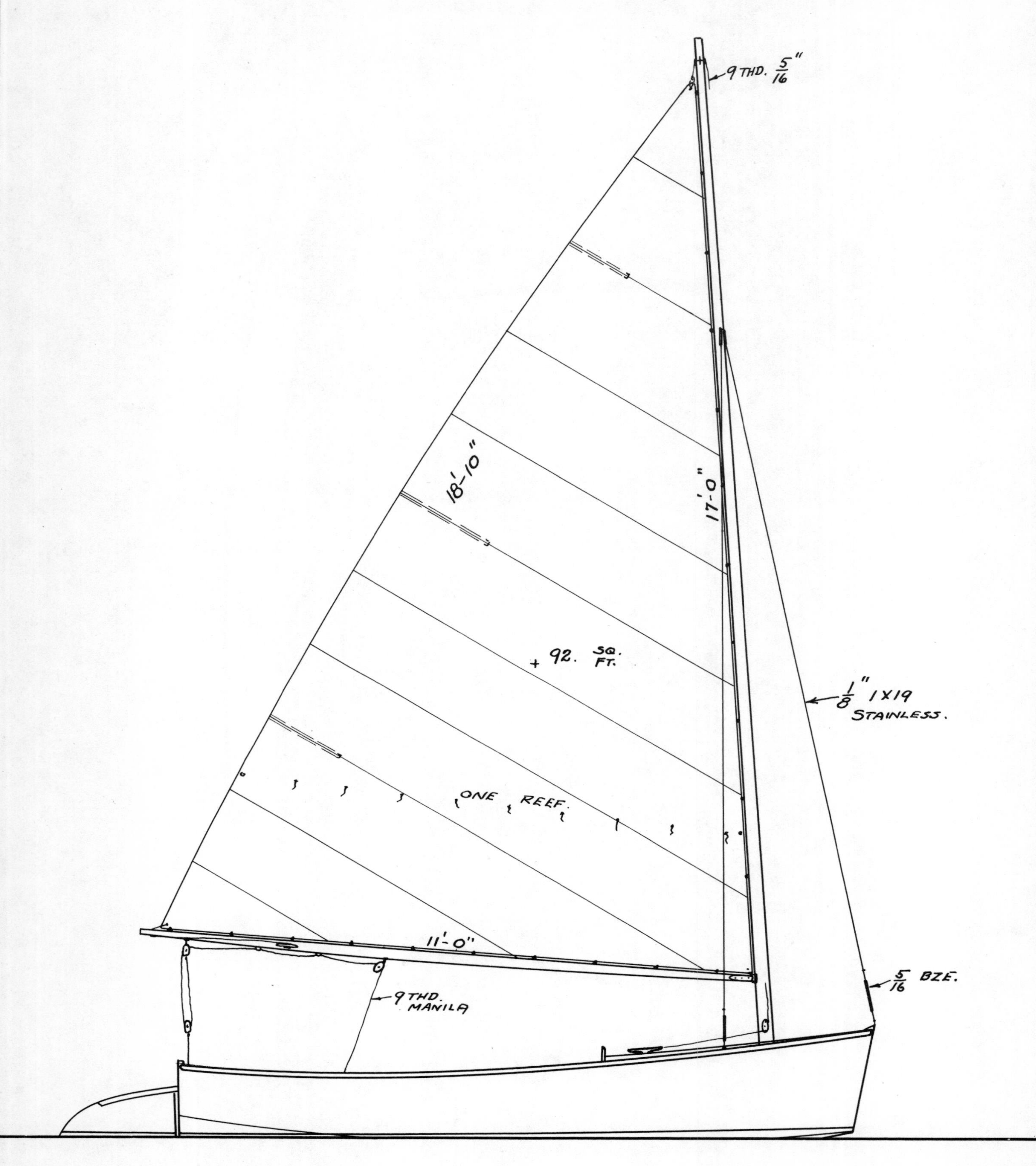

— SAIL PLAN. —

— E. B. SCHOCK & SON. —
KINGSTON, R. I.

TWELVE FOOT CAT "BEACHCOMA" SAILING

15′ KNOCKABOUT

This boat was intended as a one-design class to be built by the owners. They wanted a boat that would be easy to build, but the principal specification was speed. How well this requirement was met is shown by the fact that in handicap racing these "fifteens" give 18-foot round-bottom knockabouts a minute a mile head start, and beat them to the finish line.

They are easily built, are light enough to carry easily on a small trailer, and the material cost is within reason.

Mold Loft Work

First lay down the lines. Chapter III, page 9, gives an outline for this. Draw the stem, keel, mast step, centerboard and centerboard box, floor timbers, transom knee and rudder on the elevation.

Preliminary Construction

Details of this work are explained in Chapter IV.

Make the stem, keel, frames, transom and knee. Also make the centerboard box, the centerboard, the mast step and the chines. The stem, keel and chines can be ripped out and rabbeted on a circular saw, but if you haven't a power saw you had better have this work done at a mill. It will not cost much, and it is a long hard job to do by hand.

Framing and Planking

The procedure for this boat is exactly the same as for the 12′6″ Catboat (No. 11, page 102) and need not be repeated here.

Decking and Finishing

Follow the same directions as for the little catboat.

Paint the deck and flooring with non-skid paint, the topsides with yacht gloss, and the bottom with a good anti-fouling paint, applying the final coat of bottom paint just before launching.

Rigging

Make the mast and the boom (see Chapter IV, pages 23 to 25). Try to get good straight-grained spruce for the mast. It is expensive, but as you need only a small amount, the total cost should not be excessive. Get a piece long enough so that scarphing will be unnecessary.

Attach the rigging, the track, and the cleats to the mast.

Attach the gooseneck fitting to the mast and boom, and fit the track, sheet blocks and outhaul cleat to the boom.

Locate the jib sheet fairleads on the deck. Sailors differ in their opinions as to where these should be located, but the position shown on the plans is a good one to start with. But you may want to move it forward or aft later on; for this reason they are sometimes mounted on a short piece of sail track. They may then be moved without leaving holes in the deck.

Let her soak up for a couple of days before sailing her.

In sailing this boat you will have to learn to get the trim of the jib just right since she is very sensitive. The jib should be trimmed quite flat, and if it is poorly trimmed, she will neither balance nor sail well. So spend a little time getting the hang of trimming her sails just right. When properly tuned up, this boat is really fast. The best way to determine the efficiency of the trim of your sails is to try her out against other boats. You should soon sense whether or not she is doing her best. Lastly, keep your weight amidships, as sitting aft depresses the stern and causes a suction which will slow up any boat very markedly.

15'-0" KNOCKABOUT

ITEM	LUMBER MATERIAL	NO. PIECES REQ'D	SIZE IN INCHES	LENGTH	
STEM	OAK	1	1 3/4 X 2 1/8	2'-6"	
KEEL	OAK	1	7/8 X 6	14'-6"	
FRAMES	OAK		5/8 X 1 3/4	ABOUT 80 LINEAR FT.	
CHINES	OAK	2	1 3/8 X 1 7/8	16'-0"	
KNEES	PLYWOOD SCRAP				
FLOORS	OAK	10	7/8 X 2	1'-6"	
RUBBING STRIP	OAK	2	1 1/8 HALF ROUND		
CENTERBOARD	OAK OR HARD PINE	6	7/8 X 6	4'-0"	
C'BOARD BOX SIDES	W. PINE	2	3/4 X 17	4'-8"	
" " LEDGES	OAK	1 1	1 1/4 X 2 1/2 1 1/4 X 4	2'-2" 1'-10"	
" " BED LOG	OAK	2	1 3/4 X 5	4'-8"	
MAST STEP	OAK	1	1 1/8 X 6	2'-9"	
RUDDER	OAK	1	7/8 X 12	3'-4"	
TILLER	LOCUST	1	1 X 3	3'-0"	
TRANSOM	W. PINE	1	3/4 X 18	4'-0"	
CLAMP	SPRUCE	2	3/4 X 1 1/4	16'-0"	
DECK	FIR PLYWOOD	1	3/8 X 4	16'-0"	MAY BE BUILT OF SMALL PIECES
DECK BEAMS	SPRUCE		3/4 X 3	20 LINEAR FEET	
FLOORING	SPRUCE	12	5/8 X 4	12'-0"	
COAMING	OAK	1 2	5/8 X 9 5/8 X 8	4'-0" 9'-0"	
SEATS	W. PINE	8	5/8 X 5	4'-2"	
PLANKING	5 PLY FIR	2	3/8 X 48	16'-0"	
MAST	SITKA SPRUCE	2 2	5/8 X 3 5/8 X 1	24'-0"	1 PC-5/8 X 1 X 5'-0"
BOOM	SPRUCE	1	1 X 2 1/2	10'-6"	

PLAN 12

	HALF BREADTHS			HEIGHTS ABOVE OR BELOW WATERLINE		
STA.	DECK	CHINE	RABBET	DECK	CHINE	BOTTOM OF KEEL
1	12 5/8	6 5/8	1 1/8	22 1/4	1/4	1
2	19 3/4	14 1/8	1 3/4	20 1/4	3/8	3 1/8
3	25 3/8	20 1/8	2	18 1/2	1	5 1/8
4	29 5/8	24 5/8	2 1/8	17 1/8	1 3/8	6 1/2
5	32 1/4	27 5/8	2 1/4	15 7/8	1 5/8	7 3/8
6	33 5/8	29 1/8	2 1/4	15 1/8	1 5/8	7 5/8
7	33 3/4	29 1/2	2 1/4	14 7/8	1 1/4	7 1/4
8	32 3/4	28 5/8	2 1/4	14 7/8	3/8	6 1/4
9	30 3/4	27	2	15 1/4	3/4	4 3/4
10	28	24 3/8	1 5/8	16 1/8	2 1/2	2 1/2
T	24 1/4	20 5/8	1	17 3/8	4 1/2	0

OFFSETS FROM LOFT, E. I. SCHOCK, KINGSTON, R.I.

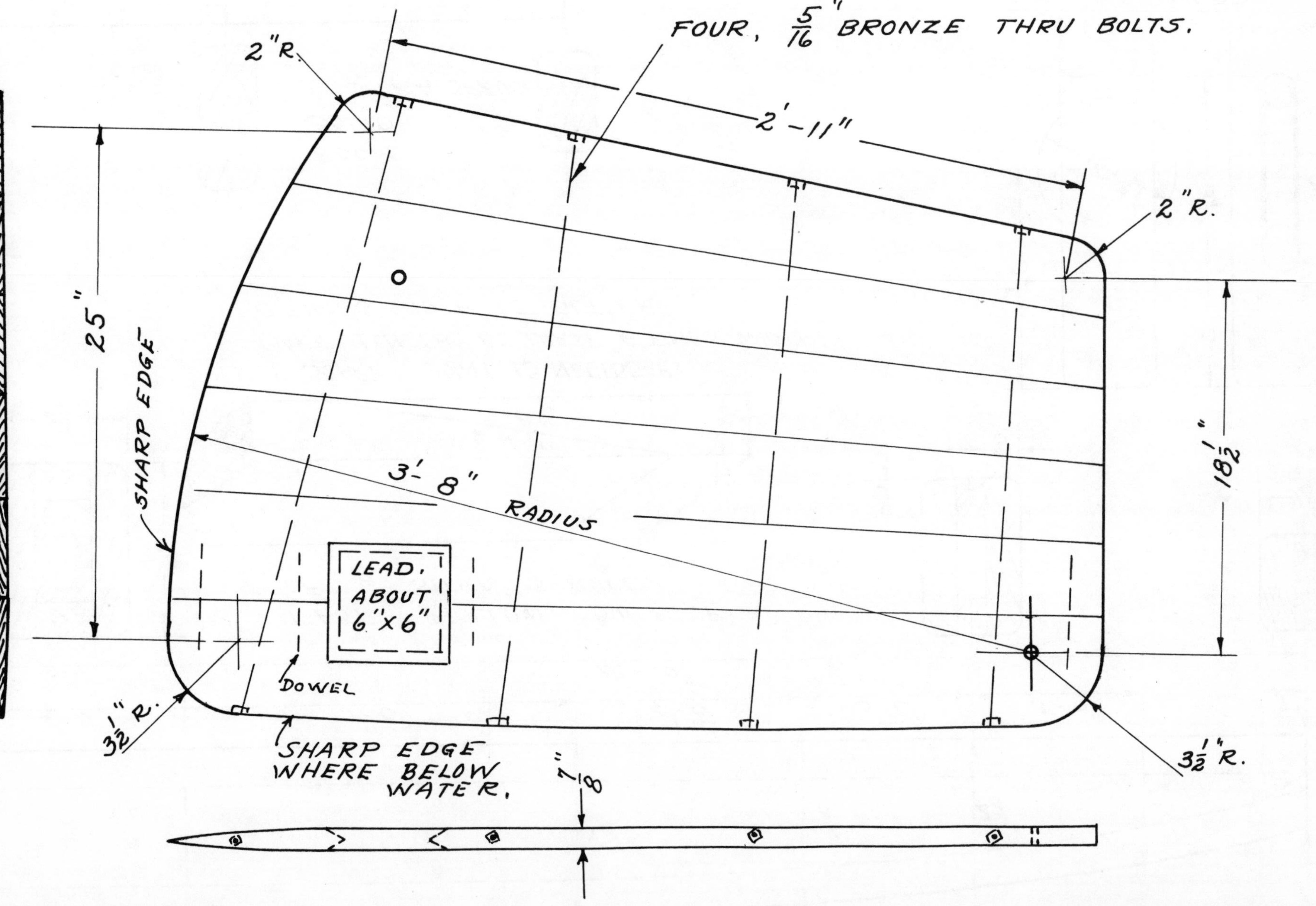

MATERIAL - OAK, OR HARD PINE.

CENTERBOARD.
E. I. SCHOCK, KINGSTON. R.I.

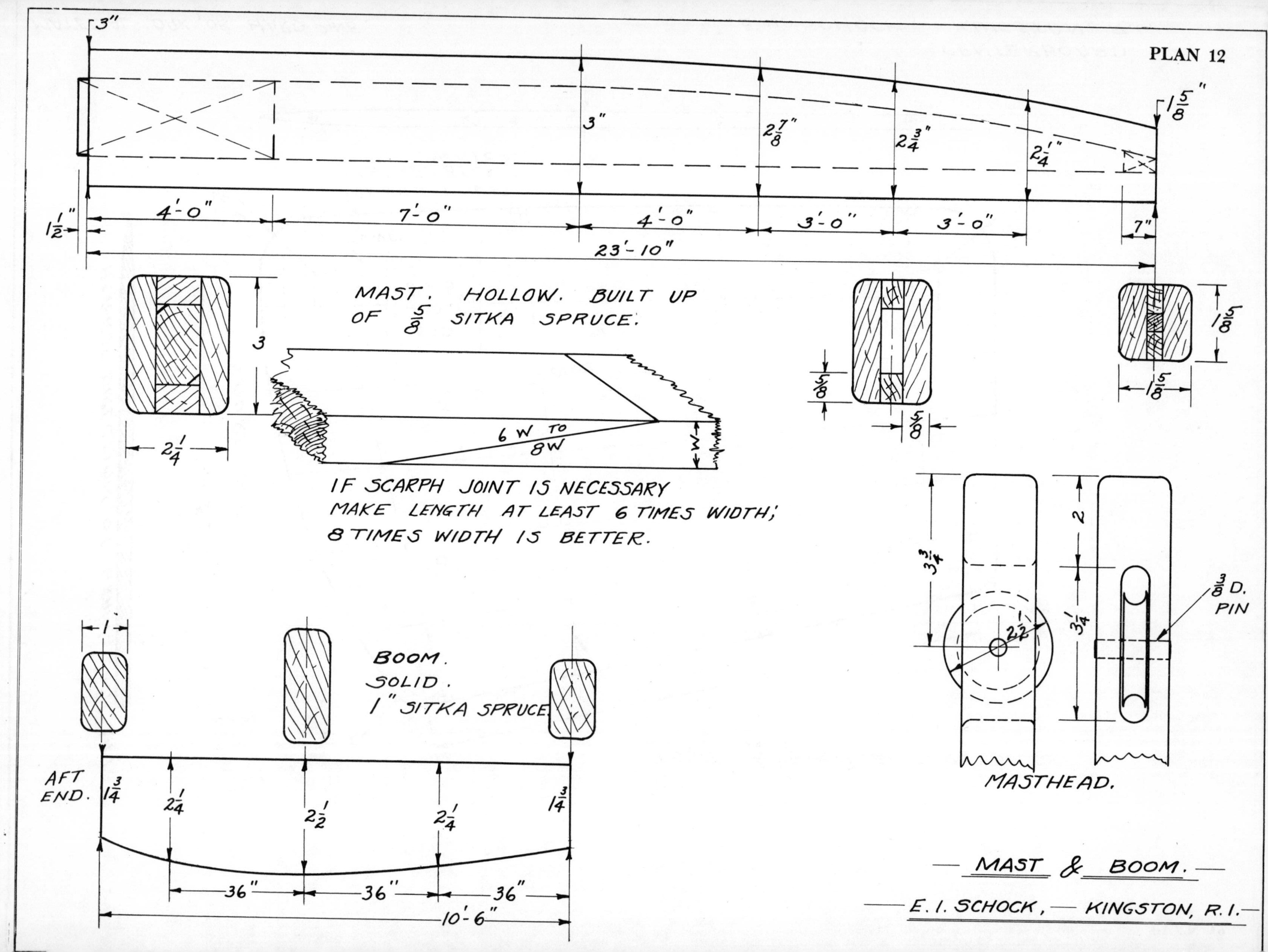
3"
3"
$2\frac{7}{8}$"
$2\frac{3}{4}$"
$2\frac{1}{4}$"
$1\frac{5}{8}$"
$1\frac{1}{2}$"
4'-0"
7'-0"
4'-0"
3'-0"
3'-0"
7"
23'-10"
MAST. HOLLOW. BUILT UP
OF $\frac{5}{8}$ SITKA SPRUCE.
3
$2\frac{1}{4}$
6 W TO
8 W
W
IF SCARPH JOINT IS NECESSARY
MAKE LENGTH AT LEAST 6 TIMES WIDTH;
8 TIMES WIDTH IS BETTER.
$\frac{5}{8}$
$\frac{5}{8}$
$1\frac{5}{8}$
$1\frac{5}{8}$
$3\frac{3}{4}$
2
$3\frac{1}{4}$
$2\frac{1}{2}$
$\frac{3}{8}$ D.
PIN
MASTHEAD.
1
BOOM.
SOLID.
1" SITKA SPRUCE
AFT
END.
$1\frac{3}{4}$
$2\frac{1}{4}$
$2\frac{1}{2}$
$2\frac{1}{4}$
$1\frac{3}{4}$
36"
36"
36"
10'-6"
MAST & BOOM.
E. I. SCHOCK, — KINGSTON, R.I.

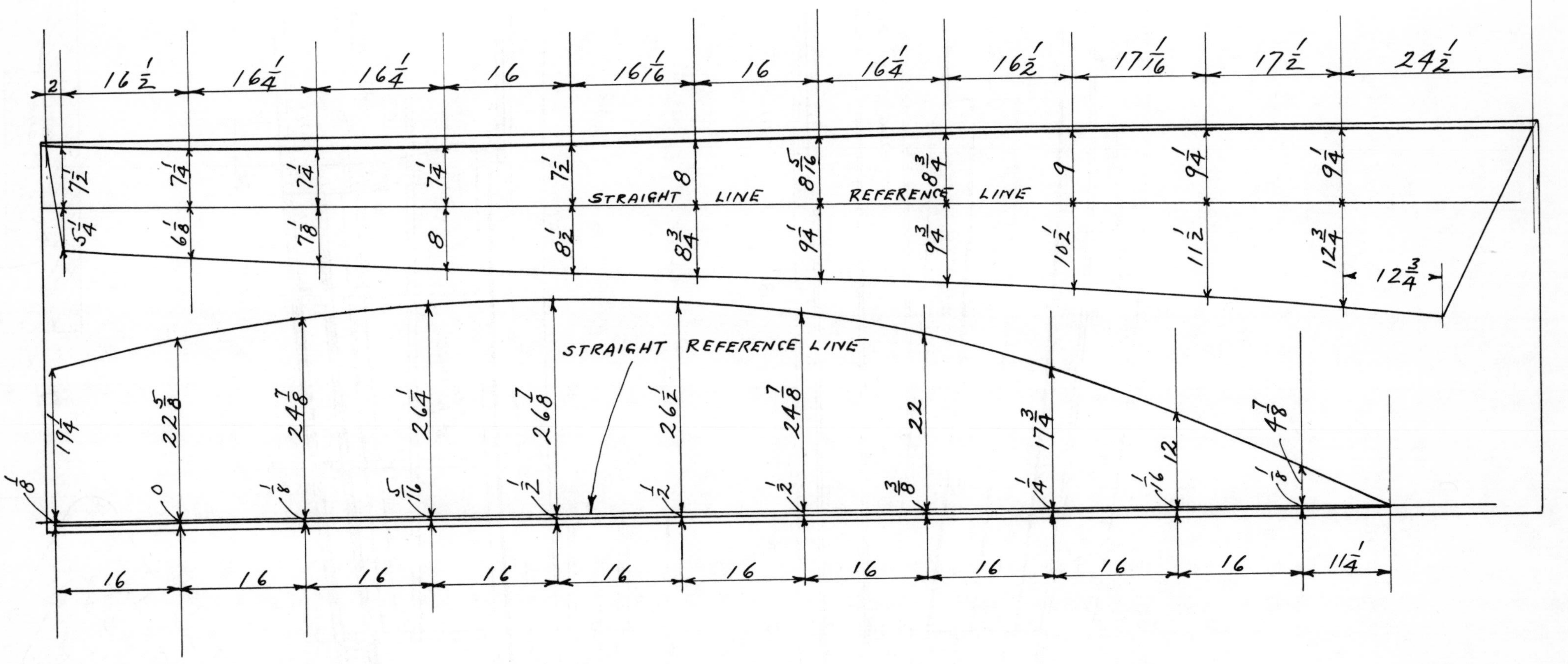

PLYWOOD PANEL $4' \times 16' \times \frac{3}{8}''$; 5-PLY.

DIMENSIONS SHOW EXACT SIZE, TAKEN FROM MOULD LOFT DRAWINGS. WHEN CUTTING PLYWOOD ALLOW $\frac{1}{8}''$ OR $\frac{3}{16}''$ EXTRA, FOR FITTING & SMOOTHING EDGES.

DEVELOPMENT OF PLYWOOD BOTTOM & SIDES.

EDSON I. SCHOCK, KINGSTON, R.I.

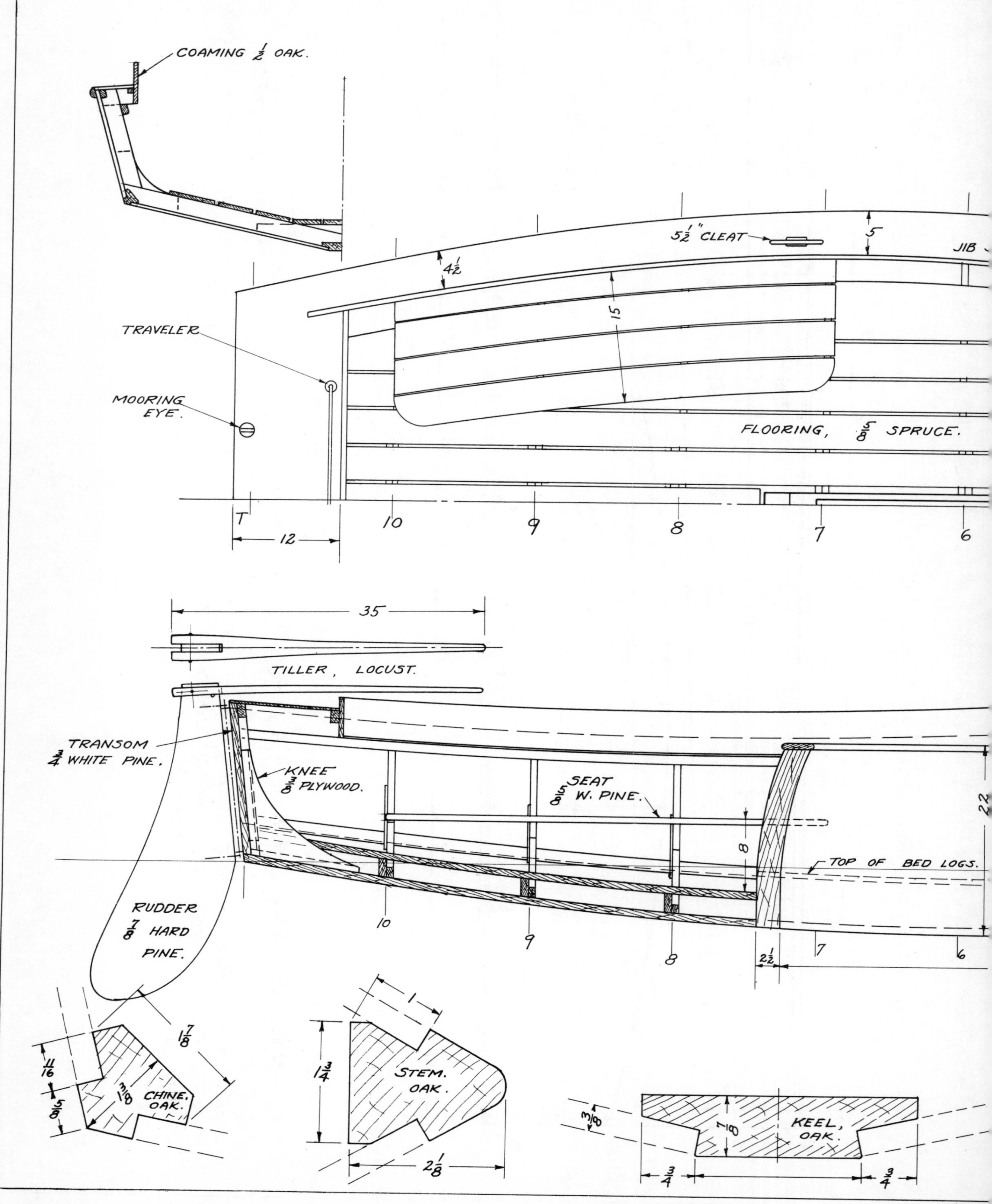

COAMING ½ OAK.
5½" CLEAT
5
JIB
4½
15
TRAVELER
MOORING EYE.
FLOORING, ⅝ SPRUCE.
T
12
10
9
8
7
6
35
TILLER, LOCUST.
TRANSOM ¾ WHITE PINE.
KNEE ⅜ PLYWOOD.
SEAT ⅝ W. PINE.
22
8
TOP OF BED LOGS.
RUDDER ⅞ HARD PINE.
10
9
8
2½
7
6
1⅞
11/16
⅝
1⅜
CHINE. OAK.
1
1¾
STEM. OAK.
2⅛
⅜
1⅛
KEEL, OAK.
¾
¾

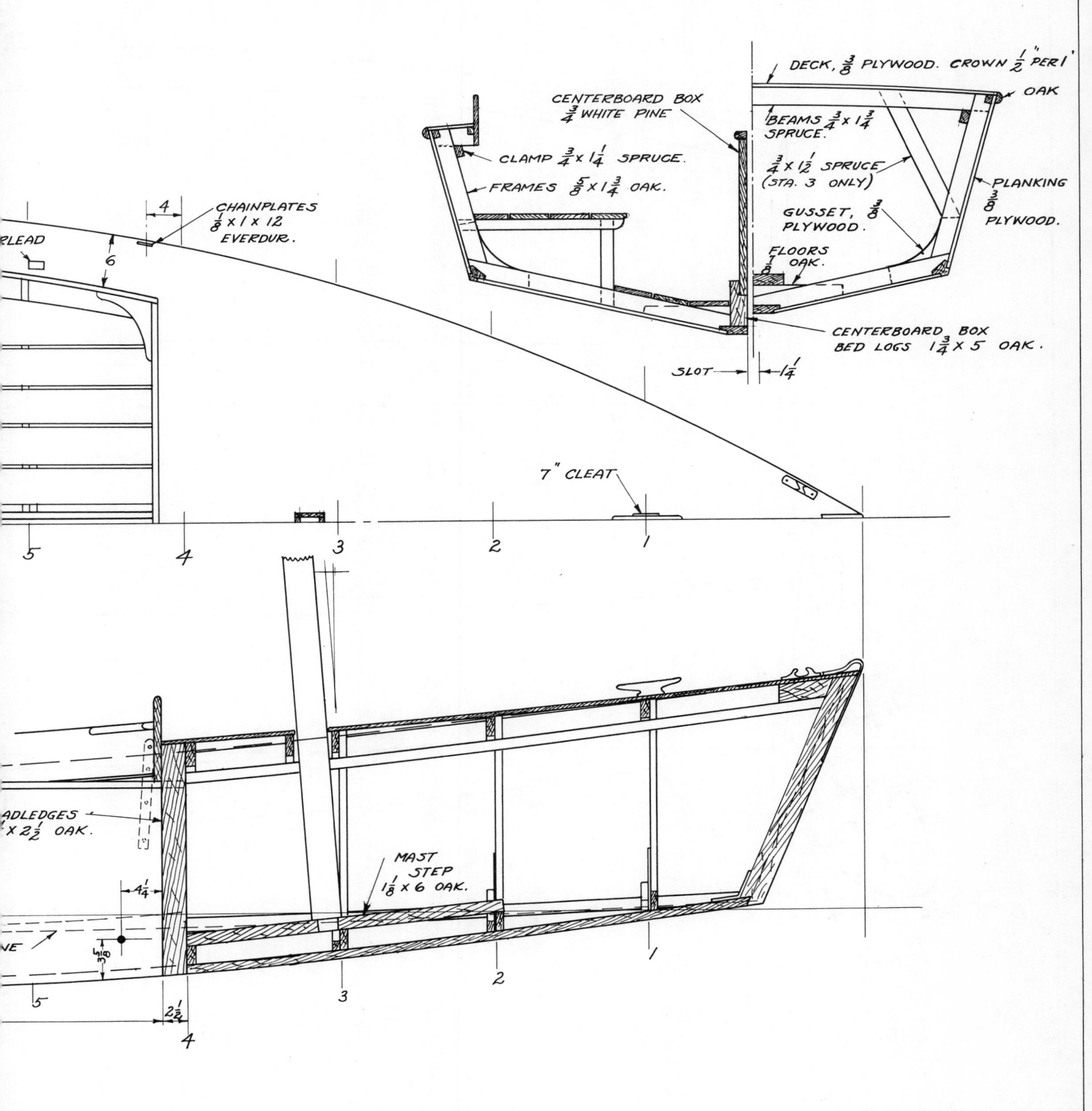
DECK, $\frac{3}{8}$ PLYWOOD. CROWN $\frac{1}{2}$" PER 1'
OAK
CENTERBOARD BOX $\frac{3}{4}$ WHITE PINE
BEAMS $\frac{3}{4}$ x 1$\frac{3}{4}$ SPRUCE.
CLAMP $\frac{3}{4}$ x 1$\frac{1}{4}$ SPRUCE.
$\frac{3}{4}$ x 1$\frac{1}{2}$ SPRUCE (STA. 3 ONLY)
FRAMES $\frac{5}{8}$ x 1$\frac{3}{4}$ OAK.
PLANKING $\frac{3}{8}$ PLYWOOD.
GUSSET, $\frac{3}{8}$ PLYWOOD.
FLOORS $\frac{7}{8}$ OAK.
CENTERBOARD BOX BED LOGS 1$\frac{3}{4}$ x 5 OAK.
SLOT
1$\frac{1}{4}$
CHAINPLATES $\frac{1}{8}$ x 1 x 12 EVERDUR.
4
6
RLEAD
7" CLEAT
5
4
3
2
1
ADLEDGES
x 2$\frac{1}{2}$ OAK.
MAST STEP 1$\frac{1}{8}$ x 6 OAK.
4$\frac{1}{4}$
3$\frac{5}{8}$
NE
2$\frac{1}{2}$
— NO. 90. —
— CONSTRUCTION. —
— E. I. SCHOCK. — KINGSTON, R. I. —
SCALE :- FEET.
0
1
2
3
4
5

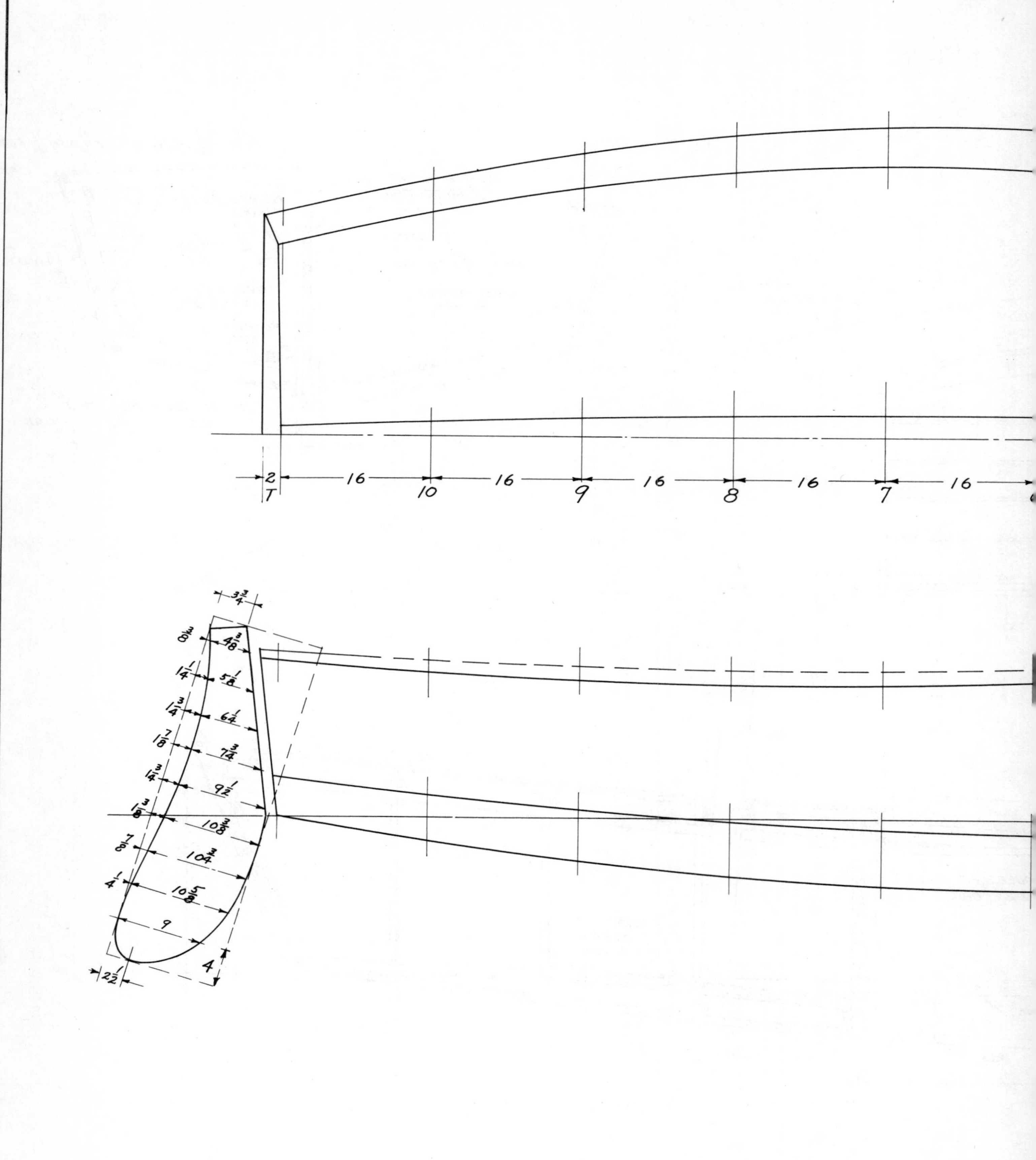

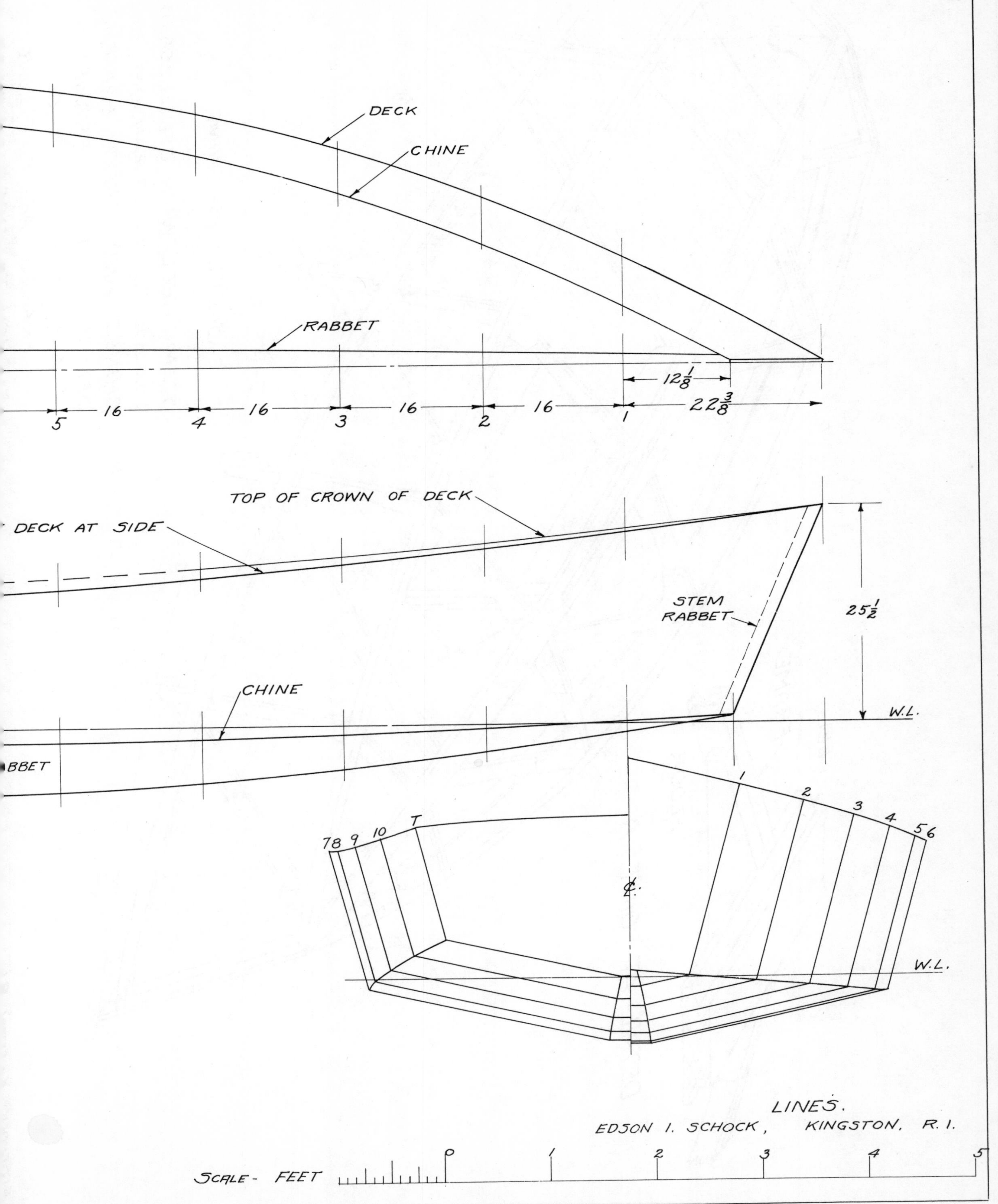

DECK
CHINE
RABBET
12 1/8
5
16
4
16
3
16
2
16
1
22 3/8
TOP OF CROWN OF DECK
DECK AT SIDE
STEM
RABBET
25 1/2
CHINE
W.L.
BBET
1
2
3
4
5 6
7 8 9 10 T
℄
W.L.
LINES.
EDSON I. SCHOCK, KINGSTON, R. I.
SCALE - FEET
0
1
2
3
4
5

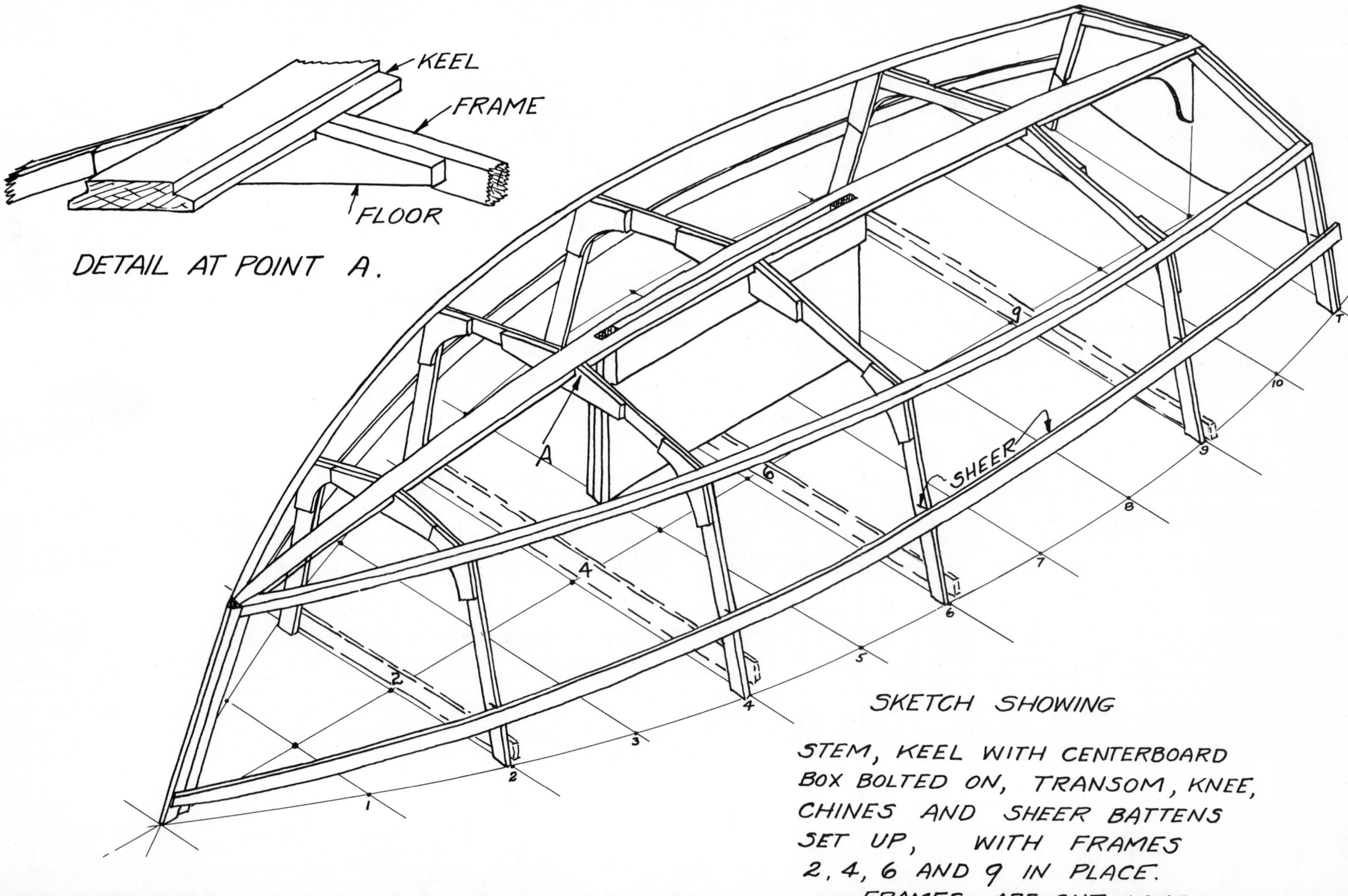

KEEL

FRAME

FLOOR

DETAIL AT POINT A.

A

SHEER

SKETCH SHOWING

STEM, KEEL WITH CENTERBOARD BOX BOLTED ON, TRANSOM, KNEE, CHINES AND SHEER BATTENS SET UP, WITH FRAMES 2, 4, 6 AND 9 IN PLACE.

FRAMES ARE CUT LONG

"SHARON POTTS" UNDER CONSTRUCTION

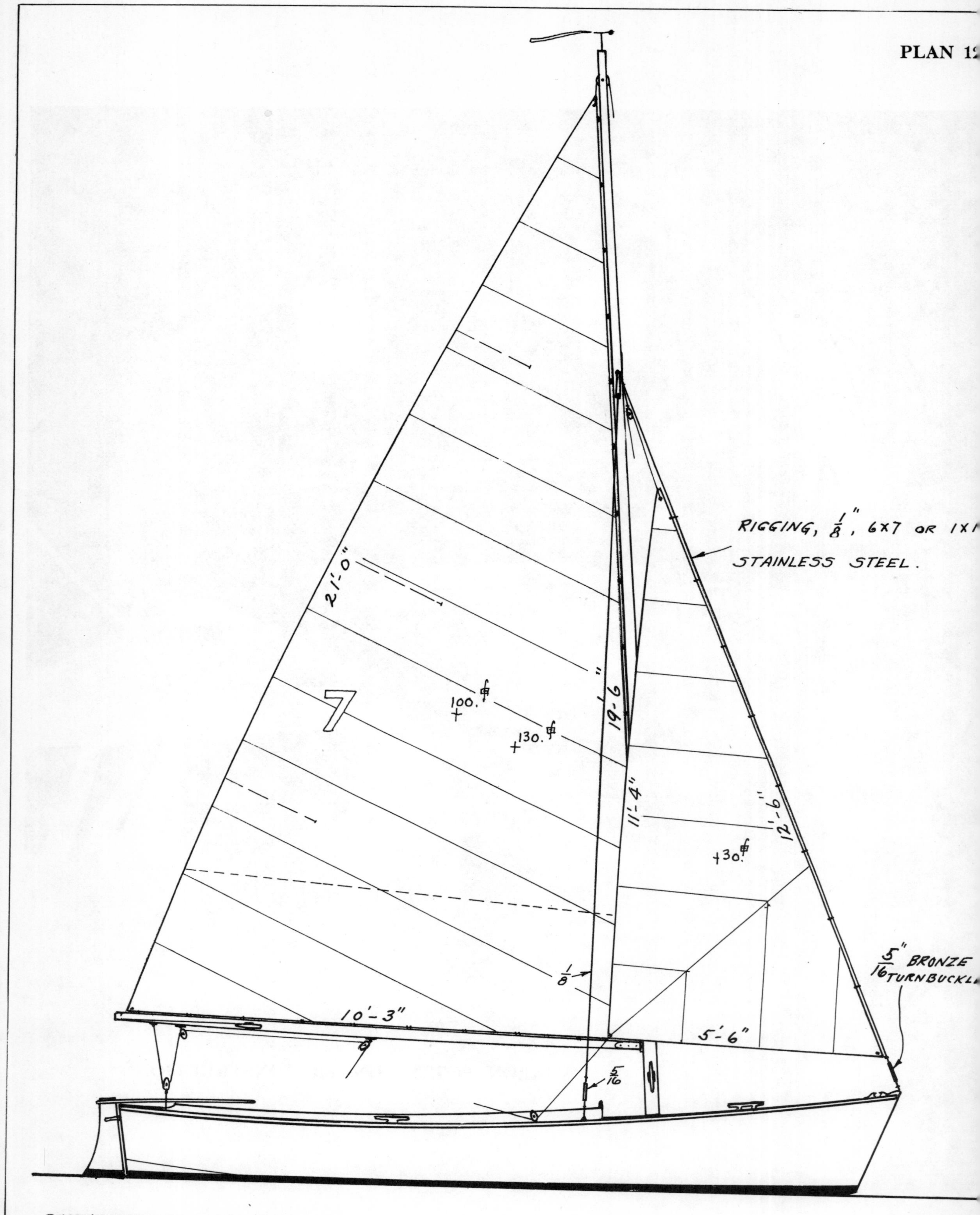
RIGGING, 1/8", 6X7 OR 1X1
STAINLESS STEEL.
21'-0"
7
100.□'
130.□'
19'-6"
11'-4"
12'-6"
30.□'
1/8
10'-3"
5'-6"
5/16
5/16" BRONZE TURNBUCKLE
DIMENSIONS OF SAILS ARE AFTER STRETCHING.
— SAIL PLAN. —
— DES. BY E. I. SCHOCK KINGSTON, R

FIFTEEN FOOT KNOCKABOUT "SHARON POTTS" SAILING

CHAPTER IX

Care and Maintenance

MUCH CAN BE SAID ABOUT TAKING CARE OF YOUR BOAT, FOR SHE NEEDS A GREAT DEAL more care than most things if she is to be kept in top shape. The first problem you will meet after she is finished is getting her overboard, or launching. If she was built some distance from the water, a trailer is the best method of transportation for her. There are many of these small boat trailers on the market, the "Little Giant" (Chauvin Industries, Worcester, Massachusetts) and the "Mastercraft" (Mastercraft Trailers, Middletown, Connecticut) are good examples of the type you will find most useful. The trailer should be low, with small wheels. Big wheels may rub against the hull, unless you block up the boat on the trailer, and the higher she is above the ground, the harder the work to get her there. If you make a trailer out of old automobile parts, make it as low as you possibly can.

Just before launching, give the bottom its last coat of copper paint. She can be launched while the paint is still wet. A very hungry worm will sometimes eat through old copper paint, but fresh copper seems to disagree with them.

Next comes the launching ceremonies. Large vessels are christened with a bottle of champagne, broken against the stem, but for a small amateur-built craft a paper cup of ginger ale seems to be just as effective, and is a lot less trouble and expense. One ambitious amateur christened his boat with a mixture of apple jack and brandy and it took the paint off the deck and stem as effectively as paint remover.

Your boat may be kept on a good heavy mooring or tied up to a pier or slip. Whatever the local practice, it is best to follow it. Other owners can advise you on the best way to tie her up to allow for local tide and wind conditions. But no matter where she moors, be sure to do a good job of making her fast, so that you can feel comfortable if it comes on to blow and you cannot get down to the water to take care of her. Every time you leave her, tie her up as though you expected a hard blow.

During the summer, watch the bottom for barnacles and grass. Do not be timid about scrubbing her often. Use a sponge or a stiff brush if necessary, every week or two. This inevitably takes off some of the copper bottom paint, and when the paint gets too thin, haul her out and give her another coat. Once a season should be often enough to repaint the bottom. Watch the varnished work. Keep it washed with fresh water, and if the varnish is thin, and before the wood shows dark under it, put on some more varnish. This may have to be done as frequently as once a month. The painted surface should only need cleaning, and a fresh coat of paint each spring.

Keep an eye on the rigging. See that the turnbuckles are tight and the cotter pins in place with their ends tucked away under adhesive tape where they cannot cut your hands or tear your sails. The new "MMM" plastic electricians' tape is fine for this. It is not dirty and gummy the way the old friction tape was. The rigging should be set up just tight enough to leave a little slack in the lee shrouds when the boat is sailing close hauled. Setting the rigging too tight strains the boat. Much harm can be done by too tight shrouds.

Keep her pumped out, washed clean, and all gear stowed in its proper place, all neat and shipshape. Keep your rope ends whipped, not knotted. Learn to splice and to whip rope neatly. Pull up the centerboard when it is not in use. If the rudder is removable, take it off. Take the sails home and dry them, if necessary, after every sail; never leave wet sails in a bag overnight. Spread them on a clean floor when you go to bed, and they will be dry by morning. If there is salt on the sails they will feel stiff. Wash it out by hand, using warm water. Never put your sails in a washing machine. Rinse them by hanging them over a line and turning a hose on them, preferably on a sunny day. Don't dry them on the grass if the lawn has been freshly cut or it may grass-stain them.

In Harvey Flint's book, *Winning Sailboat Races*, there is much good advice both on sail storage and the proper use of sails on the boat. Ratsey and de Fontaine, in *Yacht Sails, Their Care and Handling*, also offer many useful suggestions.

When it comes to winter storage, use your common sense. Be sure your sails are dry and salt-free before you fold them carefully in even layers, with as few wrinkles as possible. Wrap them in paper or put them back in their bags and store them in a dry place where rats cannot get at them. If they need repairing, send them to your sailmaker in the fall, for spring delivery.

All this may sound like a lot of housekeeping, but it is pleasant to sit in your boat and work on her, and to get things ready at home for the next day's sail. You should take a great deal of pride in a boat you built yourself, and want her to look as shipshape and Bristol fashion as the best in the fleet.

In the fall, haul her out and store her in a dry, well-ventilated building or shed. Wash her all over as soon as she is hauled out, while the bottom paint is still wet. Scrub the bottom hard; much of the old copper paint will come off, leaving the bottom clean and ready for next season's painting.

There is always a grand rush in the spring, so leave as little as possible to do then. During the winter the squirrels and chipmunks may store nuts in the boat, way up under the deck, but they do no harm, and you can brush them out.

Your mast and boom should be as carefully stored as your boat, in a dry shed, well supported at frequent intervals to prevent warping or springing. After the spars are stored, squint along them to be sure they are really straight.

The wire rigging should be washed clean of salt and dirt, and then wiped dry. The turnbuckles should be oiled, and, if they are hard to turn, freed with penetrating oil until they turn easily. New cotter pins will probably be needed next year; get them now and put them in a cloth bag tied to the turnbuckles. Little bags to keep things in are very handy for small parts. If you tie them to the boat or rigging, they are where you can find them when you want them in the spring. Don't store parts of your boat all over the house or you will have trouble locating them later on.

The trailer should be greased and stored indoors. If it needs a coat of paint, clean it up and paint it so it will be ready when wanted.

During the long winter evenings overhaul all your gear, and put everything in shape for the coming season. If you do this you will find there really are no long winter evenings; they turn out to be all too short.

When spring comes, plan your work on the boat so that she will not sit for a long time in the sun. At this time of year boats dry out badly, and their seams open, causing leaks. Get her in the water as soon as possible after she comes out of the shed. Try to spend less than a week outdoors, on fitting out and painting, before she goes overboard. When in the water, leave her for a couple of days to soak up, so that all seams will be tight, before you sail her; this is important. Whether or not this is the first time the boat has been put overboard let her soak up water for a day or two before you put any strain on the hull. This procedure is not as important with plywood-planked boats as it is with those planked in the conventional manner, but it is well to do it with any boat, and it can certainly never do them any harm.

BOATBUILDING TERMS

AFT, AFTER: The stern or back of a boat, toward the stern.

ATHWARTSHIPS: Across the boat from side to side.

BATTEN: A long slender stick or spline used to draw curved lines or to test the fairness of a curve. Also sticks used along the leach of a sail to give it a convex curve—called "roach."

BEAM: 1. The width of a boat. 2. A timber supporting the deck athwartships.

BEVEL: An angle planed on the edge of a piece of wood, to make it fit an adjoining member.

BED LOGS: The heavy fore and aft pieces of a centerboard box or trunk by which it is attached to the keel.

BLOCK: A pulley, a device for changing the direction of pull of a rope, with a rotating wheel to reduce friction.

BODY PLAN: A drawing of the cross sections of a boat's lines.

BOOM: The spar at the lower edge of a sail.

BREAST HOOK: A structural member of a boat, located at the extreme bow, and serving to hold the two sides together at the deck.

BULKHEAD: An athwartships partition in a boat, like the walls in a house.

CAULK: To fill the open seams in a boat with caulking cotton, to make her watertight.

CENTERBOARD: A movable keel, housed in the centerboard box or trunk, which may be lowered into the water to keep the boat from drifting sideways.

CENTERBOARD BOX, OR TRUNK: A box built on the center of a boat's keel, open at the bottom, into which the centerboard fits.

CENTERBOARD PENNANT: A piece of rope used to raise or lower the centerboard.

CHAINPLATE: A metal strap secured to the side of a boat to take the end of a shroud.

CHINE: A longitudinal framing member forming the junction between the bottom and the side of a V-bottom boat.

CLAMP: A longitudinal framing member between the deck and side of a boat, holding the deck beams and frames together.

CLEAT: A device of metal or wood for securing a rope by wrapping it around without knotting it. The cleats are fastened to the hull or spars of a boat.

COAMING: A raised edge or plank around an opening in the deck of a boat, to keep water from flowing from the deck into the boat.

COCKPIT: An open space in the deck in which to sit.

CONSTRUCTION PLAN: A drawing showing the principal members that make up the structure of the boat.

CROOK, NATURAL: A curved piece of wood taken from the root or a crotch of a tree, having the grain following around the bend.

DECK: A permanent covering for the interior of a boat to keep water out from above, and also to walk on.

DEVELOPMENT: The true shape of a curved piece before bending.

DOLLY: A heavy piece of metal used to back up a light member when driving nails or rivets.

DOWEL: A rod of wood or metal used to fasten two pieces of board together to make a wider board.

"EVERDUR": Trade-name for a copper-silicon alloy (bronze).

FAIR, OR FAIR CURVE: A curve or line or surface is said to be "fair" when it is evenly curved without bumps, hollows or angles.

FAYING EDGE: Edges in close contact. Also faying surfaces.

FLOOR, OR FLOOR TIMBER: Structural members of the framing of the hull, resting on and fastened to the top of the keel, and used to tie the frames together at their lower ends.

FLOORING: Boards to walk on, like the flooring of a house.

FORWARD (FOR'D): Toward the bow, or front, of the boat.

FRAME: A structural member to which the planking is fastened, extending from the keel to the deck.

GOOSENECK: A fitting attaching the boom to the mast, which allows the boom to swing freely from side to side and up or down.

GUARD, OR GUARD RAIL: A strip of hardwood around the sheer of a boat to protect her from bumps.

GUSSET: A structural piece joining the side frame to the bottom frame in a V-bottom boat.

HALF BREADTH: The width of any designated point on the boat from the centerline out, at right angles to the keel.

HALYARD: A rope used to hoist a sail.

HEADLEDGES: The posts at the ends of the centerboard box. Part of the centerboard box.

HULL: The body of the vessel, exclusive of spars and rigging.

INBOARD: Toward the center of the boat, from the sides.

INWALE: A strip running along the inside of the frames at their tops in an open boat. In a decked boat this same timber would be called the clamp.

KEEL: The backbone of the boat, along the centerline fore and aft, at the bottom of the hull.

KNEE: A piece of timber fastening and bracing two other members together where they meet at an angle, usually curved. A bracket.

"KORODLESS": The trade-name of stainless steel wire rope.

LAZYBACK: A backrest.

LIMBER HOLE: A drain hole in a frame, usually alongside the keel, to allow water to flow from one part of the boat to another. Provided to facilitate pumping.

LINES: A drawing showing by means of three projections (sheer plan, deck plan and body plan) the shape of the hull of the boat.

LOFT, OR MOLD LOFT: A large floor where the full-size drawings of a boat's lines are "laid down" or drawn.

MAST: A vertical or almost vertical spar supporting the sails.

MOLD LOFT: See LOFT.

NATURAL CROOK: See CROOK.

OFFSETS: Dimensions given for laying down the lines of a boat full size on the mold loft floor.

OUTBOARD: Toward the outside of the boat.

OUTBOARD MOTOR: A portable engine mounted on the stern or side of a boat.

OUTHAUL: A rope for pulling the sail out along the boom to make it tight.

PAINTER: The rope used to tow a boat or secure it to a dock.

PARTNERS: The block of wood which reinforces the mast hole at the deck.

PLANKING: The skin of the boat, from which she gets her strength and watertightness.

PORT: The left-hand side of a boat, looking forward. The boat's own left side.

PENNANT: A short piece of rope.

RABBET: A groove or notch in a plank or timber to receive the edge of a plank.

RISINGS: Pieces of wood extending fore and aft from frame to frame to which the seats or thwarts are fastened.

RUDDER: A device for steering a boat.

SCARPH, SCARF: A timber joint, made by sloping the ends of two pieces, and fastening them together so that they make one continuous piece usually of uniform size.

SCUPPER: A drain to allow water to run overboard.

SEALER: A paint-like preparation to fill the pores of plywood, keeping out dampness.

SHEAVE: The grooved rotating wheel of a block or pulley.

SHEER: The curve of the deckline of a boat, as seen from the side.

SHEET: A rope used to adjust the trim of a sail.

SHROUDS: Wire ropes supporting the mast at the sides.

SKEG: After part of the keel. A small triangular supplementary keel ahead of the rudder.

SOLE: Floor of the cabin.

STATION: A specified point along the keel, where a frame or mold is to be placed.

STARBOARD: The right-hand side of a boat, looking forward.

STAY: A wire rope supporting the mast in a fore and aft direction.

STEM: The foremost timber of a boat to which the planking is fastened.

STERN: The after part (or back) of a boat.

STOPWATER: A wood plug set in to prevent water from running along the joint between two timbers.

STRAIGHTEDGE: A board, straight along one edge, used for a gauge.

STRINGER: A strengthening timber running fore and aft inside the frames of a boat.

STOCK: The lumber from which a piece is to be made.

TANG: A metal strap used to connect a stay or shroud to the mast.

TELLTALE: A wind direction indicator.

THWARTS: Seats running across the boat from side to side. Often used to strengthen the boat as well as to sit on.

TILLER: The handle by which the rudder is controlled.

TRANSOM: The athwartships plank forming the stern of the boat.

WATERLINE: The line of intersection of the hull and the water when the boat is afloat. The painted waterline is usually two or more inches above this.

WHIPPINGS: Small cord wound around the end of a rope to keep it from fraying or becoming unlaid.

WIND VANE: A wind direction indicator, usually mounted on the top of the mast.

NOTE: Many of these terms have a variety of meanings and uses; the definitions given fit the use of the words in this book.